仲裁与法律

ARBITRATION AND LAW

第146辑

主办

中国国际经济贸易仲裁委员会
中国国际商会仲裁研究所

法律出版社
LAW PRESS·CHINA

仲裁与法律
第146辑

地　　　址：北京市西城区桦皮厂胡同2号国际商会大厦6层
邮 政 编 码：100035
电　　　话：(010)82217788　64646688
传　　　真：(010)82217766　64643500
电 子 信 箱：law@ cietac. org
网　　　址：http://www. cietac. org

目　　录

专论　争鸣

中伦杯获奖论文选登

域外　参考

专论 争鸣

不可抗力规则的适用
——比较法的视角

霍 伟*

摘要:在贸易往来中,不可抗力规则又开始被广泛提及。对于不可抗力(Force Majeure)制度,各国多已将其纳入立法体系,中国也不例外。相较之下,中国立法及司法实践在认定不可抗力时采取了更谨慎和保守的态度,尤其是对合同义务进行区分,对不同地区、不同行业、不同案件的影响,以及合同不能履行的因果关系和原因力大小进行综合考量。因此,不可抗力并非企业的"万能解药",也不应成为企业逃避履行合同义务/解除合同的借口或依据,中国企业仍应以积极履约、严守合同为原则,以不可抗力免责/解约为例外,审慎运用不可抗力抗辩。

关键词:新冠疫情 不可抗力 合同受挫 履行不能

一、问题的提出:不可抗力免责的认定标准

2020年1月30日,中国国际贸易促进委员会(以下简称中国贸促会)发布

---

* 中伦律师事务所合伙人,多家仲裁机构仲裁员,中国金融投资争议解决论坛(China Forum of Financial & Investment Disputes, CFFID)秘书长,先后获得对外经济贸易大学国际经济法系法学学士、硕士以及美国爱荷华大学法学硕士学位,曾在国有进出口公司及美国知名律师事务所工作多年。

通知表示,可以为受到疫情影响的企业办理与不可抗力相关的事实性证明。[①] 2020年2月2日,中国贸促会向汇大机械制造有限公司出具全国首份新冠疫情不可抗力事实性证明书。[②] 2020年2月10日,全国人大常委会法制工作委员会相关处室负责人臧铁伟表示,“当前我国发生了新冠肺炎疫情这一突发公共卫生事件。为了保护公众健康,政府也采取了相应疫情防控措施。对于因此不能履行合同的当事人来说,属于不能预见、不能避免并不能克服的不可抗力”。[③]

2020年2月7日,荷兰皇家壳牌有限公司(Royal Dutch Shell PLC)和法国道达尔公司(Total SA)声明拒绝中国海洋石油总公司(以下简称中海油)发送的不可抗力通知,反对中海油以新冠疫情构成“不可抗力”致使其无法履行液化天然气进口合同为由退出合约的主张。[④] 2020年2月13日,相关政府部门/机构已向100家中国企业签发了不可抗力证书,协助中国企业免除因未能及时履约的违约责任。[⑤]

不可抗力作为一项历史悠久的民事法律制度,已获得世界大部分国家立法的认可。[⑥] 尽管各国关于不可抗力的具体规定存在差异,但在不可抗力的构成要件、功能及其适用尺度上具有明显的同源性和趋同性。本文将通过考察中国

---

① 参见《中国贸促会扎实推进新型冠状病毒疫情防控工作》,载中国国际贸易促进委员会官网,http://www.ccpit.org/Contents/Channel_3434/2020/0130/1238889/content_1238889.htm。

② 参见《中国贸促会出具全国首份新型冠状病毒肺炎疫情不可抗力事实性证明》,载中国国际贸易促进委员会官网,http://www.ccpit.org/Contents/Channel_3434/2020/0202/1239530/content_1239530.htm。

③ 参见《企业因疫情不能正常履行合同怎么办?全国人大常委会法工委发言人臧铁伟说法律有相应规定》,载中国人大网,http://www.npc.gov.cn/npc/c30834/202002/b9a56ce780f44c3b9f6da28a4373d6c3.shtml。

④ 参见《遭遇不可抗力,中海油暂停LNG采购合同》,载国际能源网2021年2月13日,https://www.in-en.com/article/html/energy-2286788.shtml。

⑤ *China reportedly has already certified some 100 businesses to invoke so-called force majeure exemptions from contract duties, citing the coronavirus outbreak as a qualifying disaster*, https://www.law.com/international-edition/2020/02/12/general-counsel-pondering-how-to-handle-chinas-force-majeure-claims-378-134237/?kw=China%20Is%20Making%20Force%20Majeure%20Claims,%20Leaving%20General%20Counsel%20with%20Many%20Questions.

⑥ 王利明、郭明瑞、吴汉东:《民法新论》(下册),中国政法大学出版社1988年版,第474页。

在不可抗力的法律规定和司法实践上与域外立法的相似性,探寻中国法院对不可抗力免责认定的标准,以期能够协助中国企业正确行使合同权利。

二、比较法视角下的不可抗力制度

不可抗力制度起源于罗马法。罗马法将因行为人不能预见或虽能预见也无法抗拒且不可归责于债务人的外部事由而发生损害的情形称为不可抗力,债务人因此而给付不能的,不承担民事责任。① 该不可抗力制度首先被法国《民法典》所承继。随后,德国立法者通过吸收、借鉴法国的相关规定,在德国《民法典》中创设了“债务履行不能”制度。随着国际贸易的发展,英美等普通法系国家也在其判例法中确立了“合同受挫”(Frustration of Contract)等规则用以解决类似问题。《联合国国际货物销售合同公约》(United Nations Convention on Contracts for the International Sale of Goods, CISG)和《国际商事合同通则》(Principles of International Commercial Contracts, PICC)等国际统一商事规则和中国民事立法中也有关于不可抗力的规定。可见,不可抗力在各国立法上,通常都被规定为免责的条件,②且具有非常相似的构成要件。

(一)法国法中的不可抗力制度

法国《民法典》第1147条和第1148条规定,凡债务人不能证明其不履行债务系由于有不能归咎于其本人的外来原因[包含(1)不可抗力;(2)第三人的行为;(3)债权人自身的行为]时,即使在其本人方面并无任何恶意,如有必要,均因其债务不履行,或者迟延履行而受判支付损害赔偿;如债务人因不可抗力或不测事变而不能履行其承担的给付或作为之债务,或者违反约定进行对其禁止之事项,不发生损害赔偿责任。③

根据法国法院的案例和学者的学说,上述条款规定的不可抗力最初应同时具备不可预见性、不可抗拒性和外在性,但该三大要件已呈现“外在性不再被

---

① 周枏:《罗马法原论》(下册),商务印书馆1994年版,第649页。

② 王利明、郭明瑞、吴汉东:《民法新论》(下册),中国政法大学出版社1988年版,第474页。

③ 沈四宝、王军、焦津洪编著:《国际商法》,对外经济贸易大学出版社2002年版,第291页。

认定为必要条件,不可预见性和不可抵御性二者并非缺一不可”的总体趋势,即只要是债务人采取一切可能的必要措施后仍不能克服的事件,无论债务人在订立合同时能否预见,该事件仍可被认定为不可抗力。[①]

(二)德国法中的债务履行不能制度

德国《民法典》第275条和第276条规定,给付因债务关系发生后产生的不可归责于债务人的事由而致不能者,债务人免其给付义务;除另有规定者外,债务人应对其故意或过失承担责任;在交易中怠于必要注意者,为有过失。

由上述规定可知,德国《民法典》虽未单独规定不可抗力,但其创设的债务履行不能制度涵盖了不可预知、不能避免、不能克服等不可归责于债务人自身或由债务人自身过错而造成履行不能的情形,即排除了债务人对意外事故和不可抗力造成的损害后果应承担的责任。[②]

(三)英美法系确立的合同受挫理论

英美法系长期信奉“契约必须信守”原则,如“帕拉丁诉简案”(Paradine v. Jane,1635)[③]即为例证。但该等绝对义务观念致使英国合同法形成“要么履约,要么违约”的两极分化。1863年,英国法官在“泰勒诉考德威尔案”中指出,“契约应确实遵守,但由于不可抗拒之外来原因,且当事人又无故意过失,致契约履行不能时,契约应因此而解除,而当事人免除以后之履行义务”,[④]首先确立了“履约不可能”原则。随后,英国法官又在1903年的“克雷尔诉亨利案”中确立了“合同受挫”理论。[⑤] 美国判例法接受并继承了该两项原则/理论,亦认

---

① 李巾惠:《论合同法上的不可抗力制度》,华东政法大学2013年硕士学位论文,第8页。

② [德]罗伯特·霍恩等:《德国民商法导论》,楚建译,中国大百科全书出版社1996年版,第105~106、122页。

③ “帕拉丁诉简案”(Paradine v. Jane,1635)的法官认为,“当事人通过他自己订立的合同规定了自己应承担的义务和责任时,尽管由于不可避免的必然性会发生偶然事件,如可能的话,他必须履行合同规定的义务,因为他可于订立合同时对此事作出规定”,参见[英]A. G. 盖斯特:《英国合同法与案例》,张文镇等译,中国大百科全书出版社1998年版,第453页。

④ Taylor v. Caldwell, 3 Best & S. 826 (Q. B. 1863). See M. P. Funston, *Law of Contract*, Butterworths, 1986, p. 555.

⑤ Krell v. Henry [1903] 2 KB 740.

为由于某些当事人不可预见的、不能控制的事件致使合同履行已不可能,包括当事人在情况变更时并非绝对不能履约但强行履约的后果与原有合同目的不相称的情形,任何当事人都不承担违约责任。

根据英美法系中关于合同受挫制度的案例及规定,适用合同受挫制度的事件/情形通常需要具备以下要件:

(1)发生不可预见的意外事件,并且使约定的履行变得不可能或不现实,或者订立契约的目的实质上落空;①

(2)主张免责的一方当事人必须对上述合同受挫事件的发生没有过错;②

(3)当事人必须没有承担超出法律强加承担的义务。③

据此可知,英美法系的裁判者通常会从主客观两方面来判定是否构成合同受挫。具体而言:(1)客观上强调发生的意外事件必须导致合同绝对履行不能、履行极为不现实、合同目的实质性的落空;(2)主观上则重视行为人在订立合同时是否能预见、是否具有可归责性。

(四)国际统一商事规则关于不可抗力的规定

1.《联合国国际货物销售合同公约》

CISG 第 79 条第 1 款规定:"当事人对不履行义务,不负责任,如果他能证明此种不履行义务是由于某种非他所能控制的障碍,而且没有理由预期他在订立合同时能考虑到或能避免或克服该障碍或其后果。"据此,当事人要求免责需具备的要件为:(1)必须是由于他所不能控制的障碍使他不能履行合同义务;(2)此种障碍是他在订立合同时不能合理地考虑到的;(3)这种障碍的发生及其后果是没有理由预期他能够避免或克服的。换言之,这种障碍是当事人不能控制、不能预见或不能避免、不能克服的,④其适用范围更广,涵盖了情势

---

① [英]迈克尔·H. 温卡普:《合同法理论与实践——英国与欧洲大陆国家之比较》,中信出版社 2003 年版,第 306 页。

② 同上。

③ 孙美兰:《英美契约受挫制度研究》,载梁慧星主编:《民商法论丛》第 30 卷,法律出版社 2004 年版,第 268 ~ 276 页。

④ 冯大同主编:《国际货物买卖法》,对外贸易教育出版社 1993 年版,第 282 页。

变更。

与此同时,CISG第79条第3款和第4款分别规定了免责期间和通知义务,即如果履行障碍只是暂时的,则由于此种障碍的影响而不能履行义务的一方仅在该障碍存续期间得以免责,一旦障碍消除,就应恢复履行;因障碍而不履约的一方必须将其遇到的履约障碍及其影响及时通知对方,并规定此项通知应以对方收到才能生效。如果没有通知或对方未能收到通知而造成损失,应由不履行义务的一方承担赔偿责任。显然,这与不可抗力制度的相关规定也是相似的。

2.《国际商事合同通则》

PICC第7.1.7条规定:“(1)若不履行的一方当事人证明,其不履行是由于非其所能控制的障碍所致,且订立合同之时该方当事人无法合理地预见,或不能合理地避免、克服该障碍及其影响,则不履行的一方当事人应予免责。(2)若障碍只是暂时的,则在考虑到这种障碍对合同履行影响的情况下,免责只在一个合理的期间内具有效力……(4)本条并不妨碍一方当事人行使终止合同、拒绝履行或对到期应付款项要求支付利息的权利。”①

由上述规定可知,PICC关于不可抗力的规定与CISG十分相似,但其规定的适用范围较之CISG更广,涵盖了不可抗力情形在合同缔结前已经发生但当事人在订立合同时不可能知道的情况。而且,PICC采用列举的方式示明了合同当事人除赔偿请求权外终止合同、暂停履行等权利,相比CISG的规定更明确。

(五)中国现行法中的“不可抗力”

不可抗力制度在中国现行法中的规定,不仅在理论基础、内容和功能上基本一致,甚至有更严苛的适用条件,在司法实践中,中国法院也相对更审慎。

1.不可抗力相关的规定

原《民法总则》第180条规定,因不可抗力不能履行民事义务的,不承担民

① 梅明华:《国际货物买卖合同履行意外受阻之免责情形——不可抗力与艰难情事研究》,中国政法大学2002年硕士学位论文,第40页。

事责任。法律另有规定的,依照其规定。不可抗力,是指不能预见、不能避免且不能克服的客观情况。

原《合同法》第 94 条规定,“有下列情形之一的,当事人可以解除合同:(一)因不可抗力致使不能实现合同目的……”。第 117 条规定,“因不可抗力不能履行合同的,根据不可抗力的影响,部分或者全部免除责任,但法律另有规定的除外。当事人迟延履行后发生不可抗力的,不能免除责任。本法所称不可抗力,是指不能预见、不能避免并不能克服的客观情况”。第 118 条规定,“当事人一方因不可抗力不能履行合同的,应当及时通知对方,以减轻可能给对方造成的损失,并应当在合理期限内提供证明”。

2020 年 5 月 28 日通过的《民法典》中关于不可抗力制度直接沿用了原《民法总则》及原《合同法》等的相关规定。《民法典》总则第 180 条规定,“……不可抗力是不能预见、不能避免且不能克服的客观情况”。《民法典》合同编第 563 条规定,“有下列情形之一的,当事人可以解除合同:(一)因不可抗力致使不能实现合同目的……”。第 590 条规定,“当事人一方因不可抗力不能履行合同的,根据不可抗力的影响,部分或者全部免除责任,但是法律另有规定的除外。因不可抗力不能履行合同的,应当及时通知对方,以减轻可能给对方造成的损失,并应当在合理期限内提供证明。当事人迟延履行后发生不可抗力的,不免除其违约责任”。

2. 不可抗力的构成要件和法律后果

根据上述规定,中国的不可抗力制度主要由“不能预见”的主观要件和“不能避免且不能克服”的客观要件构成。具体来讲,“不能预见”作为判断当事人是否具有过错的重要因素,主要是指造成合同履行困难的客观情况是善意一般人都无法预知的。如果当事人在能够预见该等客观情况下仍然为之,则具有过错,不能主张免责,该等客观情况也不构成不可抗力。[①]“不能避免与不能克服”主要用于证明不可抗力的客观性与必然性,具体是指当事人对于不可抗力

① 刘凯湘、张海峡:《论不可抗力》,载《法学研究》2000 年第 6 期。

事件的发生虽尽了合理注意和最大努力,仍不能阻止和克服,并因此导致合同不能履行。[①]

由上述规定可知,不可抗力事件将导致如下法律后果:

(1)若造成合同完全不能履行,如标的物全部灭失导致合同履行已客观不能,则当事人免予承担违约责任;

(2)若造成合同在客观上仍可能履行,但合同目的已根本不能实现,则当事人有权解除合同;

(3)若造成合同部分不能履行或迟延履行,则当事人可免除部分不能履行/迟延履行责任。对于仍可履行的部分,双方既可以协商解除,也可继续履行。

(六)简评中国的不可抗力制度

从上述内容不难看出,不可抗力作为民法中一项具体的法律制度,尽管各国对该制度的接受路径不同,但无论是法国法中的不可抗力制度,还是德国法规定的债务履行不能制度,抑或是英美法的合同目的落空规则及两个国际统一商事规则中的规定,均与中国法律规定的不可抗力制度之间存在很高的契合度。具体而言,各国的不可抗力制度存在以下共性:(1)其理论基础均源于公平原则;(2)其构成要件非常相似:例如,均要求存在不可预见的“意外事件”,均将不可抗力与履行受阻之间的因果关系作为引起免责或解除合同等法律效果的核心;(3)其制度目的和功能亦殊途同归:即在保护无过错当事人的利益、体现意思自治理念的同时“促使人们在从事交易时,充分预测未来可能发生的风险,并在风险发生后合理地分担风险损失,从而达到合理规避风险、鼓励交易的目的”;[②](4)其法律效果相同,即都是为实现处理当事人之间不可抗力造成的风险损失的合理分配、处理债务人不履行合同的责任及合同效力等问题。可见,中国与英美等其他国家对不可抗力的规定或态度是具有一致性的。

然而,中国法界定的不可抗力事件均需同时满足不可预见、不可避免且不

---

① 刘凯湘、张海峡:《论不可抗力》,载《法学研究》2000年第6期。

② 同上。

可克服,而 CISG 等国际统一商事规则并不要求上述 3 个要素同时具备,适用范围也包括了情势变更。即从某种程度上讲,中国法律对不可抗力的规定更为严格、适用范围更狭小。

三、不可抗力制度在中国司法实践中的适用

鉴于不可抗力是基于公平原则用以缓和合同自由原则和合同严守原则的一项例外补救措施,为保障合同关系的稳定性,各国裁判者对于不可抗力的适用均较慎重、认定标准也相对严格。如前述分析,不可抗力事件与合同履行受阻之间是否存在唯一、直接的因果关系是认定能否免责或解除合同的核心。例如,在美国路易斯安那州的“Logan v. Blaxton 上诉案”中,被告主张气候恶劣导致道路无法通行属于不可抗力,应免除其交货责任。上诉法官则认为,“因被告未能证明若道路通行无阻,则其能履行契约,亦未证明该道路无法及时修复通行,同时亦未证明此项履行受阻情形无法依赖其他可能之方法解决,由于未尽此等举证责任,故无不可抗力条款之适用,被告不得免责”。[①] 可见,即使不可抗力与合同履行受阻之间存在直接的因果关系,如果不是唯一原因,债务人也不得以此免责。

具体到中国,笔者将通过列举中国各地法院最新发布的关于审理涉及新冠疫情的民商事纠纷的指导意见,分析该等指导意见在国际贸易纠纷、对赌协议纠纷及金融借款合同纠纷中的适用,以阐明中国法院对不可抗力减免责或解除合同的适用和认定标准。

(一)中国各地法院关于审理涉疫情的民商事纠纷的指导意见

中国各地各级法院就疫情期间各项审判执行工作陆续出台相关指导意见。总体来看,各地法院的指导意见对是否适用不可抗力免责均持审慎的态度,并强调要结合个案的实际情况加以具体分析。即便突发公共卫生事件构成不可抗力事件,也并非对所有合同的履行都构成阻碍,更不意味着每个案件的当事

---

① Logan v. Blaxton (1954) 71 So. 2d, 675.

人都可以此主张不可抗力免责或解除合同,关键在于判断新冠肺炎疫情或相关政府疫情防控措施是否是导致合同履行障碍的直接原因。

以浙江省高级人民法院民事审判第二庭出台的《关于审理涉新冠肺炎疫情相关商事纠纷的若干问题解答》①为例,“对于在疫情发生前签订的商事合同,当事人一方以受新冠肺炎疫情影响,导致合同不能履行为由,要求解除合同的,需要结合合同签订时间、履行期限届满的时间节点、采取替代措施的可行性及履约成本等因素,综合考量疫情对于商事合同履行的影响程度,区分具体情况,依法做出处理:

(1)疫情对合同履行没有影响的,应当按约继续履行,当事人一方以疫情属不可抗力为由,要求解除合同的,不予支持。

(2)疫情对合同履行虽有一定影响,但未导致合同不能履行或未导致履行对一方当事人明显不公平、不能实现合同目的等情形的,应当鼓励交易,可以引导当事人通过变更履行期限、履行方式、部分合同内容等方式,继续履行合同。一方当事人以疫情属不可抗力为由要求解除合同的,原则上不予支持。

(3)因疫情形势和政府及有关部门采取的疫情防控措施导致合同根本不能履行,当事人请求解除合同的,人民法院应予支持。

(4)疫情对合同履行有重大影响,继续履行合同对于一方当事人明显不公平或者不能实现合同目的,当事人请求人民法院变更或者解除合同的,应当适用公平原则,参照《最高人民法院关于适用〈中华人民共和国合同法〉若干问题的解释(二)》第二十六条和《最高人民法院关于正确适用〈中华人民共和国合同法〉若干问题的解释(二)服务党和国家的工作大局的通知》的规定予以处理”。

再以最高人民法院2020年4月16日出台的《关于依法妥善审理涉新冠肺炎疫情民事案件若干问题的指导意见(一)》为例,“三、依法妥善审理合同纠纷

① 浙江省高级人民法院民事审判第二庭关于印发《关于审理涉新冠肺炎疫情相关商事纠纷的若干问题解答》的通知(浙高法民二〔2020〕1号)规定:“2、当事人一方受新冠肺炎疫情影响,导致合同不能履行为由,要求解除合同的,如何处理?”

案件。受疫情或者疫情防控措施直接影响而产生的合同纠纷案件,除当事人另有约定外,在适用法律时,应当综合考量疫情对不同地区、不同行业、不同案件的影响,准确把握疫情或者疫情防控措施与合同不能履行之间的因果关系和原因力大小,按照以下规则处理:

(一)疫情或者疫情防控措施直接导致合同不能履行的,依法适用不可抗力的规定,根据疫情或者疫情防控措施的影响程度部分或者全部免除责任。当事人对于合同不能履行或者损失扩大有可归责事由的,应当依法承担相应责任。因疫情或者疫情防控措施不能履行合同义务,当事人主张其尽到及时通知义务的,应当承担相应举证责任。

(二)疫情或者疫情防控措施仅导致合同履行困难的,当事人可以重新协商;能够继续履行的,人民法院应当切实加强调解工作,积极引导当事人继续履行。当事人以合同履行困难为由请求解除合同的,人民法院不予支持。继续履行合同对于一方当事人明显不公平,其请求变更合同履行期限、履行方式、价款数额等的,人民法院应当结合案件实际情况决定是否予以支持。合同依法变更后,当事人仍然主张部分或者全部免除责任的,人民法院不予支持。因疫情或者疫情防控措施导致合同目的不能实现,当事人请求解除合同的,人民法院应予支持。

(三)当事人存在因疫情或者疫情防控措施得到政府部门补贴资助、税费减免或者他人资助、债务减免等情形的,人民法院可以作为认定合同能否继续履行等案件事实的参考因素”。

从最高人民法院及各地法院的审判指导意见不难看出,即便疫情或政府的相关措施对于当事人来说构成不可预知、不可避免并不可克服的客观事件,中国法院在认定当事人是否可主张不可抗力免责时,也会综合考虑合同履行的时间、方式、程度等因素以及合同义务履行障碍的具体情况,并区分合同类型。

可见,中国法院在不可抗力免责的认定和适用上同样强调不可抗力事件与合同履行障碍之间是否存在直接的因果关系,坚持“以严守合同为原则,以不可抗力免责为例外”。同时,中国法院还明确要在鼓励交易的基础上,严格适用合同解除的条件,防止违约方滥用不可抗力抗辩,损害守约方的合同利益。[①]

(二)具体案例分析

由前述全国人大常委会法制工作委员会相关处室负责人臧铁伟的表述可知,只有在政府因此而采取的疫情防控措施导致当事人完全不能履行合同的情况下才构成不可抗力的免责事由。可见,即便在中国,不可抗力免责的认定和适用也同样需要审查所涉合同主要义务的履行,以及疫情和/或政府相关措施对该等义务的履行、继续履行、合同主要目的的实现的影响。

具体来看,国际贸易合同当中,与买方的收货和付款义务相比,卖方在贸易合同项下则需承担包括备货、装货、发货等更多工作,不可抗力事件对于卖方履约行为的影响则更可能导致货物交易的合同目的不能实现。相反,在卖方已交付货物的情况下,买方因受不可抗力事件的影响而无法及时支付货款并不直接影响其接收货物,即不必然导致货物交易的合同目的落空。因此,无论本次新冠疫情和/或政府的相关措施是否构成不可抗力事件,中国法院通常不会支持国际贸易合同项下的买方以疫情导致其无法及时支付货款为由主张不可抗力免责或解除合同的请求。

关于中海油不可抗力通知遭拒事件,假使中海油与其供应商之间的纠纷适用中国法且由中国法院审理,如果中海油以新冠肺炎疫情构成不可抗力为由要求解除合同、免除其收货义务,如前述分析,根据原《合同法》及法院指导意见的规定,中国法院势必需要审查新冠肺炎疫情相关防疫措施是否导致中海油与供应商之间的合同目的不能实现。根据相关报道,中海油主张不可抗力的理由是中国"国内相关防疫措施导致收货港关键人员因自我隔离而无法到岗,超出公司正常履行合同义务的能力,并且暂时无法预估该不可抗力影响时长"。[②]

---

① 浙江省高级人民法院民事审判第二庭《关于审理涉新冠肺炎疫情相关商事纠纷的若干问题解答》规定:"……在商事纠纷的处理中,既要体现鼓励交易的原则,维护交易安全,稳定交易预期,严格合同解除的条件,防止违约方滥用不可抗力抗辩,损害守约方合同利益,又要贯彻公平原则,综合考虑疫情对于合同履行的影响程度、各方当事人的过错等因素,平衡合同各方利益。要加强调解工作,引导当事人互让互谅,合理分摊损失,共度时艰。"

② 参见《遭遇不可抗力,中海油暂停LNG采购合同》,载国际能源网2021年2月13日,https://www.in-en.com/article/html/energy-2286788.shtml。

因此，即便是在中国、适用中国法的情况下，基于现有证据和信息，中海油目前关于不可抗力免责的主张也不必然能获得中国法院的支持。

鉴于借款人在金融借款合同项下的合同义务为按期还款的"金钱债务"，根据原《合同法》第 109 条和第 110 条的规定，①"金钱债务"不存在法律上或者事实上的履行不能，即贷款人不会因受疫情或政府的防疫措施而无法履行其金融借款合同项下的还款义务。具体来讲：(1) 即便借款人因受延迟复工、政府隔离等政策的影响无法到银行还款，借款人仍可通过网上银行、手机银行、支付宝等支付平台还款；(2) 借款人仍可以通过资产变现、对外融资等方式清偿贷款。

因此，金融借款合同、融资租赁合同、股权性融资的对赌协议等涉及金钱债务的合同仅存在全面履行和迟延履行两种情形，即原《合同法》第 94 条规定的"因不可抗力致使不能实现合同目的"的合同解除情形不适用于该类合同，更何况，如前所述，对借款合同的履行之间不存在任何直接、必然的因果关系，而且也非借款人不可克服。前述各地法院的指导意见②已对此予以明确，即借款人一般不得主张适用不可抗力来免除其金钱给付义务或解除合同。

(三) 小结

根据中国的现行法及司法实践中的做法，对于买卖合同中买方收货的义务，中国各地法院在认定和适用不可抗力免责时，会综合考虑造成义务履行障碍的具体情况以及其他因素。而对于合同中的金钱给付义务，不存在履行不能

---

① 原《合同法》第 109 条规定，"【金钱债务的违约责任】当事人一方未支付价款或者报酬的，对方可以要求其支付价款或者报酬"。第 110 条规定，"【非金钱债务的违约责任】当事人一方不履行非金钱债务或者履行非金钱债务不符合约定的，对方可以要求履行，但有下列情形之一的除外：(一) 法律上或者事实上不能履行；(二) 债务的标的不适于强制履行或者履行费用过高；(三) 债权人在合理期限内未要求履行"。《民法典》第 579 条和第 580 条也作出了同样的规定。

② 北京市第一中级人民法院《新冠肺炎疫情下民营企业法律风险防范及建议》规定："涉及民营企业的融资借贷类合同主要包括金融借款合同、民间借贷合同(含企业间借贷、P2P 网络借贷)、小额贷款合同、典当合同、融资租赁合同、股权性融资的对赌协议等形式。鉴于该类合同的主要义务为'金钱给付'，新冠肺炎疫情与合同履行之'金钱给付'之间无法建立法律上的因果关系，因此，通说认为，该类合同无法主张不可抗力之抗辩。"

的情形，即无法就金钱给付义务主张不可抗力的抗辩。如前所述，《民法典》沿用了原《民法总则》及原《合同法》中关于不可抗力制度的相关规定，可以预见，各地法院对于不可抗力适用的审查标准与审慎的态度将继续延续。

四、结论

中国立法和司法实践在认定和适用不可抗力上与国际或其他法域相比，是谨慎和严格的，甚至是更加谨慎和严格的。因此，尽管中国企业履约存在一定的阻碍，仍建议中国企业，尤其是针对长期合同，要以积极履约、严守合同为原则，以不可抗力免责/解约为例外，审慎运用不可抗力，积极与交易对手沟通，通过友好协商的方式实现双方利益的平衡，在减少不利影响的同时避免承担更大的违约赔偿。

同样，建议中国企业：(1)注意审查与外国客户之间的合同是否约定了不可抗力条款，该不可抗力条款的具体约定是否涉及相关法律后果和责任分配等；(2)注意该等合同的适用法律、争议解决方式以及争议解决地等约定；(3)注意留存与相关国外客户之间的往来邮件、函件、聊天记录等书面文件以及涉及履约和/或对方违约等方面的证据材料，并及时向律师等专业法律人士咨询，必要时需要聘请律师提前介入，做好应对预案。

A Futuristic View on Mutually Agreed Solutions within the WTO Dispute Settlement System

Spyridoula Katsoni *

Abstract: The amicable settlement of disputes has made its presence in the construction of the World Trade Organization (hereinafter "WTO") dispute settlement system clear and is undoubtedly the preference of both the covered agreements and the Contracting Parties thereto. However, despite their significant contribution during the current Appellate Body crisis, there are few who raise concerns about the dangers that Mutually Agreed Solutions ("MAS") pose to the proper function of the WTO dispute settlement system. The present paper initially illustrates the evolutionary course of friendly settlements within the WTO, highlighting their gradual legalization. Subsequently, after drawing the line between MAS and similar agreements, it sets out DSU's requirements regarding the content of MAS and their notification, and discusses their legal status and binding effect. Furthermore, it addresses the question of whether MAS are a legitimate means of disputes' settlement. To this end, it analyses the main points of criticism against MAS, as the latter have been raised by academics throughout

* Ph. D Candidate at Ruhr University of Bochum; Research Associate at the Institute for International Law of Peace and Armed Conflict.

the years. Precisely, the key-issues of the potential oppression of financially weaker States through MAS and of the enforcement of MAS are addressed, as is the issue of whether the WTO legal framework can be interpreted as permitting the verification of the compatibility of MAS with the covered agreements prior to their entry into force by an objective intra-WTO forum. Eventually, such an alternative interpretation of the DSU is presented and the conclusion that MAS constitute not only an effective, but also a legitimate means of dispute settlement within the WTO is deduced.

Keywords: Amicable Settlements, Mutually Agreed Solutions, Dispute Resolution, Assurance of Legal Certainty, Dispute Settlement Understanding

1. Introduction

From its very first reading, the Understanding on Rules and Procedures Governing the Settlement of Disputes (DSU)[①] makes its favorable attitude towards the amicable settlement of disputes clear. According to DSU Article 3.7, a friendly settlement is the outcome "clearly to be preferred". Thus, it becomes apparent right from the outset that the DSU provides for a hierarchy; a commonly accepted resolution of the dispute is to be preferred to its judicial resolution.[②] Only in cases of ineffective negotiations, may the dispute at stake be brought before a WTO dispute settlement panel.[③]

In line with the aforementioned, a high percentage of disputing parties has opted for a friendly settlement of the dispute arisen; half of about 500 cases,

---

① Marrakesh Agreement Establishing the World Trade Organization, Apr. 15, 1994, 1867 UNTS 3, annex 2 (Understanding on Rules and Procedures Governing the Settlement of Disputes, Marrakesh Agreement Establishing the World Trade Organization) [hereinafter DSU].

② Wolfgang Alschner, *Amicable Settlements of WTO Disputes: Bilateral Solutions in a Multilateral System*, 13 World Trade Rev. 65, 69 (2014).

③ Peter Van Den Bossche & Denise Prevost, Essentials of WTO Law 262 - 263 (2016).

which were brought before the WTO dispute settlement system during the last twenty years, were amicably settled by the parties.① Some of the most well-known and complex cases are included among them.②

Against this background and under the light of the Appellate Body's crisis,③ which has left many appeals pending and several disputants, who want to appeal against panels' decisions, numb, the-previously ignored issue of-friendly settlements has been brought in the front light of discussions on the reform of the WTO and on the available alternatives during the dark period of this crisis.④

This will seem quite rational, if one considers that friendly settlements provide a faster and cheaper solution of disputes⑤ and a "swift and tailored solution" for the disputing parties,⑥ who are free to conclude Mutually Agreed Solutions entailing win-win provisions and terms, which are appealing to all formerly disputing sides. In this sense, MAS do constitute an effective means of dispute settlement. What remains to be seen is whether MAS are also a legitimate means of dispute settlement. It is this very question that the present article purports to explore.

Precisely, the present article aims to answer the question of whether MAS, as

---

① Wolfgang Alschner, *Amicable Settlements of WTO Disputes: Bilateral Solutions in a Multilateral System*, 13 World Trade Rev. 65 (2014); Resolving Trade Disputes Between WTO Members, https://www.wto.org/english/thewto_e/20y_e/dispute_brochure20y_e.pdf, 2 (last visited July 26, 2020).

② See for example: *Notification of a Mutually Agreed Solution, European Communities-Measures Affecting the Approval and Marketing of Biotech Products*, WTO Doc. WT/DS293/41, March 23, 2010.

③ Aditya Rathore & Ashutosh Bajpai, *The WTO Appellate Body Crisis: How We Got Here and What Lies Ahead?*, Jurist Apr. 14, 2020, https://www.jurist.org/commentary/2020/04/rathore-bajpai-wto-appellate-body-crisis/, https://voxeu.org/article/wto-dispute-settlement-and-appellate-body-crisis.

④ Geraldo Vidiga, *Living Without the Appellate Body: Multilateral, Bilateral and Plurilateral Solutions to the WTO Dispute Settlement Crisis*, 20 JWIT 862, 883 (2019); Joost Pauwelyn, *WTO Dispute Settlement Post* 2019: *What to Expect?* 22 J. Int. Econ. Law 297, 305 (2019).

⑤ Wolfgang Alschner, *Amicable Settlements of WTO Disputes: Bilateral Solutions in a Multilateral System*, 13 World Trade Rev. 79 (2014).

⑥ Ibid., at 66.

a means of dispute settlement, are capable of overcoming the hurdle posed to dispute settlement by the Appellate Body crisis and of providing the parties with an enforceable solution, compatible with the legal framework of the WTO. To this end, the paper will initially provide a brief overview of the progressive evolution of the amicable settlement of trade disputes since the 1947 General Agreement on Tariffs and Trade (GATT 1947),[①] as well as an analysis of the provisions regulating the conclusion of MAS and of the key elements, which distinguish MAS from other agreements within the framework of the WTO dispute settlement system. Subsequently, a presentation and an assessment of the validity of the main points of criticism imposed on MAS will take place. Specifically, the key-issues of the potential oppression of financially weaker States through MAS and of the enforcement of MAS will be addressed, as will the issue of whether the WTO legal framework, as it stands, can be interpreted as permitting verification of the compatibility of MAS with the covered agreements prior to their entry into force by an objective intra-WTO forum. Eventually, a conclusion as to whether MAS, as regulated by the current legal framework, are indeed an efficient means of dispute settlement will be deduced.

2. Amicable Settlements and MAS in the WTO

This Section will discuss the amicable settlements and MAS in the WTO in general and the function of MAS within the WTO dispute settlement system in particular. To this end, it will initially highlight the gradual legalization of friendly settlements within the WTO and it will address the issue of MAS' definition. Subsequently, it will analyze the DSU's requirements regarding the content of MAS and their notification and, finally, it will explore their legal status and

---

① General Agreement on Tariffs and Trade, Oct. 30, 1947, 55 U. N. T. S. 194 [hereinafter GATT].

binding effect.

2.1 The Evolution of Amicable Settlements in the WTO

The WTO dispute settlement system has only gradually settled to the way as it is known today. This shall seem quite expected, if one considers, that from the entry into force of the GATT 1947 to the formation of the WTO in 1995 the world trading system underwent a gradual "legalization",① turning from a "power-oriented" to a "rule-oriented" diplomacy.② Such a shift could not have left amicable settlements unaffected.

The dispute settlement procedure was initially regulated by Articles XXII and XXIII of the GATT 1947. According to the latter, if the parties' negotiations, aiming at a satisfactory solution for both disputing sides, did not meet the said desirable objective, the dispute would be referred to all Contracting Parties as a subject matter of negotiations for the sake of mutual concessions' balance. The mechanism envisaged in the GATT 1947 was-according to the provisions of Article XXIII and contrary to the current provisions on the matter-a process based on diplomacy.③

Things changed radically during the Tokyo Negotiation Round, when the WTO members adopted the 1979 Understanding regarding Notification, Consultation, Dispute Settlement and Surveillance,④ which codified the customary GATT dispute settlement practice and added certain new elements and clarifications. The shift of the system's approach from a purely diplomatic procedure to a legalized, rule-oriented means of disputes' settlement by a

---

① Judith Goldstein & Lisa L. Martin, *Legalization, Trade Liberalization, and Domestic Politics: A Cautionary Note*, 54 Int'l Organization 603, 604 – 605 (2000).

② John Howard Jackson, The World Trading System: Law and Policy of International Economic Relations(2nd ed. 1997), Cambridge, The MIT Press, p. 109 – 110.

③ Joost Pauwelyn, *The Transformation of World Trade*, 104 Michigan L. Rev. 1, 14 (2005).

④ World Trade Organization, Understanding of November 28 1979 Regarding Notification, Consultation, Dispute Settlement and Surveillance, WTO Doc L/4907, 26 BISD 210 (1979).

competent body became a reality. However, even though the 1979 Understanding named itself a codification work of customary practice, many noted the "artistic reconstruction of the GATT history"① effected through this pact and the indirect emergence of the friendly settlement of disputes as a primary purpose through its provisions. ②

Against this background, particular emphasis was placed on the resolution of disputes through MAS, as the parties to the GATT expressed vivid concerns about the so-called "wrong cases" that could end up being brought before WTO panels seeking resolution. ③ Precisely, their concerns focused primarily on the sensitive political or economic interests that certain cases comprised, on the inefficiency of their putative arbitral resolution and on the efficiency of the amicable settlement of such disputes through MAS. Specifically, some WTO members urged that such cases should not be subject to resolution by WTO panels, as they feared that some parties would get away with neglecting to comply with panels' rulings. Such an event would ultimately lead to the undermining of the system's validity and functionality. ④

For the effective appeasement of such worries, emphasis was placed on the conclusion of MAS even after the initiation of proceedings and thus pursuant to a more extensive negotiation between the parties. Particular emphasis was also placed on the adoption of a more active mediatory role of the panels to this end. ⑤

---

① Robert E. Hudec, *GATT Dispute Settlement after the Tokyo Round: An Unfinished Business*, 13 Cornell Int'l L. J. 145, 186 – 187 (1980).

② Ibid., at 186; World Trade Organization, Understanding of November 28 1979 Regarding Notification, Consultation, Dispute Settlement and Surveillance, WTO Doc L/4907, 26 BISD 210 (1979), Annex Art. 41.

③ Wolfgang Alschner, *Amicable Settlements of WTO Disputes: Bilateral Solutions in a Multilateral System*, 13 World Trade Rev. 80 (2014).

④ Robert E. Hudec, *GATT Dispute Settlement after the Tokyo Round: An Unfinished Business*, 13 Cornell Int'l L. J. 159 – 163 (1980).

⑤ Ibid., at 177, 185 – 188.

Moreover, Article 19 of the 1979 Understanding introduced a further step towards transparency, as it allowed third-non disputant-WTO members to request and receive information on an amicable agreement concluded between other members before a WTO panel, provided that this agreement was related to trade matters. However, this possibility was greatly limited, not only due to the restriction as to the subject matter of these agreements, but also due to the fact that Article 19 did not cover bilateral agreements reached at the negotiations' stage.

In 1989, significant progress regarding the protection of the collective interest of the Contracting Parties to the GATT was provided by the 1989 GATT decision on "Improvements to the GATT Dispute Settlement Rules and Procedures",① which included provisions underlining the necessity of MAS' conformity with GATT, as well as MAS' mandatory notification. Such provisions were later incorporated in DSU Articles 3. 5 and 7 with minor adjustments.② Thus, MAS were actually formed in the Uruguay Round, gaining the appropriate procedural and substantive safeguards, so as to confer the effective protection of all the parties to the multilateral trading system of the WTO.③

Nowadays, the DSU offers the disputing parties a number of opportunities for reconciliation; DSU Article 11 provides that, even when consultations fail and a panel is established, the latter is still obliged to give the parties a sufficient opportunity to find a satisfactory solution. Thus, only when the parties fail to reach a MAS, may the panel submit its legal findings to the Dispute Settlement

---

① World Trade Organization, Ministerial Decision of 12 April 1989 on Improvements to the GATT Dispute Settlement Rules and Procedures, WTO Doc L/6489, 36 GATT BISD 61 (1989).

② Wolfgang Alschner, *Amicable Settlements of WTO Disputes: Bilateral Solutions in a Multilateral System*, 13 World Trade Rev. 81 (2014).

③ Ibid.

Body (hereinafter "DSB") ① for adoption. Moreover, the parties involved can forego a DSB's final decision by reaching a MAS up to the last minute. ② After all, as the Appellate Body has underlined, MAS can take place even after the issuance of recommendations and rulings by the DSB. ③

Indeed, MAS can take place prior to the panel and Appellate Body proceedings, as was the case in *Colombia-Customs Measures on Importation of Certain Goods from Panama*, ④ or pursuant to such proceedings, as was the case with the Softwood Lumber MAS ⑤ on the basis of the text of DSU Article 22.8. ⑥ Most of all, it should be noted that MAS can also take place even while the proceedings before the panels or the Appellate Body have been initiated and the case is pending. ⑦ In line with the aforementioned, MAS constitute a realistic means of even resolving disputes that-at least for the time being-cannot be brought before the Appellate Body, or are still pending before the latter.

Lastly, according to DSU Article 3.7, MAS must be in conformity with the covered agreements, while, transparency is nowadays better ensured through DSU

---

① Marrakesh Agreement Establishing the World Trade Organization, Apr. 15, 1994, 1867 UNTS 3, annex 2 (Understanding on Rules and Procedures Governing the Settlement of Disputes, Marrakesh Agreement Establishing the World Trade Organization), Art. 12.7.

② Ibid., at Art. 12.7, Ibid., at Art. 15; Armin Steinbach, *The DSU Interim Review-Need for Its Elimination or Extension to the Appellate Body Stage*, 12 J. Int'l Econ. L. 417, 417 – 434 (2009 Wolfgang Alschner, *Amicable Settlements of WTO Disputes: Bilateral Solutions in a Multilateral System*, 13 World Trade Rev. 66 (2014)).

③ A Handbook on The WTO Dispute Settlement System 170 (Legal Affairs Division and Rules Division of the WTO Secretariat and the Appellate Body Secretariat eds, 2nd ed. 2017).

④ Request for Consultations, *Colombia-Customs Measures on Importation of Certain Goods from Panama*, WTO Doc WT/DS348/1 G/L/782 G/VAL/D/8 (July 25, 2006).

⑤ Notification of Mutually Agreed Solution, *United States-Reviews of Countervailing Duty on Softwood Lumber from Canada* (US-Softwood Lumber), WTO Doc. WT/DS311/2 (Nov. 16, 2006).

⑥ Alberto Alvarez-Jiménez, *Mutually Agreed Solutions under the WTO Dispute Settlement Understanding: An Analytical Framework after the Softwood Lumber Arbitration*, 10 World Trade Rev. 343, 346 (2011).

⑦ A Handbook on The WTO Dispute Settlement System 170 (Legal Affairs Division and Rules Division of the WTO Secretariat and the Appellate Body Secretariat eds, 2nd ed. 2017).

Article 3. 6, which requires the notification of the MAS reached to the DSB and the relevant Councils and Committees, where any WTO member may raise any point relating thereto.

2. 2 The Definition of "MAS"

Given the absence of a definition of the term "MAS" within the DSU, many attempts for the repletion of this gap have been made. Initially, it was suggested that all agreements, which have been notified by the contracting parties as such, in accordance with DSU Article 3. 6, fall under the scope of the term "MAS". ① However, the said suggestion was not wholeheartedly accepted, since many noted that the said notification is not a prerequisite for the conclusion and/or the entry into force of a MAS, according to the provisions of the said DSU Article; as will be indicated in the following Section, it is rather the omission of such a notification that may lead to a violation of DSU Article 3. 6. ②

Notably, the later trends of state practice added more complexity to the issue of MAS' definition. The more *de facto*, unregulated by the DSU and unexpectedly introduced to the WTO dispute settlement system interim agreements were concluded, ③ the more complex the approach of MAS' definition became. Precisely, instead of concluding the traditional form of MAS, which implies a prior notification to the DSB and the relevant Councils and Committees, States have in certain cases chosen to conclude Memoranda of Understanding (hereinafter "MoU"), the latter being a first step towards the final conclusion of MAS. On such occasions, MoU would eventually be notified in accordance with DSU

---

① Wolfgang Alschner, *Amicable Settlements of WTO Disputes: Bilateral Solutions in a Multilateral System*, 13 World Trade Rev. 81 (2014).

② Appellate Body Report, *European Communities-Regime for the Importation, Sale and Distribution of Bananas-Second Recourse to Article* 21. 5 *of the DSU by Ecuador*, WTO Doc. WT/DS27/AB/RW2/ECU (adopted Dec. 11, 2008), para. 222.

③ Wolfgang Alschner, *Amicable Settlements of WTO Disputes: Bilateral Solutions in a Multilateral System*, 13 World Trade Rev. 72 (2014).

Article 3.6, if/when they ever turned into a *strictosensu* MAS. Additionally, other forms of *sui generis* agreements have been also preferred to the traditional form of MAS by WTO members amicably settling disputes. ①

Such agreements highlight a blank spot within the WTO dispute settlement system, since it is quite likely that-pursuant to their conclusion-an actual MAS will not be eventually concluded. Even when the provisions of such alternative agreements are actually implemented, the formal subsequent conclusion (and proper communication) of MAS is not certain. As a result, these disputes are considered as pending, although they may be deemed as solved by the formerly disputant parties, whereas the terms of these disputes' resolutions remain unknown to other WTO Members. Hence, on such occasions, the rest of the WTO Members cannot raise their putative concerns on the terms of the said MoU or *sui generis* agreements and cannot verify their compatibility with the covered agreements. It has, thus, been argued that an important step in addressing this "*lacuna*" of the DSU, which leaves MoU and *sui generis* agreements unregulated, will be the insertion of a two-step process, according to which such interim agreements will entail the obligation of their notification on one hand, and the compulsory notification of the final MAS after the interim agreement's implementation on the other. ②

The irregularity described above certainly raises the question of whether these interim agreements fall within the ambit of MAS. To this question, the answer must be negative, as the term "MAS" must be interpreted narrowly. The said

① Joint Communication from Brazil and the United States, *United States-Subsidies on Upland Cotton*, WTO Doc. WT/DS267/45 (Aug. 31, 2010); *Communication from Brazil*, *Colombia*, *Costa Rica*, *Ecuador*, *European Union*, *Guatemala*, *Honduras*, *Mexico*, *Nicaragua*, *Panama*, *Peru*, *and the Bolivarian Republic of Venezuela*, *Geneva Agreement on Bananas*, WTO Doc. WT/L/784 (Dec. 15, 2009).

② Wolfgang Alschner, *Amicable Settlements of WTO Disputes: Bilateral Solutions in a Multilateral System*, 13 World Trade Rev. 86 (2014).

negative answer does not solely follow from the interpretation of the third sentence of DSU Article 3. 7, based on its context, as the customary rule① enshrined in VCLT② Article 31. 1 suggests,③ but is also the response given by the WTO dispute settlement fora themselves. Indeed, the said answer has been already reaffirmed by the panel and the Appellate Body, when they were asked to clarify the nature of the European Communities-United States, Ecuador agreement. ④The said fora clarified that for the conception of an agreement as a MAS, the very agreement must be the actual solution to the dispute and not its declaration, introducing an objective criterion, which directly precludes the classification of interim agreements as MAS. ⑤

The term "MAS" is, thus, used to define agreements, which settle differences between WTO members effectively. ⑥ Hence, agreements that constitute early-stage understandings for the subsequent conclusion of *strictosensu* MAS are not themselves MAS. ⑦ Nor are the settlement agreements, through

---

① Anthony Aust, Modern Treaty Law and Practice 12 – 13 (2nd ed. 2007).

② Vienna Convention on the Law of Treaties, May 23, 1969, 1155 UNTS 331.

③ Alberto Alvarez-Jiménez, *Mutually Agreed Solutions under the WTO Dispute Settlement Understanding: An Analytical Framework after the Softwood Lumber Arbitration*, 10 World Trade Rev. 347 – 348 (2011).

④ Notification of Mutually Agreed Solution, *European Communities-Regime for the Importation, Sale and Distribution of Bananas*, WTO Doc. WT/DS27/58 (July 2, 2001).

⑤ Panel Report, *European Communities-Regime for the Importation, Sale and Distribution of Bananas, Second Recourse to Article* 21. 5 *of the DSU by Ecuador*, WTO Doc. WT/DS27/RW2/ECU, (adopted April 7 2008), para. 7. 107; Appellate Body Report, *European Communities-Regime for the Importation, Sale and Distribution of Bananas, Second Recourse to Article* 21. 5 *of the DSU by Ecuador*, WTO Doc. WT/DS27/AB/RW2/ECU-WT/DS27/AB/RW/USA paras. 214 – 219, (adopted Nov. 26, 2008).

⑥ Alberto Alvarez-Jiménez, *Mutually Agreed Solutions under the WTO Dispute Settlement Understanding: An Analytical Framework after the Softwood Lumber Arbitration*, 10 World Trade Rev. 348 (2011).

⑦ Appellate Body Report, *European Communities — Regime for the Importation, Sale and Distribution of Bananas*, WTO Doc. WT/DS27/AB/RW2/ECU-WT/DS27/AB/RW/USA, paras. 217 – 220 (adopted Nov. 26, 2008).

which the disputant parties finally agree to a friendly settlement of a case concerning violations of several legal provisions (among which WTO legal provisions are included), which was brought before an extra-WTO competent judicial body seeking resolution. ①

2.3 The Multilateral Elements of MAS

The DSU sets two requirements regarding the content of MAS and their notification. The said two requirements have been also described as their "multilateral elements". ② These two elements are as follows:

Firstly, according to DSU Article 3.5, MAS "shall be consistent with the WTO covered agreements and shall not nullify or impair benefits accruing to any Member under those agreements, nor impede the attainment of any objective of those agreements". ③

Secondly, according to DSU Article 3.6, MAS "shall be notified to the DSB and the relevant Councils and Committees, where any Member may raise any point relating thereto". ④

Pursuant to the statement of the abovementioned two conditions, as set out in the DSU, what should be considered is, whether they are of an "absolute nature", namely whether the partial inconsistency with (one of) them, renders the conducted agreement void-or whether it at least divests the agreement of its characterization as a MAS. It has been argued, that a partial inconsistency of a

---

① Alberto Alvarez-Jiménez, *Mutually Agreed Solutions under the WTO Dispute Settlement Understanding: An Analytical Framework after the Softwood Lumber Arbitration*, 10 World Trade Rev. 347-348 (2011).

② Panel Report, *European Communities-Regime for the Importation, Sale and Distribution of Bananas*, Second Recourse to Art. 21.5 of the DSU by Ecuador, WTO Doc WT/DS27/RW2/ECU, para. 7.102 (adopted Oct. 7, 2008).

③ Marrakesh Agreement Establishing the World Trade Organization, Apr. 15, 1994, 1867 UNTS 3, annex 2 (Understanding on Rules and Procedures Governing the Settlement of Disputes, Marrakesh Agreement Establishing the World Trade Organization), Art. 3.5.

④ Ibid., at Art. 3.6.

MAS at stake with the covered agreements should not immediately lead to the conclusion that the MAS is wholly invalid, provided that some of its clauses stand valid, effective in resolving the dispute and-hence-applicable. ①

Furthermore, with regard to the second element, namely the compulsory notification of MAS, it should be noted that a thorough analysis of the issue took place in *European Communities-Bananas* Ⅲ. The European Communities (Respondent in the dispute) informed the DSB that an agreement with Ecuador and the United States had been achieved. ② Subsequently, the complainants argued that the necessary notification of DSU Article 3.6 had not been preceded. The panel placed particular emphasis on the importance of the MAS' notification, in accordance with DSU Article 3.6, as this notification safeguards the opportunity of any Contracting Party to raise its concerns. Subsequently, the Appellate Body noted that primary emphasis should be placed on the substance of the agreement and the expressed intention of the parties thereto and, secondarily, on their subsequent statements. ③ It seems that the Appellate Body avoided encouraging the subsequent arbitrary sabotage of the MAS by its parties. It also seems quite probable, that the Appellate Body would not have followed the same line, if a third party had contested that certain interests had been plagued due to lack of proper notification. At any rate, the Appellate Body suggested that skipping the notification provided for in DSU Article 3.6 does not *per se* deprive the conducted agreement of its classification as a MAS.

---

① Alberto Alvarez-Jiménez, *Mutually Agreed Solutions under the WTO Dispute Settlement Understanding: An Analytical Framework after the Softwood Lumber Arbitration*, 10 World Trade Rev. 352 (2011).

② Notification of Mutually Agreed Solution between the European Communities and the United States and Ecuador, WTO Doc. WT/DS27/58 (July 2, 2001).

③ Appellate Body Report, *European Communities — Regime for the Importation, Sale and Distribution of Bananas*, WTO Doc. WT/DS27/AB/RW2/ECU-WT/DS27/AB/RW/USA, para. 222 (adopted Nov. 26, 2008).

As a result, the conclusion to be reached is that the conditions imposed under the DSU with respect to MAS are not of an "absolute nature" and that deviations are-under certain circumstances-permitted.

2.4 The Legal Status and Binding Effect of MAS

Surprising though it may seem, the classification of MAS as part of the WTO law has been questioned. On this matter, it should be emphasized that three arguments① support the indisputable abolition of the aforementioned speculation. Initially, it has been noted that MAS are provided for by a specific covered agreement, namely the DSU. Secondly, they are inextricably linked to WTO rights and obligations, as they are concluded by WTO members to resolve disputes over such rights and obligations. Lastly, the fact that MAS are part of WTO law is also evinced by their mandatory alignment with the covered agreements.② This very last observation is the greatest opposition to those who would try to designate MAS as *leges speciales*. Hence, even though MAS are indeed not part of the WTO covered agreements, they should be deemed as comprised within the wider WTO legal framework.③

Lastly, reference should be had to the silence of the DSU on the binding or non-binding effect of MAS. This silence could be seen as a deliberate flexibility, allowing the MAS parties at stake to decide themselves on the (non) elasticity of the provisions of the concluded MAS.④ Indeed, it has been noted that MAS, which include provisions encouraging their parties to commit or abstain from a particular act and, which, thus, do not include a "functional language delimiting

---

① Alberto Alvarez-Jiménez, *Mutually Agreed Solutions under the WTO Dispute Settlement Understanding: An Analytical Framework after the Softwood Lumber Arbitration*, 10 World Trade Rev. 353 (2011).

② Ibid.

③ Ibid.

④ Ibid., at 348.

the extent of the obligation", [1] are not binding. Adversely, parties may choose to impose a binding force on the MAS to be concluded. [2] Hence, it would be rather paradoxical to *a priori* conclude that MAS are binding nor non-binding. [3] Conversely, their binding effect should be rather determined on a *de facto* basis. And even though the existing case-law on the matter does not seem to have cleared the landscape on MAS' binding effect, [4] having only confirmed the possibility of MAS creating rights and obligations, [5] as well as having only acknowledged that MAS entail at least procedural obligations, [6] practice under the WTO seems to indicate a strong preference of WTO Members for the conclusion of binding MAS. [7]

As the analysis presented above evinces, the friendly settlement of disputes within the WTO has undergone a gradual legalization process throughout the years. Furthermore, the term "MAS" should be used restrictively to describe agreements, which settle differences between WTO members altogether. In this sense, MoU and interim *sui generis* agreements should not be seen as falling

---

① Panel Report, *European Economic Community-Imposition of Anti-Dumping Duties on Imports of Cotton Yarn from Brazil*, WTO Doc. BISD 42S/17, para. 582 (adopted Oct. 30, 1995).

② MAS, *India-Measures Affecting the Automotive Sector*, WTO Doc WT/DS96/8 (Nov. 25, 1997).

③ Alberto Alvarez-Jiménez, *Mutually Agreed Solutions under the WTO Dispute Settlement Understanding: An Analytical Framework after the Softwood Lumber Arbitration*, 10 World Trade Rev. 348 (2011).

④ Panel Report, *India-Measures Affecting the Automotive Sector*, WTO Doc. WT/DS146/R-WT/DS175/R, para. 7. 115 (adopted Dec. 21, 2001). India's appeal against this report was subsequently withdrawn.

⑤ Notification of Mutually Agreed Solution, *European Communities — Regime for the Importation, Sale and Distribution of Bananas*, WTO Doc. WT/DS27/58, para. G (July 2, 2001); Understanding on Bananas between Ecuador and the European Communities, *European Communities — Regime for the Importation, Sale and Distribution of Bananas*, WTO Doc. WT/DS27/60, para. G (July 9, 2001).

⑥ Alberto Alvarez-Jiménez, *Mutually Agreed Solutions under the WTO Dispute Settlement Understanding: An Analytical Framework after the Softwood Lumber Arbitration*, 10 World Trade Rev. 349 (2011).

⑦ Ibid.

within the ambit of MAS. Most importantly, as was indicated above, MAS can be concluded prior to or after the initiation of proceedings before the panels or the Appellate Body or while the dispute is still pending before the latter and even before or after the issuance of a decision by the DSB. In this sense, MAS constitute a realistic means of even resolving disputes that-at least for the time being-cannot be brought before the Appellate Body, or are still pending before the latter. Furthermore, although the compatibility of MAS with the covered agreements and their communication to the DSB and the relevant Councils and Committees is explicitly required by the DSU, a deviation of some of a MAS' provisions with the WTO legal framework does not render the whole MAS void, whereas the lack of proper notification is not a prerequisite for the conclusion and/or the entry into force of a MAS. Finally, as was underlined above, MAS are comprised within the wider WTO legal framework, while the DSU allows its parties to decide on the binding or non-binding effect of the MAS at stake.

3. The Legitimacy of MAS as a Means of Dispute Settlement

Having already analyzed, how MAS function within the WTO dispute settlement system, the present paper will proceed to a further assessment of their legitimacy as a means of dispute settlement, especially against the background of the current malfunction of the Appellate Body and the inefficiency of the appellate review of decisions. For the purposes of this Section, MAS will be deemed as a legitimate means of dispute settlement, if-aside from being capable of overcoming the hurdle posed to dispute settlement by the Appellate Body crisis-they provide the parties with an enforceable solution, compatible with the legal framework of the WTO.

These remarks having been made, this Section will enumerate the main points of criticism that have been elaborated throughout the years with regard to MAS.

Most of all, it will further attempt to combat these points of criticism, on the basis of relevant instances of existing arbitral and academic practice, so as to evaluate whether MAS are indeed capable of maneuvering around the skepticism arisen and whether they can indeed be seen as a legitimate means of disputes' resolution. Precisely, this Section will explore, whether MAS is-from a legal point of view-a means of oppression of the financially weaker States, whether their enforcement can be demanded under the supervision of a WTO forum and finally whether they actually constitute a lawful means of WTO dispute resolution, namely a means of solving disputes in accordance with the applicable law, i. e. the covered agreements.

3.1 Oppression of Financially Weaker Contracting Parties

From time to time, concerns have been raised as to the danger imposed on financially weaker Members through MAS. Precisely, it has been held that MAS are a way of oppression of the said WTO Members,① which (fearing what the WTO's judicial bodies might adjudicate or even doubt the compliance of the financially stronger party with the decision to be issued) will compromise easily with whatever the wealthier party is willing to offer. It is true that the aforementioned speculations are not unfounded. Indeed, if one considers firstly that in case the dispute is settled by a WTO forum, a certain period of time will elapse for the procedures envisaged in DSU Article 22. 2 to take place, and secondly that the WTO legal framework does not-at least according to the

① Johan Lindeque & Steven McGuire, *The United States and Trade Disputes in the World Trade Organization: Hegemony Constrained or Confirmed?*, 47 Management Int'l Rev. 725, 729, 734 – 735 (2007); Daya Shanker, *Argentina-US Mutually Agreed Solution, Economic Crisis in Argentina and Failure of the WTO Dispute Settlement System*, 44 Idea: J. of L. & Technology 565, 571 566 (2004); Wolfgang Alschner, *Amicable Settlements of WTO Disputes: Bilateral Solutions in a Multilateral System*, 13 World Trade Rev. 75 (2014).

prevailing view[①]-provide retrospective remedies, which would effectively relieve the financially weaker parties during the whole period, that the wealthier disputant party did not comply with its obligations, then the insecurity of the financially weaker disputant parties seems quite understandable.

However, it should be highlighted that respecting the sovereignty of States[②] within the framework of international law entails respecting their choices, whichever these may be. Hence, even if a State's decision to "compromise" may be perceived by some as a form of oppression exercised by the financially stronger to the finically weaker party to the MAS reached, merely due to the fact that it might run counter to some of the latter party's interests, it should be recalled that no State needs paternalism or guidance as to its choices. After all, sacrificing the satisfaction of certain interests with a view to the satisfaction of more crucial ones' is the outcome of almost every negotiation. Thus, MAS should not be *a priori* condemned as pandering States' inequality and suasion among States. It should be rather seen as entailing the dangers inherent in any inter-State negotiations.

3.2 The Enforcement of MAS' Provisions

Furthermore, it has been argued that the enforcement of MAS' provisions, namely the assurance of the implementation of their provisions in cases that the latter are not voluntarily implemented by one of the parties amicably settling a dispute, cannot be effectively ensured. This point of view underlines that MAS actually constitute means of figuratively solving disputes; virtual solutions, which-regardless of the legality of their provisions-will eventually not be implemented. It is this point of criticism that attention will be now turned to. It shall be, however, at this point noted that any discussion regarding MAS' enforcement requires the

① Alberto Alvarez-Jiménez, *Mutually Agreed Solutions under the WTO Dispute Settlement Understanding: An Analytical Framework after the Softwood Lumber Arbitration*, 10 World Trade Rev. 372 (2011).

② James R. Crawford, Brownlie's Principles of Public International Law 384, 447 (8th ed. 2012).

existence of a binding MAS. Indeed, if a non-binding MAS is at stake, then such discussions could only revolve around procedural obligations,[①] stemming from its conclusion.

Undoubtedly, the panels' and the Appellate Body's findings, once adopted by the DSB, create an obligation of bringing the measure(s) recognized as incompatible with the covered agreements to compliance with the latter.[②] Contrary to the possibilities offered by the DSU in cases of non-executed decisions,[③] the WTO legal framework does not provide for such an assurance, in cases of non-voluntary implementation of MAS' provisions by the parties thereto. It at least does not provide for such a compulsory enforcement explicitly. Thus, a debate as to whether the WTO dispute settlement system has jurisdiction to resolve disputes emerging from MAS-or the lack of the latter's provisions' implementation-has arisen. The subject-matter of this debate is closely linked to the enforceability of MAS, as if the jurisdiction of WTO fora over MAS-relatcd disputes is adequately contended, then disputes stemming from the violation of MAS' provisions or from the lack of MAS' provisions' implementation, will be permissibly brought before the said fora. In this sense, the acknowledgment of a breach of a MAS' provisions by means of a report, will inevitably lead the DSB to adopt the said report and the respondent Member to bring its measure(s) into conformity with the MAS. On

---

① Alberto Alvarez-Jiménez, *Mutually Agreed Solutions under the WTO Dispute Settlement Understanding: An Analytical Framework after the Softwood Lumber Arbitration*, 10 World Trade Rev. 349 (2011).

② Wolfgang Alschner, *Amicable Settlements of WTO Disputes: Bilateral Solutions in a Multilateral System*, 13 World Trade Rev. 88 (2014).

③ Marrakesh Agreement Establishing the World Trade Organization, Apr. 15, 1994, 1867 UNTS 3, annex 2 (Understanding on Rules and Procedures Governing the Settlement of Disputes, Marrakesh Agreement Establishing the World Trade Organization), Art. 21.5, 22.

such occasions, DSU Articles 21 and 22 will be accordingly applicable,① eventually ensuring the enforcement of the provisions of the MAS at stake.

According to the first view on the mentioned debate-that being Prof. Alvarez-Jiménez' view-WTO panels have jurisdiction over any dispute stemming from MAS and not just over disputes stemming from MAS, which explicitly provide for the panels' jurisdiction. This point of view is based on the teleological interpretation of DSU Articles 3. 3 and 3. 7,② as well as on jurisprudential pronouncements of several panels and of the Appellate Body, which have not rejected the WTO fora's jurisdiction over disputes arising from MAS. ③

Indeed, the line of reasoning followed by Prof. Alvarez-Jiménez, views DSU Article 3.3 as the legal basis of the said WTO fora's jurisdiction over MAS-related disputes, since it implies the existence of advantages deriving *indirectly* from the covered agreements. ④ The third paragraph of DSU Article 3. 7 is further seen as providing contextual support to the said interpretative outcome, whereas, the interpretation of the DSU in a way, which does not confer jurisdiction to the WTO dispute settlement system over its preferred way of dispute settlement, is also marked as rather absurd, since the very purpose of the dispute settlement mechanism, according to DSU Article 3.6, is to ensure a "positive solution to the dispute". ⑤

---

① Alberto Alvarez-Jiménez, *Mutually Agreed Solutions under the WTO Dispute Settlement Understanding: An Analytical Framework after the Softwood Lumber Arbitration*, 10 World Trade Rev. 359 – 360 (2011).

② Ibid., at 358.

③ Panel Report, *India — Measures Affecting the Automotive Sector*, WTO Doc. WT/DS146/RWT/DS175/R (adopted Dec. 21, 2001), paras. 7. 114 – 7. 115; Panel Report, *European Communities-Regime for the Importation, Sale and Distribution of Bananas*, Second Recourse to Art. 21. 5 of the DSU by Ecuador, WTO Doc WT/DS27/RW2/ECU, paras. 7.85 – 7.96 (adopted Oct. 7, 2008).

④ Alberto Alvarez-Jiménez, *Mutually Agreed Solutions under the WTO Dispute Settlement Understanding: An Analytical Framework after the Softwood Lumber Arbitration*, 10 World Trade Rev. 354 (2011).

⑤ Ibid., at 355.

Undoubtedly, the interpretative route presented above, reinforces the security and foreseeability of the global trading system and strengthens the central character of the WTO dispute settlement system. After all, it should be borne in mind that when the parties wanted to exclude certain disputes from the jurisdiction of the panels and the Appellate Body, they did so explicitly.① An *a contrario* and contextual interpretative argument can, thus, be raised to highlight that, since the Contracting Parties have not similarly excluded MAS-related disputes from the jurisdiction of WTO fora, the latter do enjoy it. Lastly, the WTO system's evolution and its adaptability to new challenges, that the issue concerning the enforcement of the MAS resolving the *Softwood Lumber* case brings to mind,② seems to provide additional support to the above interpretative conclusion. After all, WTO jurisdictional extensions akin to the one suggested by this side of the debate have also occurred in the past.③

Conversely, the other side of the debate, which questions the jurisdiction of WTO fora over MAS-related cases,④ points out that as the word "indirectly", spotted in DSU Article 3.3,⑤ is not included in the text of DSU Article 1.1, the jurisdiction of WTO fora seems to be limited to disputes pertinent to the WTO covered agreement.⑥ This point of view, however, overemphasizes the textual

---

① See e.g. Marrakesh Agreement Establishing the World Trade Organization, Apr. 15, 1994, 1867 UNTS 3, annex 2 (Understanding on Rules and Procedures Governing the Settlement of Disputes, Marrakesh Agreement Establishing the World Trade Organization), Art. 17.4.

② Alberto Alvarez-Jiménez, *Mutually Agreed Solutions under the WTO Dispute Settlement Understanding: An Analytical Framework after the Softwood Lumber Arbitration*, 10 World Trade Rev. 359 (2011).

③ Appellate Body, *Brazil-Export Financing Programme for Aircraft-Recourse by Canada to Article 21.5 of the DSU*, WTO Doc WT/DS46/AB/RW (adopted Aug. 4, 2000).

④ Wolfgang Alschner, *Amicable Settlements of WTO Disputes: Bilateral Solutions in a Multilateral System*, 13 World Trade Rev. 89 - 90 (2014).

⑤ Ibid., at 89.

⑥ Wolfgang Alschner, *Amicable Settlements of WTO Disputes: Bilateral Solutions in a Multilateral System*, 13 World Trade Rev. 89(2014).

interpretation of DSU Article 3.3 and neglects the adverse interpretative outcome, to which the contextual and teleological interpretation of the said provision leads. In this sense, it fails to interpret the said DSU provision in a holistic fashion.① After all, even from a textual interpretative point of view, the interpretation of DSU Article 1.1 as including the meaning of the word "indirectly" cannot be precluded, since this provision itself does not clearly preclude such an interpretation and does not include the word "directly" either.

Firstly, in an attempt to contradict the first debated side presented above, proponents of the view that WTO fora do not have jurisdiction over MAS-related disputes argue that the Appellate Body, placing particular emphasis on the intention of the parties, leaves it up to them to provide the MAS at issue with recognition of its jurisdiction to resolve future disputes.② This argument is however highly self-referential, as it does not actually contradict the opposite point of view and rather bases its validity on elements extrinsic to the legal framework regulating WTO dispute settlement and intrinsic to MAS. In other words, it seems to hold that the WTO fora do have jurisdiction over disputes stemming from a putative MAS only when its parties consent to that via a MAS provision, whereas what is unclear is whether WTO Members have already consented to WTO fora's jurisdiction over MAS-related disputes during the drafting of the DSU.

Secondly, as a criticism to the first debated side presented above, the Softwood Lumber MAS is used to emphasize that a customized transnational arbitration vehicle is in a much better position to manage specific issues than a WTO panel, underlining that the said MAS resolved 20 issues in total arising from national law,

① Appellate Body Report, *Continued Existence and Application of Zeroing Methodology*, WTO Doc. WT/DS350/AB/R, para. 268 (adopted June 2, 2009).

② Ibid., at 90.

NAFTA[①] and WTO law.[②] A counterweight to this criticism is the exclusive jurisdiction of WTO's dispute settlement mechanism over WTO-related issues and the lack of a need of a hierarchy of international courts and arbitration bodies.

Thirdly, with regard to Prof. Alschner's point, that other types of agreements, not falling within the ambit of MAS (namely MoU and other *sui generis* agreements amicably settling WTO disputes) escape the system's jurisdiction, until they transform into MAS, the only adequate response seems to be the adoption of the system of a mandatory conversion of interim agreements into MAS, as he suggested himself.[③] Finally, as far as the assumption that the Appellate Body, would much rather leave the matter to be resolved by the parties, given the sensitive issue of the implementation of the MAS's terms,[④] it can be noted that the Appellate Body should be called to fulfil its purpose as a dispute settlement forum by following the correct interpretation of the covered agreements and by avoiding denial of justice.

Inductively, as the argumentation above indicates, the WTO fora do have jurisdiction over disputes stemming from MAS and their enforcement. The following Section will explore the most serious point of criticism on MAS, namely the speculations questioning MAS' lawfulness.

3.3 The Lawfulness of MAS

To the points of criticism analyzed (and contradicted) above, the following question should be added: "*What should be the fundamental objective of the [multilateral trading] system-to solve the instant dispute (by conciliation,*

---

① North American Free Trade Agreement, Can.-Mex.-U.S., Dec. 17, 1992, 32 I.L.M. 289 (1993) [hereinafter NAFTA].

② Wolfgang Alschner, *Amicable Settlements of WTO Disputes: Bilateral Solutions in a Multilateral System*, 13 World Trade Rev. 90 (2014).

③ Ibid., at 86.

④ Ibid., at 90.

obfuscation, power-threats, or otherwise), or to promote certain longer term systemic goals such as predictability and stability of interpretations of treaty text?"[①] The quoted question, raised by Prof. Jackson, highlights yet another disadvantage of MAS, namely their potential adverse effect on the legal certainty within the WTO dispute settlement system. Precisely, the quoted question seems to be suggesting that MAS, which primarily purport to settle a dispute to the mutual satisfaction of the parties, may entail various deviations from the applicable law or flawed interpretations of treaty texts, which-however convenient for the MAS' parties at stake-are capable of eventually agitating the harmonic waters of lawfulness and foreseeability within the WTO dispute settlement system. From this point of view, MAS could be described as the ideal legal yet unlawful means of dispute settlement; their parties may end their dispute through a means, which is prescribed by the WTO legal framework and yet deviate from the applicable law by agreeing on terms, which are not (wholly) compatible with it.

Such "flawed" MAS can easily escape the collective assessment of the WTO Members, which may abstain from raising points in accordance with DSU Article 3.6, even in situations where MAS' provisions are incompatible with the covered agreements. This might be the case, either because they would like to conclude similar MAS in the future themselves, or because they want to gain the favor of the contracting parties to the MAS reached, or simply because it is not their primary concern to safeguard MAS' compliance with the covered agreements. After all, it is apparent that, if a MAS is not properly communicated and/or if the two-step system[②] regarding interim agreements is not adopted, so that the latter are mandatorily incorporated into a subsequent MAS, then third WTO Members

---

① John H. Jackson, *Dispute Settlement and the WTO: Emerging Problems*, 1 J. Int'l Econ. L. 329, at 331 (1998).

② Wolfgang Alschner, *Amicable Settlements of WTO Disputes: Bilateral Solutions in a Multilateral System*, 13 World Trade Rev. 86 (2014).

will not have the opportunity to detect such irregularities in the first place.

Against this background, the referenced question seems to be hitting MAS to their very core: the purpose of their existence, the "positive solution"[①] of disputes. This will seem quite rational, if one considers that under the WTO system, a system of reciprocal concessions, in which the breach of the contractual framework by one Member is presumed affect the rest of the Members,[②] it is not the parties amicably settling a dispute through MAS that are affected by the latter's incompatibility with the covered agreements but rather the WTO system *in globo*. Thus, if the harm done to the WTO long-term systemic goals is so major as to put the legal certainty, the foreseeability and the trustfulness of the WTO dispute settlement at stake, then any conversation on the legitimacy of MAS as a means of dispute settlement will seem inane.

Under these circumstances, the assurance of the long-term systemic objectives ofthe WTO seems to be only effectively assured through the assurance of MAS' compliance with the already stable and predictable WTO legal framework. And in turn the MAS' compliance with the covered agreements seems to be only effectively ensured through the establishment of a previous assessment of its compatibility with the covered agreements by an objective forum as a precondition for its entry into force. Hence, the search for a possible interpretation of the DSU-as it stands[③]-that allows a WTO forum to exercise jurisdiction over MAS,

① Marrakesh Agreement Establishing the World Trade Organization, Apr. 15, 1994, 1867 UNTS 3, annex 2 (Understanding on Rules and Procedures Governing the Settlement of Disputes, Marrakesh Agreement Establishing the World Trade Organization), Art. 3.7.

② Appellate Body Report, European Communities-Regime for the Importation, Sale and Distribution of Bananas, WTO Doc. WT/DS27/AB/R, paras. 136 – 138 (adopted Sept. 9, 1997).

③ For an alternative approach, which suggests a reform to the amicable dispute settlement system and the establishment of a WTO Secretariat for the assistance in the monitoring and management of the enforcement of WTO rules in disputes resolved by MAS see: Di Hao, *Compliance Problems Under WTO Disputes Settled by Mutually Agreed Solution* 49 Geo. J. Int'l Law 887, 923 – 927 (2018).

verifying the compatibility of its provisions with the covered agreements is a one-way course for the efficient answer to the question quoted above. At this point, it should be clarified that the following will focus on the search of a possibility of a WTO forum enjoying jurisdiction over MAS' assessment, however not in terms of MAS' substantial content, but solely in terms of conformity of the MAS at stake with the covered agreements; the potentially competent forum will not assess the appropriateness of the MAS, or whether it is in fact advantageous for each of the parties, or whether it would be more efficient to resolve the dispute in a different way; it will rather suffice itself in checking whether or not the agreement reached is in conformity with the covered agreements. Most of all, as the partial deviation from the covered agreements, does not *per se* render the MAS concluded void, the potentially competent forum will also assess, whether the putative deviation is determinative for the annulment of the agreement.

Pursuant to the analysis of Section 4.2 above, the assumption of the WTO dispute settlement system's jurisdiction over MAS-related disputes, will be taken as granted in the present Section as well. That being said, attention should be turned to DSU Article 2.1, which sets the role of the DSB straight, providing that "*the DSB is hereby established to administer these rules and procedures and, except as otherwise provided in a covered agreement, the consultation and dispute settlement provisions of the covered agreements*". To this end, "*the DSB shall have the authority to establish panels, [...] and authorize suspension of concessions and other obligations under the covered agreements*".[①] Hence, it would appear from the outset that the DSU does not exempt the DSB from its authority to establish panels aiming to verify the legality of the notified (according

① Marrakesh Agreement Establishing the World Trade Organization, Apr. 15, 1994, 1867 UNTS 3, annex 2 (Understanding on Rules and Procedures Governing the Settlement of Disputes, Marrakesh Agreement Establishing the World Trade Organization), Art. 2.1.

to DSU Article 3. 6) MAS. In fact, the DSB is not obstructed by any other provision of the DSU to transfer the compatibility assessment of a MAS into a panel. In this hypothetical scenario, potential claims raised by WTO Members (in line with DSU Article 3.6) regarding the MAS in question could be transmitted to the panel, which will have been established for the verification of the MAS's legality by the DSB. As one of MAS' objectives is the avoidance of long-term proceedings, the deadlines set for the assessment of the MAS and any claims should-in this scenario-be as short as possible, so that the suggested procedure will indeed be effective.

However, the fact that the panels are not already established (i. e. they are not standing bodies) and that their establishment is itself too time-consuming for the short-term demands of the contracting parties to a MAS, is definitely a strong counterpart to their effectiveness and seems to indirectly enhance Prof. Jackson's implied view that speed and longer-term systemic goals do not go hand in hand.① Thus, one would rationally wonder, whether the panels' establishment could be detoured and-consequently-whether this otherwise short process of examining the legality of MAS would be feasible by the DSB itself.

Although it has been adequately argued that the interpretation of DSU Article 23 provides a basis for the existence of DSB's jurisdiction, once a dispute regarding the compliance with a MAS arises,② it is not self-evident that the same holds true for the verification of a MAS' legality. However, DSB is established to administer the rules and procedures of WTO law. Thus, it could be rather difficult for one to uphold, that the term "administer" of DSU Article 2, broadly

---

① John H. Jackson, *Dispute Settlement and the WTO: Emerging Problems*, 1 J. Int'l Econ. L. 329, at 331 (1998).

② Alberto Alvarez-Jiménez, *Mutually Agreed Solutions under the WTO Dispute Settlement Understanding: An Analytical Framework after the Softwood Lumber Arbitration*, 10 World Trade Rev. 365 (2011).

interpreted, in the light of DSU's object and purpose, does not entail the assessment of the agreement of MAS with the rest of the rules and procedures of WTO law. The interpretation of DSU Article 2, in accordance with VCLT Article 31.1 at least does not preclude that conclusion from being drawn, whereas contextual support of the aforementioned interpretation is provided by DSU Article 3.7, which states that "[*t*] *he aim of the dispute settlement mechanism is to secure a positive solution to a dispute*". ①The determination of the solution to be found as "positive" could not be conceived as otherwise than "lawful"; for so positive a solution to be secured by the WTO dispute settlement mechanism, the prior verification of its legality by the competent WTO forum is necessary.

Meanwhile, contextual support is also provided by DSU Articles 3.5 and 3.7, which state that MAS must be in conformity with the covered agreements. It is, thus, quite paradoxical for one to accept that the WTO dispute settlement mechanism's jurisdiction to determine the legality of MAS is contrary to the provisions of the DSU, unless they manage to subvert the interpretational presumption that the provisions of a treaty are *per se* not incompatible with each other. Namely, it would seem irrational, if the DSU set legality as a prerequisite for the validity of MAS on one hand and prohibited the previous verification of their legality on the other, since the latter would be the most efficient way to achieve the aforementioned prerequisite.

Lastly, what should be underlined is that for the purpose of *ex ante* assessment of MAS by the panels or the DSB, no additional consent of the Contracting Parties is needed, since the aforementioned jurisdiction, the panels'/

---

① Marrakesh Agreement Establishing the World Trade Organization, Apr. 15, 1994, 1867 UNTS 3, annex 2 (Understanding on Rules and Procedures Governing the Settlement of Disputes, Marrakesh Agreement Establishing the World Trade Organization), Art. 3.7.

DSB's jurisdiction to affirm the compatibility of MAS' provisions with the covered agreements stems from the interpretation of the DSU, which is already binding for the Contracting Parties. After all, it should be underlined that even MAS clauses barring the initiation of panel proceedings pursuant to their conclusion, will not actually prevent the said proceedings, since the aim of such MAS clauses is simply to avert the parties from referring the dispute to the dispute settlement bodies for solution; they do not seek to exempt MAS' provisions from the assessment of their compatibility to the covered agreements.

Thus, the argumentation elaborated above leads to the conclusion that the interpretation of the DSU in accordance with the customary rules on treaty interpretation, acknowledges the jurisdiction of the WTO's dispute settlement mechanism to test the legality of MAS in advance, namely immediately after their notification and before their entry into force. Even though the approach described above could be marked as quite innovative-if not groundbreaking-or quite far-fctched instead, it is certainly in line with the WTO's constantly evolving① and flexible② system. Moreover, this approach is the only way to the assurance of the predictability and stability of interpretations of the covered agreements, as well as to the efficient answer to the question raised by Prof. Jackson. This approach is, in other words, a step forward, which must be taken for legal certainty to be ensured and for the process of MAS' legality assessment to be refined. This way, the MAS will be elevated from being a merely effective means of dispute settlement to being a lawful one, which does not only guarantee a quick, mutually favorable solution of a dispute but also the compatibility of the

① A. L. C. De Mestral & M. Auerbach-Ziogas, *A Proposal to Introduce an Advocate General's Position into WTO Dispute Settlement System*, *in* Law in The Service of Human Dignity: Essays in Honour of Florentino Feliciano 13 (Steve Charnovitze et. al. eds., 2005).

② Claus-Dieter Ehlermann, *Reflections on the Appellate Body of the WTO*, 6 J. Int'l Econ. L. 695, 701 (2003).

said solution to the legal framework of the WTO. The fact that concerns about the expanding jurisdictional ambitions and the judicial activism of the WTO dispute settlement fora are multiplying, seems to be the beginning of a different conversation.

Inductively, the argumentation raised in this Section managed to contradict the main points of criticism elaborated against MAS (namely that they foster the oppression of financially weaker parties, that enforcement of their provisions is not certain and that the lawfulness of their provisions cannot be ensured) and highlighted that the latter do constitute a legitimate means of disputes settlement within the WTO.

4. Conclusions

As the analysis of the Sections above evince, the question of whether MAS constitute an efficient means of dispute settlement, under the light of the ongoing Appellate Body crisis, which the present article purported to explore, should be answered affirmatively. Indeed, pursuant to the brief overview of the progressive evolution of the amicable settlement of disputes in the WTO and its gradual legalization, the paper proceeded to an analysis of the provisions regulating the function of MAS and of the key elements, which distinguish the latter from other agreements within the framework of the WTO dispute settlement system, which do not actually bring the dispute to an end. This analysis highlighted that, since MAS can be concluded prior to or after the initiation of proceedings before the panels or the Appellate Body or while the dispute is still pending before the latter and even before or after the issuance of a decision by the DSB, MAS constitute a realistic means of resolving disputes that-at least for the time being-cannot be brought before the Appellate Body, or are still pending before the latter. Furthermore, having noted that MAS are comprised within the wider WTO legal framework and that their binding or non-binding effect depends on the parties' will, the paper highlighted that, although the compatibility of MAS with the covered agreements and their communication to the DSB and the relevant Councils and Committees is explicitly required by the DSU, a deviation of some of a MAS' provisions with the WTO legal framework does not render the whole MAS void, whereas the lack of proper notification is not a prerequisite for the conclusion and/or the entry into force of a MAS.

Against this background, which suggests permissible derogation from the covered agreements via the conclusion of MAS, points of criticism on the legitimacy of MAS as a means of dispute settlement started seeming rational. The main points of criticism, elaborated in academic writings pertinent to the matter, highlight the potential oppression of financially weaker States through MAS, the uncertain enforcement of even binding MAS and the latter's doubtful lawfulness. The analysis of the third Section above contradicted the said criticisms and underlined that sovereign States do not need paternalism over their MAS-related moves, as well as that the enforcement of MAS can actually be ensured by the WTO fora. Most of all, the paper suggested an interpretation of the DSU that acknowledges WTO panels'/DSB's jurisdiction to assess the compatibility of MAS with the covered agreements, before their entry into force. As through this interpretation, the lawfulness of MAS is also achieved and the last point of criticism is also contradicted, the present paper is led to the conclusion that MAS constitute a legitimate means of dispute settlement, capable of effectively assisting the WTO Members, which are willing to seek an amicable end to disputes pending before the Appellate Body or disputes that would be brought before it, during these uncertain times of the ongoing crisis.

中伦杯获奖论文选登

编者按：

为进一步推进中国商事仲裁的发展，中国国际经济贸易仲裁委员会与中国人民大学法学院、中华全国律师协会、北京律师协会联合发起了“中国仲裁周”活动，“中国仲裁周”旨在打造一个全国性、国际性、开放性的仲裁宣传、交流和研讨的平台，每年举办一届。在2018年和2019年举办的“中国仲裁周”活动期间，“中国仲裁周”活动组委会分别举办了第六届和第七届“中伦杯”全国国际商事仲裁征文大赛活动，面向有志于研究国际商事仲裁理论与实践的教师、学生和实务工作者征文。

征文活动得到了广泛的欢迎和热烈的响应。经“中国仲裁周”活动组委会邀请多位国内知名专家通过公开、公平、公正的程序进行评审，第六届最终评选出30篇获奖论文，第七届评选出30篇获奖论文。获奖论文对国际商事仲裁理论与实践中存在的问题进行了翔实地解读和深度地思考，提出的意见和建议对我国商事仲裁的未来发展不乏参考和借鉴价值。

国际商事仲裁司法审查中“超裁”认定的实证研究

——基于5个最高人民法院复函样本分析

陈建华*

摘要:通过分析最高人民法院5个复函发现,中国法院对国际商事仲裁协议司法审查中“超裁”的认定存在如下问题:一是“超裁”的含义不明确;二是部分法院在国际商事仲裁“超裁”司法审查案件中未履行内部请示报告制度;三是司法审查的启动与认定的情形不统一;四是司法裁决的可分性存在争议。针对上述问题,建议采取如下措施予以解决:一是明确不予承认与执行国际商事仲裁裁决的“超裁”情形;二是严格落实内部请示报告制度;三是统一司法审查标准,确定审查仲裁标准;四是积极支持国际商事仲裁。

关键词:国际商事仲裁　司法审查　超裁

2019年4月,中共中央办公厅、国务院办公厅印发了《关于完善仲裁制度提高仲裁公信力的若干意见》,①对完善仲裁制度、提高仲裁公信力提出了明确的要求。据统计,2019年,全国253家仲裁委员会共受理传统商事仲裁案件

---

* 法学博士,湖南省郴州市中级人民法院执行局副局长。主要研究方向:司法制度。

① 中共中央办公厅、国务院办公厅《关于完善仲裁制度提高仲裁公信力的若干意见》,载《武汉仲裁》2019年第1期。

281,411件,比2018年增加93,883件,增长50%;仲裁案件标的额总计为7598亿元,比2018年增加648亿元,增长率为9.3%。[①] 这在一定程度上表明,国际商事仲裁是国际商事纠纷解决中最常用的方式之一,对于改善中国贸易投资环境、保障贸易投资活动的正常开展、促进中国对外开放和经济发展具有非常重要的作用。中国法院对于国际商事仲裁裁决的司法审查,有利于确保国际商事仲裁的公正性、权威性、公信力。在司法实践中,是否"超裁"属于人民法院对于仲裁进行司法审查的重要内容,也是人民法院司法监督仲裁的重要表现。

"超裁"在法学理论界存在较大争议,如有学者认为,"超裁"的标准产生了很多争议。[②] 在司法实务界也存在较大分歧,如有学者对司法审查"超裁"问题提出不同的看法:有的学者认为,在关于"超裁"的认定上,中国法院对仲裁庭管辖权的审查过于宽容;而有的学者则认为,"在关于超裁的认定上,中国法院对仲裁庭管辖权的审查有过于严格之嫌"。[③] 理论认识的不一致也带来司法实践的不统一。

为了完善国际商事仲裁司法审查中"超裁"的认定,笔者基于自身的理论观察和实务经验,拟就"超裁"认定的现状和问题进行分析,并为解决这些问题提出相应建议。

一、中国法院对国际商事仲裁裁决中"超裁"的认定

党的十八届四中全会明确提出,要加强和规范司法解释和案例指导,统一法律适用标准。2016年,最高人民法院周强院长在最高人民法院司法案例研究院揭牌暨"中国司法案例网"开通活动上强调,加强司法案例研究,以促进严格公正司法。[④] 为响应周强院长的这一号召,现就最高人民法院5个复函样本

---

① 参见中国国际经济贸易仲裁委员会主编:《中国国际商事仲裁年度报告(2019-2020)》,法律出版社2020年版,第8页。

② 张毅:《仲裁超裁裁决司法监督的问题研究》,西南政法大学2012年硕士学位论文,第12页。

③ 刘敬东、王路路:《"一带一路"倡议下我国对外国仲裁裁决承认与执行的实证研究》,载《法律适用》2018年第5期。

④ 2016年最高人民法院院长周强在最高人民法院司法案例研究院揭牌暨"中国司法案例网"开通活动上的重要讲话。

分析中国法院对国际商事仲裁裁决中"超裁"的认定。

(一)5 个最高人民法院复函样本

样本 1:船舶建造合同的买方西特福公司以卖方作为被申请人提起仲裁,要求返还已支付款项。西特福公司同时请求,如果两名被申请人没有返还上述款项,西特福公司有权要求中国银行按照保函返还并支付利息。最高人民法院复函[①]指出:对于该仲裁裁决,除其 A 部分第 5 项[②]因超出仲裁协议范围而不予承认和 A 部分第 6 项[③]因申请人撤回承认申请而不予审查外,其他裁决事项应予承认。关于涉案仲裁裁决是否存在超出仲裁协议范围裁决的问题,即为 A 部分第 5 项是否因超出仲裁协议范围而不应予以承认,最高人民法院指出,虽然中国银行山东分行为涉案船舶建造合同下买方预付款的返还提供还款保函,但该银行不是涉外船舶建造合同的一方当事人,也没有与合同当事人共同签订书面仲裁协议,不是涉案仲裁裁决的申请人或者被申请人。保函的权利义务关系不应作为涉案仲裁的裁决事项,伦敦仲裁庭作出的 A 部分第 5 项裁决超出了仲裁协议的范围,故该项裁决不应予以承认,但并不影响对其他可分事项裁决的承认。[④]

样本 2:最高人民法院对"济南永宁制药股份有限公司与合资公司济南——海慕法姆制药有限公司之间的租赁合同纠纷仲裁案"的复函中指出:Hemofarm DD、MAG 国际贸易公司、苏拉么媒体有限公司与济南永宁制药股份有限公司在《济南——海慕法姆制药有限公司合资合同》中约定的仲裁条款仅约束合资

① 最高人民法院《关于西特福船运公司申请承认英国伦敦仲裁庭作出的"HULL XXK06 - 039"号仲裁裁决案件请示的复函》[(2015)民四他字第 48 号],参见刘炯、汤旻利、吴慧洁:《中国法院认定外国仲裁裁决违反中国公共政策之标准及实例分析》,载锦天城律师事务所官网 2018 年 2 月 9 日,https://www.allbrightlaw.com/SH/CN/10475/b1e51fcd893a059a.aspx。

② 涉案仲裁裁决 A 部分第 5 项为"若卖方未能向买方返还该等款项,买方将有权要求中国银行山东分行支付"。

③ 涉案仲裁裁决 A 部分第 6 项为"在收到买方终止合同的通知后,卖方应毫不拖延地向买方返还全部款项 16,392,000 美元加上由此产生的利息"。

④ 参见(2015)民四他字第 48 号最高人民法院《关于西特福船运公司申请承认英国伦敦仲裁庭作出的"HULL XXK06 - 039"号仲裁裁决案件请示的复函》,载贺荣主编、最高人民法院民事审判第四庭编:《涉外商事海事审判指导》2016 年第 1 辑,人民法院出版社 2016 年版,第 257 页。

合同当事人就合资事项发生的争议，不能约束济南永宁制药股份有限公司与合资公司济南——海慕法姆制药有限公司之间的租赁合同纠纷。国际商会仲裁院在该仲裁案件中对济南永宁制药股份有限公司与合资公司济南——海慕法姆制药有限公司之间的租赁合同纠纷进行了审理和裁决，超出了合资合同约定的仲裁协议的范围。[①]

样本3：最高人民法院关于王某林申请撤销贸仲华南分会裁决的复函中认为，在该案中，吴某琛系以案涉合同有效并要求王某林支付股权转让余款为请求提起仲裁，仲裁庭有权主动对案涉合同的效力进行审查并作出认定。但是，仲裁庭在未向当事人释明合同无效的后果以及未给予当事人变更仲裁请求机会的情况下，直接对合同无效后的返还以及赔偿责任作出裁决，确实超出了当事人的请求，属于"超裁"。[②]

样本4：最高人民法院关于"香港七好（集团）有限公司申请部分撤销〔2002〕深仲裁字第641号裁决案"的请示的复函中指出，金乌公司在仲裁过程中撤回了部分反请求所直接依据的证据，但其并未表示变更其反请求事项以及具体的请求数额，仲裁庭裁决支持该部分反请求没有超出仲裁协议约定的仲裁事项的范围和金乌公司仲裁反请求的范围，不构成"超裁"。[③]

样本5：最高人民法院关于"浙江省天河房地产联合发展公司申请撤销中国经济贸易仲裁委员会上海分会仲裁裁决案"的复函中指出，该案所涉仲裁裁决书对天河公司与合资公司关于土地使用面积是80亩还是68亩的争议、我国台湾地区宁诚公司的购房款应付给谁、远湖公司的出资是否到位等问题有所论及，但并没有对这些问题作出裁决，且裁决书中明确表示我国台湾地区宁诚公司与天河公司之间的有关约定系另一法律关系，以及合资公司与远湖公司、天河公司之间的争议系另一法律关系、不属于该案仲裁的范围。因此，不能认为该案仲裁裁决超出了仲裁庭应当裁决的范围。[④]

---

① 参见（2008）民四他字第11号。

② 参见（2013）民四他字第8号。

③ 参见（2004）民四他字第26号。

④ 参见（2003）民四他字第19号。

（二）对5个最高人民法院复函样本的分析

在中国司法实践中，法院主要是根据《承认及执行外国仲裁裁决公约》（以下简称《纽约公约》）的相关规定对国际商事仲裁裁决进行司法审查。有学者统计，截至2019年2月，中国法院审理的申请承认和执行外国仲裁裁决的司法审查裁判文书共有215篇，其中以超裁拒绝或部分承认的案件共9宗。[①] 根据笔者统计分析，目前，因超裁被拒绝承认执行的仲裁裁决主要有如下3种情形：第一，裁决列明的责任主体并非仲裁协议当事人而被认定超裁；第二，仲裁裁决超出仲裁协议约定的范围；第三，仲裁裁决超出仲裁申请人请求的范围。

上述前3个最高人民法院复函样本代表了不同情形，具体而言，样本1反映的是裁决列明的责任主体并非仲裁协议当事人，而被认定超裁。样本2反映的是仲裁裁决超出仲裁协议约定的范围。样本3反映的是仲裁裁决超出仲裁申请人的请求范围。出现上述3个样本的原因主要是因为"超裁"的含义不明确。同时，导致上述3个样本的原因还有：部分法院在对国际商事仲裁进行司法审查时未履行内部请示报告制度和部分法院司法审查标准与内容不统一以及对仲裁裁决的可分性存在争议等。这3个样本所展现的认定"超裁"问题在国际商事仲裁司法审查中具有普遍性、代表性。样本4因为仲裁庭裁决支持该部分反请求没有超出仲裁协议约定的仲裁事项的范围和金乌公司仲裁反请求的范围，不构成超裁。样本5因为不能认为该案仲裁裁决超出了仲裁庭应当裁决的范围，不构成超裁。故样本4、样本5的司法审查结论是不构成"超裁"。

二、仲裁司法审查中"超裁"认定中存在的主要问题

习近平总书记在2016年召开的全国哲学社会科学工作座谈会上指出，"坚持问题导向是马克思主义的鲜明特点"。研究国际商事仲裁"超裁"现象，应先掌握当前对国际商事仲裁司法审查中"超裁"认定中存在的主要问题。总体而

① 王好：《外国仲裁裁决司法审查中"超裁"认定的实证分析》，载《法律适用》2019年第4期。

言,目前中国仲裁司法审查中“超裁”认定存在的主要问题有四个方面:一是“超裁”的含义不明确;二是部分法院在国际商事仲裁“超裁”司法审查案件中未履行内部请示报告制度;三是部分法院司法审查标准与内容不统一;四是对司法裁决的“超裁”部分与未“超裁”部分是否可分存在争议。

(一)“超裁”的含义不明确

对国际商事仲裁“超裁”进行司法审查,要准确把握“超裁”的内涵。然而,当前“超裁”的含义不够明确,理论界与实务界对该问题是仁者见仁、智者见智,莫衷一是。

从理论上看,“超裁”又称越权,是指仲裁庭超越权限作出裁决。① 对于“超裁”还有学者从广义和狭义上进行界定。狭义上的“超裁”,主要是指超越仲裁协议约定的范围和超越当事人仲裁请求的范围。广义上的“超裁”不仅包括超越仲裁协议约定的范围和超越当事人仲裁请求的范围,而且包括未适用当事人关于管辖权的约定②、仲裁庭没有适用任何国际法、仲裁庭显然漠视法律。③ 国际公约、示范法和各国法律均规定,“超裁”或越权作出裁决,是裁决被撤销或不予执行的重要理由。④ 例如,1996 年英国《仲裁法》第 103 条第 2 款⑤规定:“被寻求承认或执行裁决的一方当事人,如能证明以下情况,则裁决可被拒绝……裁决解决的并非当事人约定或交付仲裁之条款所包含的争议,或包含超出提交仲裁范围的事项的决定(第 4 款除外)。”1999 年瑞士《仲裁法》作出规定,撤销或不予执行仲裁裁决的其中一项理由是“裁决涉及的争议不属于提交仲

---

① 林一飞:《仲裁裁决抗辩的法律与实务》,武汉大学出版社 2008 年版,第 151 页。

② 这里的管辖权是指仲裁庭的管辖权。

③ 陈文君、宋连斌:《因“超裁”拒绝承认与执行仲裁裁决的案例分析》,载《北京仲裁》2006 年第 3 期。

④ 1958 年《纽约公约》作出了类似规定。

⑤ 1996 年英国《仲裁法》第 103 条第 2 款:“被寻求承认或执行裁决的一方当事人,如能证明以下情况,则裁决可被拒绝:(a) 仲裁协议的一方当事人(根据适用于他的法律)无行为能力;(b) 根据当事人选择适用于仲裁协议的法律,或未指明适用的法律时根据裁决作出地国家的法律规定,仲裁协议是无效的;(c) 其未得到委任仲裁员或进行仲裁程序的适当通知,或因他故不能陈述案件;(d) 裁决解决的并非当事人约定或交付仲裁之条款所包含的争议,或包含超出提交仲裁范围的事项的决定(第 4 款除外);(e) 仲裁庭组成或仲裁程序未依当事人的约定,或无约定而未依仲裁进行地国家的法律;(f) 仲裁裁决尚未对当事人产生约束力,或已被裁决作出地国或裁决所依据法律之国家有权机构撤销或中止。”

裁的范围或包含的裁定超过仲裁协议范围”。

从实务角度来看,不同法院对“超裁”的理解和认定也并不一致。“部分法院将纽约公约第5条第1款[①](丙)项所指的‘超裁’与该条第2款(甲)项规定的可仲裁性问题混为一谈;对将未签署仲裁协议的一方作为仲裁被申请人,并且仲裁其承担责任,有的法院认为属于超裁,有的法院则认为属于公约第5条第1款(甲)项规定的情形,还有的法院认为属于裁决尚无拘束力的情形。”[②]从实例来看,关于何为“超裁”,不同案例存在不同认定。如在“史某芸与甘肃省食品股份有限公司申请撤销仲裁裁决案”[(2016)甘01民特11号]中,兰州市中级人民法院即认为,“超裁是指仲裁裁决的事项超出了仲裁协议的范围”。不同意见则如在“常州市鑫溢铂晶大酒店有限公司、吕某刚等申请撤销仲裁裁决案”[(2014)常商仲审字第6号]中,常州市中级人民法院即指出,“超裁是指仲裁庭作出的仲裁裁决事项部分超出了其管辖权的范围,该范围不仅限于当事人提交仲裁协议的范围,还受限于当事人提请仲裁的争议范围”。

由于司法实务界对“超裁”问题的理解、解释和适用各不相同,法官在对国际商事仲裁裁决进行司法审查过程中大多通过自由裁量作出认定。这导致仲裁员对于国际商事仲裁裁决“超裁”问题“诚惶诚恐”,犹如“惊弓之鸟”,在案件审理、合议和裁决的过程中如履薄冰,出现“避裁”或者“不裁”,不仅影响迅速解决纠纷,而且也影响对当事人合法权益的有效保护。

(二)未履行内部请示报告制度

为了避免下级法院因把握不准审查国际商事仲裁案件的法律政策,而导致的司法裁判不统一的情况,保障司法审查质量,统一司法审查的标准和尺度,最

---

① Article V 1. Recognition and enforcement of the award may be refused at the request of the party against whom it is invoked, only if that party furnished to the competent authority where the recognition and enforcement is sought, proof that (a)...(e) The award... has been set aside or suspended by a competent authority of the country in which, or under the law of which, that award was made. 该条对应的中文为:“只有在请求承认和执行裁决中的被诉人向请求地管辖机关证明下列情况的时候,才可以根据被诉人的请求,拒绝承认和执行裁决:(a)……(e)仲裁(裁决)对当事人没有拘束力,或者仲裁(裁决)已经被仲裁地国或裁决据以进行的那个缔约国的指定国的管理机关撤销或命令停止执行。”

② 王好:《外国仲裁裁决司法审查中“超裁”认定的实证分析》,载《法律适用》2019年第4期。

高人民法院先后下发了《关于人民法院处理与涉外仲裁及外国仲裁事项有关问题的通知》(法发〔1995〕18 号)①、《关于人民法院撤销涉外仲裁裁决有关事项的通知》(法〔1998〕40 号)②以及《关于承认和执行外国仲裁裁决收费及审查期限问题的规定》(法释〔1998〕28 号)③3 个文件,④要求受理案件的人民法院对于涉外、涉我国港澳台地区和外国的仲裁司法审查案件,如要作出否定性结论(认定仲裁协议无效、不予承认和执行仲裁裁决、撤销仲裁裁决的),均需要逐级呈报到最高人民法院审定。

有学者提出,针对"超裁"问题不必适用内部请示报告制度。⑤ 理由在于:内部请示报告制度有违审判独立。笔者对此不敢苟同,理由在于:无论是拒绝

---

① 该通知两个条款均涉及内部请示报告制度,例如,"一、凡起诉到人民法院的涉外、涉港澳和涉台经济、海事海商纠纷案件,如果当事人在合同中订有仲裁条款或者事后达成仲裁协议,人民法院认为该仲裁条款或者仲裁协议无效、失效或者内容不明确无法执行的,在决定受理一方当事人起诉之前,必须报请本辖区所属高级人民法院进行审查;如果高级人民法院同意受理,应将其审查意见报最高人民法院。在最高人民法院未作答复前,可暂不予受理。二、凡一方当事人向人民法院申请执行我国涉外仲裁机构裁决,或者向人民法院申请承认和执行外国仲裁机构的裁决,如果人民法院认为我国涉外仲裁机构裁决具有民事诉讼法第二百六十条情形之一的,或者申请承认和执行的外国仲裁裁决不符合我国参加的国际公约的规定或者不符合互惠原则的,在裁定不予执行或者拒绝承认和执行之前,必须报请本辖区所属高级人民法院进行审查;如果高级人民法院同意不予执行或者拒绝承认和执行,应将其审查意见报最高人民法院。待最高人民法院答复后,方可裁定不予执行或者拒绝承认和执行"。其中,该通知中的第2条已被最高人民法院《关于调整司法解释等文件中引用〈中华人民共和国民事诉讼法〉条文序号的决定》(2008 年 12 月 16 日发布, 2008 年 12 月 31 日实施)调整。

② 该通知两个条款均涉及内部请示报告制度,例如,"一、凡一方当事人按照仲裁法的规定向人民法院申请撤销我国涉外仲裁裁决,如果人民法院经审查认为涉外仲裁裁决具有民事诉讼法第二百六十条第一款规定的情形之一的,在裁定撤销裁决或通知仲裁重新仲裁之前,须报请本辖区所属高级人民法院进行审查。如果高级人民法院同意撤销裁决或通知仲裁庭重新仲裁,应将其审查意见报最高人民法院。待最高人民法院答复后,方可裁定撤销裁决或通知仲裁庭重新仲裁。二、受理申请撤销裁决的人民法院如认为应予撤销裁决或通知仲裁庭重新仲裁的,应在受理申请后三十日内报其所属的高级人民法院,该高级人民法院如同意撤销裁决或通知仲裁庭重新仲裁的,应在十五日内报最高人民法院,以严格执行仲裁法第六十条的规定"。其中,该通知中的第1条已被最高人民法院《关于调整司法解释等文件中引用〈中华人民共和国民事诉讼法〉条文序号的决定》(2008 年 12 月 16 日发布, 2008 年 12 月 31 日实施)调整。

③ 该通知一个条款涉及内部请示报告制度,例如,"当事人依照纽约公约第四条规定的条件申请承认和执行外国仲裁裁决,受理申请的人民法院决定予以承认和执行的,应在受理申请之日起两个月内作出裁定,如无特殊情况,应在裁定后六个月内执行完毕;决定不予承认和执行的,须按最高人民法院法发〔1995〕18 号《关于人民法院处理与涉外仲裁及外国仲裁事项有关问题的通知》的有关规定,在受理申请之日起两个月内上报最高人民法院"。该通知已失效。

④ 涉及内部请示报告制度的 3 个文件,均为最高人民法院颁布施行的。

⑤ 王好:《外国仲裁裁决司法审查中"超裁"认定的实证分析》,载《法律适用》2019 年第 4 期。

承认和执行外国仲裁裁决，还是因部分“超裁”对仲裁予以部分承认和执行，根据最高人民法院《关于人民法院处理与涉外仲裁及外国仲裁事项有关问题的通知》，凡一方当事人向人民法院申请承认和执行外国仲裁机构的裁决，人民法院在裁定拒绝承认和执行之前，必须报请本辖区所属高级人民法院进行审查；如果高级人民法院同意拒绝承认和执行，应将其审查意见报最高人民法院；待最高人民法院答复后，方可裁定拒绝承认和执行。2017 年 12 月 26 日，最高人民法院《关于仲裁司法审查案件报核问题的有关规定》进一步明确了地方法院的报核义务，将报核要求以司法解释的形式予以确定，并将报核制度扩大适用于国内商事仲裁裁决的司法审查。既然内部请示报告制度是所有撤销或不予执行涉外仲裁裁决都需要遵守的程序，那么对于因“超裁”问题而不予承认(认可)和执行仲裁裁决或者撤销仲裁裁决的，当然也需要遵守内部请示报告制度，需要由上级人民法院乃至最高人民法院予以认定是否正确。故笔者认为，针对“超裁”问题需要适用内部请示报告制度。

相关资料显示，自从该内部请示报告制度建立以来，全国各高级人民法院向最高人民法院报请的拟否定仲裁协议和仲裁裁决效力的案件，30% ~40% 的案件未得到最高人民法院批准。加上高级人民法院不同意中级人民法院的意见未向最高人民法院请示的案件，否定仲裁协议和仲裁裁决效力的请示未被批准的比例会更高。① 然而，在拒绝承认与执行国际商事仲裁裁决的司法审查案件中，有少数法院未按照最高人民法院的内部请示报告制度的规定履行报批义务，即使在最高人民法院要求所有能够公开的裁判文书一律上网公开的情形之下，仍有少数法院出现了这种情形。②

---

① 于喜富：《国际商事仲裁市场竞争机制下国内法院对国际商事仲裁的支持》，载《东岳论丛》2014 年第 4 期。

② 如“北京恒元信业信息技术有限公司与范某龙合同纠纷案”中，申请执行人北京恒元信业信息技术有限公司于 2018 年 1 月 24 日向甘肃省定西市中级人民法院申请执行某国内仲裁裁决，定西市中级人民法院于 2018 年 2 月 9 日即以没有仲裁协议为由作出不予执行裁定。在北京恒元信业信息技术有限公司向甘肃省高级人民法院提起申诉，高级人民法院查明定西市中级人民法院未按要求报核后撤销了中级人民法院的裁定书。详情见(2018)甘执监 14 号。

(三)司法审查的启动与认定的情形不统一

在“超裁”认定上,目前存在司法审查的启动与认定的情形不统一的问题。不同法院在是否依职权启动司法审查上存在不同做法。虽然《纽约公约》第5条第1款对“超裁”进行了规定,并且认为是依当事人申请进行司法审查,而不是依职权进行司法审查,但少数法院对违反《纽约公约》第5条第1款规定的“超裁”情形是依职权进行司法审查,而非依当事人申请进行司法审查。[①] 同时,对于《纽约公约》第5条第2款规定的违反可仲裁性和公共政策情形,人民法院需要依职权积极主动进行审查,有些法院却违反《纽约公约》第5条第2款的规定,依当事人申请进行审查。同时,在仲裁实践中,“超裁”是被执行人较常援引的主张案件仲裁裁决应不予承认与执行的理由。有的法院援引《纽约公约》第5条第1款(甲)项;有的法院援引《纽约公约》第5条第1款(丙)项;有的法院则援引我国《仲裁法》不具有可仲裁性。

(四)仲裁裁决的可分性存在争议

“超裁”问题还涉及裁决的可分性,而各地法院在对裁决的可分性上存在较大分歧。2006年9月8日起施行的最高人民法院《关于适用〈中华人民共和国仲裁法〉若干问题的解释》第19条规定,当事人以仲裁裁决事项超出仲裁协议范围为由申请撤销仲裁裁决,经审查属实的,人民法院应当撤销仲裁裁决中的“超裁”部分;但“超裁”部分与其他裁决事项不可分的,人民法院应当撤销仲裁裁决。在司法实践中,不同法院对于部分“超裁”与部分不“超裁”的裁决的处理方式存在重大分歧。[②] 有的法院对“超裁”部分可与未“超裁”部分分开时,

① 最高人民法院在其就湖北省高级人民法院请示的“申请人保罗·赖因哈特公司、申请人来宝资源有限公司与被申请人湖北清河纺织股份有限公司(以下简称‘清河公司’)申请承认和执行外国仲裁裁决”所作的批复中,明确了该项规定的适用前提,即该项规定只能依当事人的申请而适用,不能由法院依职权主动援引。

② 张毅:《仲裁超裁裁决司法监督的问题研究》,西南政法大学2012年硕士学位论文,第36页。

对未"超裁"部分予以承认及执行;[①]而有的法院则不进行区分,对凡是有部分"超裁"的情形,一律不予承认及执行。[②] 通过仲裁裁决司法审查的实践可知,不同的法院在下列问题上存在分歧:一是部分"超裁"与部分不超裁能否进行区分;二是假如部分"超裁"与部分不超裁能够进行区分,未"超裁"部分能否予以承认及执行。[③] 正如实务部门的专家所认为的,"在实践中,不仅是否超裁属于司法审查中的难点,判断"超裁"部分是否可分也存在较大争议,不同的法院做法并不相同,有待进一步统一司法观点"。[④]

三、司法审查中"超裁"认定的未来路径

"徒法不足以自行。"法院对国际商事仲裁"超裁"问题进行司法审查,有赖建立一套符合中国国际商事仲裁实际情况的司法审查制度。2018 年 9 月 7 日,第十三届全国人大常委会将《仲裁法》修订列入二类立法规划。在此契机下,可以通过完善《仲裁法》来解决司法审查中"超裁"认定存在的问题,具体有如下 3 点主要对策。

(一)明确不予承认与执行国际商事仲裁裁决的"超裁"情形

"一个探索者在任何领域中的工作总是从创造该领域中的有用的语言和

---

① 在"成可化学工程和咨询公司案"中,河南新乡中级人民法院的裁定最终表述为:对国际商会仲裁院 18046/JHN/GFG 号《最终裁决书》第(414)项中"只要多氟多公司继续使用成可公司的技术,则应在接下来每个月的 23 日向成可公司支付月罚金 100,000 欧元"的部分,第(415)项"多氟多公司不得使用成可公司的技术,直到本《最终裁决书》第 414 自然段所裁决的款项全部付清为止"的裁项以及第(417)项中"此后的每月到期的罚金,也按年利率 5% 计息,利息计算至付款完成"的部分不予承认和执行。从该案裁定来看,似乎可以对同一裁项中的部分内容单独予以承认。详情见(2015)新中民三初字第 53 号。

② 在"JESSSMITH & SONSCOTTON"与"无锡市天然纺织实业有限公司等仲裁裁决申请案"中,法院认为,裁决文书已写明天然纺织公司和绿色纤维公司对于与卖家杰斯史密斯公司之间签订的、编号为 PME-10032 的合同的履行承担共同连带责任,裁决主文中亦通篇使用"买方"这个称谓通常是指天然纺织公司和绿色纤维公司,但对于这两家公司承担的责任没有明确区分,因此法院对于仲裁庭有权裁决部分和"超裁"部分亦无法区分,故对于无法区分的该涉案仲裁裁决应全部不予承认和执行。从这个案件来看,最高人民法院并未将裁决主文中未超裁的部分单独予以承认,而是认定裁决不可分。详情见(2013)锡商外仲审字第 0007 号。

③ 王好:《外国仲裁裁决司法审查中"超裁"认定的实证分析》,载《法律适用》2019 年第 4 期。

④ 同上。

概念开始的。"[①]在众说纷纭的背景之下,科学界定"超裁"是十分必要的。面对"超裁"定义模糊的情况,我们非常有必要明确不予承认与执行国际商事仲裁裁决的"超裁"情形。在笔者看来,不予承认与执行国际商事仲裁裁决的"超裁"情形就是"超裁"的含义。根据《纽约公约》和《仲裁法》的规定,如下3种情形是属于国际商事仲裁裁决上的"超裁"情形:

第一种情形,是指仲裁裁决超出仲裁协议的范围。有学者对"超裁"大数据进行分析,发现在适用《纽约公约》第5条第1款的10件案例中,8件案例由于仲裁裁决超出了仲裁协议的范围而被拒绝承认和执行。[②]《纽约公约》第5条第1款(甲)项明确规定了可以拒绝承认和执行外国仲裁裁决的两种情况,即当事人无行为能力,或者仲裁协议无效。当事人无行为能力的直接后果,往往是不存在有效的仲裁协议,在实践中,通常将《纽约公约》第5条第1款(甲)项总结为不存在有效的仲裁协议。[③] 意思自治是仲裁制度存在的前提与基础。法院对于国际商事仲裁裁决是否承认与执行,都是基于对当事人处分权利的尊重与支持。换言之,国际商事仲裁裁决是否得到中国法院的承认与执行,往往要判断仲裁裁决是否超出了双方当事人约定交付仲裁解决的事项范围。一旦超出了仲裁协议约定范围(一般情况下,此类仲裁协议会被裁定无效),或者当事人之间未能就仲裁协议达成一致(实质上等同于无有效的仲裁协议),因为仲裁协议无效导致依据该无效仲裁协议所作出的国际商事仲裁裁决得不到法院的承认与执行。

第二种情形,就是仲裁裁决超出仲裁请求范围。根据有学者对"超裁"大数据分析,在适用《纽约公约》第5条第1款(丙)项的10件案例中,2件案例是由于超出申请人提出的仲裁请求范围。[④]《纽约公约》第5条第1款(丙)项明确规定了,裁决涉及仲裁协议所没有提到的,或者不包括在仲裁协议规定之内

---

① [美]E.霍贝尔:《原始人的法》,严存生等译,贵州人民出版社1992年版,第17页。

② 杜越、贡正:《近20年194个案例!大数据分析我国法院对外国仲裁裁决的承认和执行情况》,载微信公众号"国际贸易与金融法律研究"2020年7月30日,http://www.deheng.com.cn/about/info/19115。

③ 同上。

④ 同上。

的争执;或者裁决内含有对仲裁协议范围以外事项的决定时,法院可以在作为裁决执行对象的当事人提出证明的时候拒绝承认和执行该裁决。换言之,《纽约公约》第5条第1款(丙)项允许缔约方管辖机关在裁决含有"对提交仲裁协议范围以外"事项时,拒绝或部分拒绝承认与执行仲裁裁决。从民事诉讼法原理上看,当事人具有自由处分权。根据这点,人民法院在裁判案件的时候,实行"不告不理",审理范围仅限于原告的诉讼请求。同样,在国际商事仲裁司法审查实践中,法院需要审理当事人之间是否存在有效的仲裁协议、仲裁庭的审理范围是否超出申请方申请仲裁的范围。曾经出现一起被申请人以仲裁裁决超出申请人请求范围进行抗辩并且抗辩成功的案例。申请人丸万株式会社向中国法院申请承认和执行根据日本商事仲裁协议作出的仲裁裁决,该案仲裁裁决书因其内容超出仲裁请求的范围而不被承认和执行。①

第三种情形,是仲裁事项不具有可仲裁性。有专家指出,除超出仲裁协议和仲裁请求的范围外,"超裁"还包括审查仲裁事项是否具有可仲裁性。② 根据《纽约公约》第5条第2款第1项的规定,若仲裁事项不具有可仲裁性,法院可以拒绝承认与执行仲裁裁决。从国内仲裁司法审查相关规定来看,"超裁"还包括审查仲裁事项不具有可仲裁性。《仲裁法》将裁决事项不具有可仲裁性进行了规定。《仲裁法》第58条③规定的撤销仲裁裁决的事由中,将"裁决的事项

---

① 被申请人北京德霖高尔夫体育发展有限公司提出:"申请人提出仲裁申请时的第2项仲裁请求是:自2010年12月28日起,申请人对于由销售代理合同产生的任何债务和负债,均不承担任何责任。该项仲裁请求不涉及对销售代理合同效力的评价,也不涉及被申请人在销售代理合同项下的债务承担问题。但是仲裁裁决相应的裁决内容是:2009销售代理合同已经终止,申请人和被申请人均不再负有2009销售代理合同项下的任何后续义务。申请人并没有请求解除销售代理合同或确认该合同的状态,但仲裁庭却裁决该协议'已经终止'。显然,仲裁裁决内容已经超出了申请人仲裁申请的范围,其所裁并非申请人所请。"详情见(2013)二中民特字第12593号。

② 狄建庆、姚强、王丽平:《国际商事仲裁超裁的司法认定》,载《人民司法(案例)》2016年第20期。

③ 《仲裁法》第58条规定:"当事人提出证据证明裁决有下列情形之一的,可以向仲裁委员会所在地的中级人民法院申请撤销裁决:(一)没有仲裁协议的;(二)裁决的事项不属于仲裁协议的范围或者仲裁委员会无权仲裁的;(三)仲裁庭的组成或者仲裁的程序违反法定程序的;(四)裁决所根据的证据是伪造的;(五)对方当事人隐瞒了足以影响公正裁决的证据的;(六)仲裁员在仲裁该案时有索贿受贿,徇私舞弊,枉法裁决行为的。人民法院经组成合议庭审查核实裁决有前款规定情形之一的,应当裁定撤销。人民法院认定该裁决违背社会公共利益的,应当裁定撤销。"

不属于仲裁协议的范围”与“仲裁委员会无权仲裁”进行了规定。而“仲裁委员会无权仲裁”的其中一个情形是争议事项不具有可仲裁性。《仲裁法》在不予执行仲裁裁决的规定中,作出了上述同样的规定。从国际商事仲裁裁决的实践上来看,正如前面所列举的实例,的确存在“超裁”还包括审查仲裁事项不具有可仲裁性的情形。

综合上述分析,笔者建议,把国际商事仲裁中的“超裁”界定为:仲裁裁决超出仲裁协议的范围或超越仲裁请求的范围,或所审查事项不具有可仲裁性。《纽约公约》是规范承认与执行外国仲裁裁决的公约。有专家对大数据下不予承认和执行外国仲裁裁决的7类理由进行分析后发现,“超裁”是其中一类重要理由。① 换言之,只要国际商事仲裁裁决“超裁”,将会导致仲裁裁决不予承认和执行。据此,建议在《仲裁法》相应条款中明确对“超裁”作出界定。具体而言,可在《仲裁法》新增一条“不予承认和执行外国仲裁裁决的三种情形”,即为“约定的仲裁事项超出法律规定的仲裁范围的和超越当事人仲裁请求的范围以及审查仲裁事项不具有可仲裁性”。同时,为了确保中国法律规定的一致性,对于“超裁”相关的法律法规与司法解释的内容也应予以修正,规定上述内容。

(二)严格落实内部请示报告制度,统一司法审查标准

实际上,学界和实务界专家都对内部请示报告制度提出了质疑。譬如,有学者认为,内部请示报告制度与司法审查“一裁终局”的原则相悖,是一种司法审判制度的倒退现象,故应取消该制度。② 又如,有实务部门的专家指出了内部请示报告制度的缺陷,认为内部请示报告制度违反审判独立原则、不符合诉讼原理、与正在进行的司法改革方向相悖。③ 尽管存在上述问题,并且有专家

---

① 杜越、贡正:《近20年194个案例!大数据分析我国法院对外国仲裁裁决的承认和执行情况》,载微信公众号“国际贸易与金融法律研究”2020年7月30日,http://www.deheng.com.cn/about/info/19115。

② 刘想树:《中国涉外仲裁裁决制度与学理研究》,法律出版社2001年版,第239~240页。

③ 朱科:《中国国际商事仲裁司法审查制度完善研究》,法律出版社2018年版,第288~289页。

针对上述问题提出了建立有限上诉制度的建议,[①]笔者依然认为,在审查“超裁”问题上,各级法院需要严格落实内部请示报告制度。这主要是基于以下理由:

一是有利于统一司法审查标准。“没有据以遵循的规则,任何法官都不应当拥有裁判的权力,否则,诉讼当事人将受制于他的反复无常。”[②]在《仲裁法》实施之后,由于全国各地法官对国际商事仲裁案件的司法审查的业务能力和水平参差不齐,一些中级人民法院在审查国际商事仲裁案件时,出现把握政策不准的情况。为了统一国际商事仲裁司法审查的标准和尺度,最高人民法院先后下发了《关于人民法院处理与涉外仲裁及外国仲裁事项有关问题的通知》(法发〔1995〕18 号)、《关于人民法院撤销涉外仲裁裁决有关事项的通知》(法〔1998〕40 号)及《关于承认和执行外国仲裁裁决收费及审查期限问题的规定》(法释〔1998〕28 号),上述 3 个文件要求下级法院对于不予承认和执行的国际商事仲裁裁决案件,必须逐级呈报最高人民法院审查。正如有专家指出,“内部请示报告制度在实践中起到了非常重要的积极效果,大量地方法院拟拒绝承认和执行的案件通过报核程序得到纠正,最高人民法院也通过公开复函的方式表明中国法院对待仲裁的支持态度,以司法指导的方式统一司法尺度”。[③]

二是内部请示报告制度运行良好。中国 20 多年内部请示报告制度的实践证明,内部请示报告制度确保了仲裁司法审查案件质量,有利于提高基层法官的办案能力和水平,维护了中国司法审查的权威和司法公信力,彰显中国对《纽约公约》的高度重视,得到了国内外仲裁界的高度好评。倘若不存在内部请示报告制度,将会影响司法的统一性和国际商事仲裁司法审查案件的质量。

总之,在国际商事仲裁裁决的“超裁”认定上,内部请示报告制度有利于统一司法审查的标准,因此有必要继续坚持这一制度。具体而言,凡属于一方当事人向人民法院申请和承认国际商事仲裁裁决,人民法院在作出拒绝承认和执行裁定之前,必须要呈报所属的省高级人民法院进行审查,如果省高级人民法

---

① 朱科:《国际商事仲裁司法审查案件内部请示报告制度的转型》,载《法学杂志》2017 年第 6 期。

② [美]史蒂文 · 苏本等:《美国民事诉讼的真谛——从历史、文化、实务的视角》,蔡彦敏等译,法律出版社 2002 年版,第 60 页。

③ 王好:《外国仲裁裁决司法审查中“超裁”认定的实证分析》,载《法律适用》2019 年第 4 期。

院同意拒绝承认和执行,应当将审查意见呈报最高人民法院,等候最高人民法院答复之后,作出拒绝承认和执行裁定的人民法院方可裁定拒绝承认和执行。当然,倘若人民法院一开始就对国际商事仲裁裁决作出承认和执行裁定,也即不是否认国际商事仲裁裁决的裁定,不需要向上级法院和最高人民法院进行呈报。由于内部请示报告制度属于内部问题,不需要在《仲裁法》新修正的时候有所体现。

同时,针对国际商事仲裁裁决是否可分的问题。在笔者看来,部分"超裁"与部分不超裁共同组成的裁决,对于"超裁"部分,可以拒绝承认与执行;对于不"超裁"的部分,可以予以承认与执行。这一点也是属于人民法院对国际商事仲裁裁决进行司法审查的内部问题,不需要在《仲裁法》新修正的时候有所体现。

(三)确定审查仲裁标准,积极支持国际商事仲裁

正如刘敬东教授所言,目前中国法院对于国际商事仲裁"超裁"的司法审查过于严格。尤其是"对仲裁庭管辖权范围的审查,由于涉及到对仲裁庭裁决实质内容的审查,从而极易侵犯仲裁庭的自裁管辖权"。① 当前,对于国际商事仲裁司法审查标准主要有两种:第一种是诉讼标准,也即对仲裁全面审查;第二种是仲裁标准,也即仅审查仲裁程序。究竟是坚持诉讼标准还是仲裁标准,存在较大分歧。在司法实务界,一些法官认为既然案件到了法院,就应当按照诉讼标准来审查与处理,自然应根据诉讼标准来审查仲裁案件。在笔者看来,选择仲裁标准是可行的,具体理由如下:

一是尊重当事人意思自治的需要。众所周知,当事人意思自治是仲裁的灵魂。一旦选择仲裁,意味着当事人排除法院管辖,不愿意走诉讼救济之路。

二是有利于缓解法院案多人少矛盾。"支持仲裁的正当性并非完全取决于逻辑,更不是因为仲裁绝对不会损害程序正义或实体正义,支持仲裁来源于人们对多元争端解决机制的理性认识。"②近年来,中国法院案多人少矛盾日益

---

① 刘敬东、王路路:《"一带一路"倡议下我国对外国仲裁裁决承认与执行的实证研究》,载《法律适用》2018年第5期。

② 宋连斌:《理念走向规则:仲裁法修订应注意的几个问题》,载《北京仲裁》2004年第2期。

突出,尤其是在员额制改革背景之下,法官人数变少,然而案件数量却不断增长,从而导致案多人少矛盾日益突出。根据有关报道,全国法院受理的案件数从 1978 年的 61 万件增加到 2015 年的 1952 万件,是 1978 年的 32 倍。而法官人数从 1978 年的 6 万人仅增加到目前的 20 万人,法官增长的倍数仅占案件增长倍数的 1/10。[①] 如何缓解案多人少矛盾,在笔者看来,多元化纠纷解决机制的构建非常必要。仲裁作为多元化纠纷解决机制的重要组成部分,应予以支持。

三是顺应新时代发展的需要。《纽约公约》对不予承认与执行外国仲裁裁决规定了比较严格的条件,体现了"尽量认定仲裁协议有效""赞成仲裁""支持执行"等精神,充分体现对仲裁宽容的态度。当前,世界上有 150 多个国家或地区加入了《纽约公约》,目标是共同构建一张互相承认与执行国际商事仲裁裁决的巨大网络,使国际商事仲裁裁决能够在公约成员方得到承认与执行。最高人民法院周强院长指出:"法院支持仲裁的作用并不是仅仅表现为执行仲裁协议、提供临时措施,协助组建仲裁庭和强制执行仲裁裁决,更为重要的是,法院对仲裁程序和公共政策的监督,对社会公平正义最后一道防线的守护,保障了仲裁裁决的正当性,增强了当事人对仲裁公平公正解决争议的信心,从而推动仲裁业长期有序发展。"[②]目前,中国提出了"一带一路"伟大倡议目标,"十三五"规划纲要中提出要健全对外开放新体制,积极参与全球经济治理,积极承担国际责任和义务。《中华人民共和国国民经济和社会发展第十四个五年规划和 2035 年远景目标纲要》("十四五"规划)在"推进基础设施互联互通"小节中特别强调,有序推动重大合作项目建设,将高质量、可持续、抗风险、价格合理、包容可及目标融入项目建设全过程。这也为未来"一带一路"项目开展提供了指引。有学者指出,"从近年来仲裁制度的实践看,对仲裁法进行修改是

---

① 王梦遥:《最高法推进案件繁简分流》,载《新京报》2016 年 9 月 14 日,A20 版。

② 周强:《亚太新时代的国际仲裁、司法与法治——在 2013 年亚太区域仲裁组织大会开幕式上的主旨演讲》,载贺荣主编、最高人民法院民事审判第四庭编:《涉外商事海事审判指导》,人民法院出版社 2014 年版,第 3 页。

大势所趋，仲裁法修改中的司法审查也是一个必要改进的焦点问题”。[①] 在这一背景之下，需要我们在《仲裁法》修改过程中，尤其是确定审查仲裁标准、积极支持国际商事仲裁上，需要坚定“中国立场”，体现“中国表达”，发出“中国声音”，贡献“中国智慧”。将来在《仲裁法》新修改时，在《仲裁法》第9条之后新增加“兼顾效率”“当事人的意思自治为主，适时适当限制为补充原则”等基本原则。

四、结语

在中国实施“一带一路”倡议背景之下，笔者选择国际商事仲裁裁决“超裁”认定问题进行研究，目的是统一司法审查标准，让更多符合域内外法律规定的国际商事仲裁裁决能够在中国得到承认和执行。本文基于对最高人民法院5个复函样本的司法实践的考察发现，中国法院对国际商事仲裁协议司法审查中“超裁”的认定存在如下问题：一是“超裁”的含义不明确；二是部分国际商事仲裁“超裁”司法审查案件未履行内部请示报告制度；三是司法审查的启动与认定的情形不统一；四是司法裁决的可分性存在争议。针对上述问题，采取如下措施加以解决：一是明确不予承认与执行国际商事仲裁裁决的“超裁”情形；二是严格落实内部请示报告制度；三是统一司法审查标准，确定审查仲裁标准；四是积极支持国际商事仲裁。笔者希冀本文的探索有助于建立一套完善、规范和高效的国际商事仲裁司法审查制度，确保司法认定质量，竭力维护好国际商事仲裁当事人的合法权益。

---

① 韦伟强：《〈仲裁法〉的修改与完善——从一起仲裁执行异议之诉案件所进行的实证分析》，载《社会科学家》2018年第5期。

网络仲裁司法审查的实证研究

谢金钗*

摘要:信息网络化的环境催生了人们对于效率与成本的更高需求,网络仲裁应运而生。然而,在网络仲裁发展中,困难与机会并存,因此对网络仲裁司法审查进行实证分析非常必要。通过对172件网络仲裁的司法审查案件分析发现,不予执行网络仲裁裁决等消极司法审查结果超过七成,影响因素也是多元的,其中包括程序事由、合法依据事由、网络仲裁合意事由以及公共利益事由。对此,应该通过完善网络仲裁法律制度、构建网络仲裁运行规则、改善网络仲裁合意达成以促进网络仲裁不断发展。

关键词:网络仲裁　司法审查　仲裁程序

一、引言

在信息时代,人们将网络视为赖以生存的一部分,凭借网络手段实现更高效率与付出更低成本也成为人们的重要追求。互联网正在无形中推动更符合时代特征的争议解决方式的发展。其中,网络仲裁(又称"网上仲裁"或"在线仲裁")即为一个典型代表。

网络仲裁的概念有广义与狭义之分。广义的网络仲裁对网络载体的利用

* 华东政法大学国际法学院硕士研究生,主要研究方向:国际私法、国际仲裁。

要求并不那么高,可具体细分为"涉及说"与"封闭机构说"。[①] "涉及说",系指某一环节涉及或者利用网络的仲裁,其只要求仲裁流程中某一环节涉及网络。相比之下,"封闭机构说"利用网络程度相对较高,系指一个封闭的在线仲裁系统,该系统由一个在线争议解决(Online Alternative Dispute Resolution,ODR)提供者维持,通过密码(password)和用户身份卡(userID)安全连接而进行访问。狭义的网络仲裁,[②]系指所有环节均在网络上进行的仲裁,这种仲裁"利用现代电子技术和因特网,即从仲裁协议的订立、仲裁程序的进行,以及仲裁裁决的作出,均通过电子邮件、网上聊天室以及与因特网配套的音像设施软件,使通过仲裁解决争议的全过程,均在因特网上进行"。笔者认为,对网络仲裁的界定,关键在于是否把网络作为依托载体,网络在仲裁中扮演何种角色。上述概念对网络利用要求要么过高、要么过低。笔者认为,界定网络仲裁应当以"网络参与仲裁的核心环节"作为标准。何为核心环节?即仲裁证据的提交、仲裁当事人之间信息的处理和交换、仲裁中的质证与辩论、裁决的作出。因此,本文把网络仲裁界定为,以传统仲裁原理为基础,核心环节需要依托网络进行的争议解决办法。值得注意的是,中国国际经济贸易仲裁委员会(以下简称贸仲)在疫情期间发布了《关于新冠肺炎疫情期间积极稳妥推进仲裁程序指引(试行)》(以下简称《指引》)。从形式上看,《指引》所采用的网上仲裁属于网络仲裁的一种,但由于是特殊时期为克服不可抗力而出台的,具有临时性,也并未有相关配套的仲裁规则,故不予纳入本文"网络仲裁"的研究范围。

近年来,网络仲裁发展迅速。2014年11月4日,贸仲发布了《网上仲裁规则》。[③] 随后于2015年9月24日,中国广州仲裁委员会牵头发起设立互联网仲裁联盟。[④] 从2017年起,网络仲裁以其快捷的优势得到应用,网络仲裁的司法

① 钟丽:《在线仲裁的界定及其仲裁地问题探讨》,载《社会科学》2002年第3期;钟丽学者总结了"涉及说"以及"封闭机构说"。

② 赵秀文:《国际商事仲裁及其适用法律研究》,北京大学出版社2002年版,第356页。

③ 中国国际贸易促进委员会:《网上仲裁规则》,载贸仲官网,http://www.cietac.org/index.php?m=Page&a=index&id=19&l=cn。

④ 《中国互联网仲裁联盟在广州成立》,载中国新闻网,http://www.chinanews.com/sh/2015/09-24/7542643.shtml。

审查案件数量也随之增长。①

但作为新型的争议解决方式，其在发展过程中自然会面临一些问题：在法律制度相对滞后的情况下，超前发展的网络仲裁是否具有合法地位？目前对网络仲裁的司法审查处于何种状态？网络仲裁的实体与程序规则如何安排才能保障正义？上述问题均与网络仲裁的司法审查紧密相关。但由于网络仲裁仍处于初步发展过程，相关实证研究几乎没有。为了探究网络仲裁目前在中国的实践现状，有必要对网络仲裁司法审查开展实证研究。

二、网络仲裁司法审查之内涵

网络仲裁作为一种仲裁形式，具有仲裁本身的私力性，其需要公力的支持与审查以保障仲裁裁决的执行力。公力审查需平衡公与私，以协调私人利益与公共利益的博弈。此种形式的体现即网络仲裁的司法审查。

为使研究结果更加直观，本文按照网络仲裁的司法审查结果不同分为积极的司法审查结果与消极的司法审查结果。

网络仲裁积极的司法审查结果，系指一国的司法机关对网络仲裁的合法性进行审查，作出肯定网络仲裁及网络仲裁裁决的司法审查结果，其中包括但不限于认定网络仲裁合意有效、驳回网络仲裁管辖权异议、承认与执行网络仲裁裁决、驳回撤销网络仲裁裁决的申请、驳回不予执行网络仲裁的申请等。

网络仲裁消极的司法审查结果，系指一国司法机关对网络仲裁的合法性进行审查，作出否定网络仲裁或网络仲裁裁决的司法审查结果，其中包括但不限于认定网络仲裁合意无效、认定网络仲裁管辖权异议有效、不予承认或执行网络仲裁裁决、撤销网络仲裁裁决等。

片面追求网络仲裁积极或者消极司法审查结果并无意义。若只追求网络仲裁司法审查得到积极结果，网络仲裁难以成熟发展；若绝对追求网络仲裁司

① 根据本文案件数据统计，2017 年开始，集中出现网络仲裁审查案件 63 件，从一定程度上反映了网络仲裁在 2017 年开始快速发展。

法审查得到消极结果,网络仲裁在实践中更是难有立足之地。因此,本文的实证分析着眼于把握二者的平衡,在此基础上,主要分析网络仲裁获得消极审查结果的原因,并就改善网络仲裁运行机制提出有关建议。

三、网络仲裁司法审查裁判案例的数据分析

网络仲裁的司法审查结果意味着当下司法实务界对新兴网络仲裁所秉持的态度,对网络仲裁机构本身甚至于该行业未来发展均有重要影响。因此,本文分别以"网络仲裁""网上仲裁""在线仲裁""互联网仲裁"为关键词在"无讼"平台①检索,获得2019年6月前当事人向法院申请执行、不予执行、撤销网络仲裁裁决等网络仲裁司法审查案件,整理去除重复部分,可得案件172件。本文通过分析样本案件,提取法院对网络仲裁的司法审查结果作为因变量。因变量可分为积极的司法审查结果、消极的司法审查结果与其他裁定结果等情形。

(一)样本案件的整体统计

总体而言,消极的司法审查结果比率(77.91%)远高于积极的司法审查结果比率(19.18%),意味着司法对新兴的网络仲裁裁决效力的支持作用并未得到充分发挥,详见表1。②

表1 网络仲裁司法审查的总体情况

裁定结果		数量/件	比率/%
支持	终结执行	22	12.80
	准许执行	4	2.33
	驳回不予执行	3	1.74
	执行裁定:冻结银行账户	2	1.16
	驳回管辖权异议,认可网络仲裁	1	0.58
	驳回撤销申请	1	0.58

① 参见无讼官方网站,www. itslaw. com/。

② 如无特别说明,本文表格中的数据均由笔者根据样本案件统计而成。

续表

裁定结果		数量/件	比率/%
反对	不予执行	75	43.60
	驳回	59	34.30
其他	冻结(准许保全)	4	2.33
	指定下级法院受理	1	0.58
总计		172	100.00

（二）样本案件的分类统计

本文对172个案件进行归类、因自变量抽取与统计分析，分析各自变量因素对因变量审查结果的影响。

由于网络平台案件库和法院公开的案件数量有限，全面掌握网络仲裁司法审查的结果存在一定困难，但目前公开的网络仲裁的司法审查结果也能提供一定的参考。下面笔者将从争议类别、年份、法院、仲裁委员会等方面对搜集到的172个案例进行分析。

1. 争议类别

从仲裁争议本身类别看，绝大部分法院会对网络仲裁司法审查案件写明案由，也有不到5%的法院并不写明案由。案由出现频率由高至低排列分别为借款合同纠纷、金融借款合同纠纷、追偿权纠纷、民间借贷纠纷、财产损害赔偿纠纷，所占172件案件比例分别为43.29%、27.44%、21.95%、6.71%、0.61%。通过梳理争议类别可以发现：

第一，追偿权纠纷源于P2P网络借贷平台回购出借人的债权，利用平台申请仲裁从而申请执行。一般而言，P2P平台作为一个纯信用信息居间方，并无权利起诉违约借款人。但其可以通过事先在出借人、借款人、居间方三方协议中设置债权回购条款或事后另行签订债权转让条款等一系列方式获得出借人的授权，并且约定以网络仲裁的方式解决纠纷，从而代多个出借人参与仲裁（本文称为集团仲裁）。前文已述网络仲裁的快捷性，此时再结合集团仲裁的高效率，P2P平台此种维权模式便具有更多的速度优势和资源优势。

第二,就纠纷本身性质而言,进行司法审查的网络仲裁目前仅限于简单的借贷纠纷或小范围的金融投资纠纷,并未扩展到其他纠纷领域。由于各地法院对案件类别的划分各不相同,我们需要分析上述案件的客观事实进而得出争议类别。网络仲裁涉及案件绝大多数为有关借款合同的纠纷,其中包括P2P网络借贷平台引起的平台与借款人的追偿权纠纷、金融机构与借款人的金融合同纠纷、金融机构或者P2P网络借贷平台纯参与居间的出借人与借款人的民间借贷纠纷、贵金属买卖引起的财产损害赔偿纠纷,所占涉案纠纷比例分别为49.42%、32.56%、17.44%、0.58%。显然,网络仲裁目前仅限于简单的借贷纠纷或小范围的金融投资纠纷,适用范围十分有限。同时,这也意味着网络仲裁并不一定只适用于与互联网有关的纠纷,也同样适用于一些线下纠纷,例如,金融机构与借款人的金融合同纠纷、金融机构参与居间的出借人与借款人的民间借贷纠纷、贵金属买卖引起的财产损害赔偿纠纷。这是因为各仲裁委员会将网络仲裁的功能与目标定位于主要处理网络上的纠纷,小范围涉及其他关联或者相似纠纷。

2. 年份

从年份上来看,仲裁委员会作出网络仲裁裁决时间集中于2017年、2018年,分别为67件、103件。据此可知,网络仲裁在2016年以前并未成为当事人所青睐的仲裁形式。直至2017年,网络仲裁才得以快速发展。由前文已知,样本中网络仲裁主要的争议类别为借款纠纷,其中P2P纠纷在样本纠纷中的占比超过一半(66.28%)。这是因为近年来宽松的投资环境、个人流动现金增加、互联网平台的崛起等因素使人们开始将投资方向转向网贷平台,而由于网贷平台的最大特点是利用网络的高效性,仲裁作为一种高效的争议解决方式,与网贷平台的这一特点不谋而合,网贷平台提供的争议解决条款也就多为网络仲裁条款。因此,网贷平台上产生的纠纷更多地适用网络仲裁方式予以解决,从而不可避免地导致网络仲裁司法审查的案件增多。

3. 法院

根据《民事诉讼法》第224条的规定,①受理网络仲裁裁决执行申请的法院遍布各地。通过法院的角度可看出以下特点:

第一,网络仲裁裁决的司法审查结果与法院本身存在密切联系。同一法院审查多个网络仲裁裁决所作出的裁定结果高度一致,并且裁定理由基本一致。例如,在本文实证研究的样本中,受理网络仲裁案件最多的是长沙市中级人民法院,其对38个仲裁裁决进行司法审查的结果均为不予执行,详见表2。

表2　样本中各人民法院的倾向

倾向(比例/%)	法院(网络仲裁裁决司法审查案件数量/件)	省、自治区、直辖市(法院个数/个)
消极(76.27)	长沙市中级人民法院(38)、肇庆市中级人民法院(21)、重庆市第三中级人民法院(15)、百色市中级人民法院(1)、崇左市中级人民法院(1)、德庆县人民法院(1)、毕节市中级人民法院(1)、河池市中级人民法院(1)、揭阳市中级人民法院(1)、临朐县人民法院(1)、三门峡市中级人民法院(1)、汕尾市中级人民法院(1)、韶关市中级人民法院(1)、万源市人民法院(1)、信阳市中级人民法院(1)、玉林市玉州区人民法院(1)、玉林市中级人民法院(1)、湛江市中级人民法院(1)、张家界市中级人民法院(1)	广东(6)、广西(5)、湖南(2)、贵州(1)、山东(1)、河南(2)、四川(1)、重庆(1)
积极(22.03)	河源市中级人民法院(7)、阜阳市中级人民法院(6)、潮州市中级人民法院(4)、广州市中级人民法院(1)、海南省第二中级人民法院(1)、杭州市中级人民法院(1)、兰州市西固区人民法院(1)、松原市中级人民法院(1)、泰兴市人民法院(1)、无锡市中级人民法院(1)、运城市中级人民法院(1)、中卫市中级人民法院(1)	广东(3)、江苏(2)、安徽(1)、海南(1)、浙江(1)、甘肃(1)、吉林(1)、山西(1)、宁夏(1)
其他(1.69)	佛山市顺德区人民法院(1)、广东省高级人民法院(1)	广东(2)

① 《民事诉讼法》(2017年6月27日第十二届全国人民代表大会常务委员会第二十八次会议修正)第224条规定:"发生法律效力的民事判决、裁定,以及刑事判决、裁定中的财产部分,由第一审人民法院或者与第一审人民法院同级的被执行的财产所在地人民法院执行。"

第二,由表2不难看出,对网络仲裁裁决的司法审查秉持消极态度的法院数量多于秉持积极态度的法院,且前者作出的裁判数目也多于后者。由此可见,目前对网络仲裁裁决的司法审查更倾向秉持消极态度。

第三,以省为类别,广东省对网络仲裁裁决作出的司法审查案件居于首位,这是由于广州仲裁委员会是国内首个"一站式"网络仲裁服务平台线上机构,同时牵头建立互联网仲裁联盟,其作出的网络仲裁案件自然多。基于此,居住于广东省的当事人适用网络仲裁解决纠纷的机会自然多于其他省份,根据地域管辖,也意味着广东省法院对网络仲裁裁决申请司法审查,尤其是执行立案的案件,会多于其他省份。另外,作为毗邻广东省的省份——广西壮族自治区,其法院受理的网络仲裁案件数目位列第二。由表2可知,除广东省外,其他省份内部对网络仲裁的司法审查态度均保持一致。

4. 仲裁委员会

从仲裁委员会来看,被申请司法审查的网络仲裁裁决主要来自以下仲裁委员会:广州仲裁委员会(46.51%)、衢州仲裁委员会(36.63%)、衡水仲裁委员会(12.21%)、湛江仲裁委员会(3.49%)、保定仲裁委员会(1.16%)。由此可见,虽在中国国内采取网络仲裁方式的委员会分布各地,但实际网络仲裁裁决的作出限定于特定的几个仲裁委员会,尤其是2014年作为牵头设立中国互联网仲裁联盟的广州仲裁委员会,[①]申请司法审查的网络仲裁案件约占一半。

而各仲裁委员会作出的网络仲裁裁决的司法审查结果比例情况,在各仲裁委员会内部各不相同,详见表3。广州仲裁委员会作为中国互联网仲裁联盟牵头机构,受理网络仲裁案件不容小觑,但其作出的网络仲裁裁决经过司法审查最后得到有效执行的比例(1.25%)较低。背后的原因较复杂,该数据比例可能需要同时考虑司法在整体上对于网络仲裁裁决的否定倾向。

① 《中国互联网仲裁联盟在广州成立》,载中国新闻网,http://www.chinanews.com/sh/2015/09-24/7542643.shtml。

表 3 各仲裁委员会作出的网络仲裁裁决的司法审查情况

各仲裁委员会名称	积极的司法审查结果		消极的司法审查结果		其他	
	件数/件	比率/%	件数/件	比率/%	件数/件	比率/%
广州仲裁委员会	1	1.25	79	98.75	0	0
衢州仲裁委员会	18	28.57	44	69.84	1	1.59
衡水仲裁委员会	10	47.62	6	28.57	5	23.81
湛江仲裁委员会	2	33.33	4	66.67	0	0
保定仲裁委员会	1	50.00	1	50.00	0	0

四、网络仲裁司法审查的消极结果事由分布

如前文所述，消极的司法审查结果的案件为 134 件，占总数 172 件案件的 77.91%。下文将针对消极的司法审查结果案件进行消极事由分析。

根据《民事诉讼法》第 237 条第 2 款、第 3 款的规定，被申请人提出证据证明仲裁裁决有下列情形之一的，经人民法院组成合议庭审查核实，裁定不予执行：(1)当事人在合同中没有订立仲裁条款或者事后没有达成书面仲裁协议的；(2)裁决的事项不属于仲裁协议的范围或者仲裁机构无权仲裁的；(3)仲裁庭的组成或者仲裁的程序违反法定程序的；(4)裁决所根据的证据是伪造的；(5)对方当事人向仲裁机构隐瞒了足以影响公正裁决的证据的；(6)仲裁员在仲裁该案时有贪污受贿、徇私舞弊、枉法裁决行为的。人民法院认定执行该裁决违背社会公共利益的，裁定不予执行。

从检索取得的样本来看，不予执行网络仲裁的事由分布并不均匀，仅集中在几项事由中。首先，以第 3 项理由——“仲裁庭的组成或者仲裁的程序违反法定程序的”为不予执行事由的案件最多，有 119 件，约占样本中网络仲裁司法审查消极结果的裁定总数的 88.81%。其次，以网络仲裁缺失正当法律依据①

① “网络仲裁缺失正当法律依据”为判决书中直接出现的不予执行事由，有关法院并未在判决书中指出网络仲裁违反《民事诉讼法》第 237 条之规定，笔者猜测可能是法院认为网络仲裁缺失正当法律依据，从而不予适用《民事诉讼法》第 237 条。此外，网络仲裁由于缺少正当法律依据，法院不予执行。

为由不予执行网络仲裁的案件,有28件,占总数20.90%。与前者案件数量接近的为涉及第1项理由的案件,即未达成网络仲裁合意的案件,有22件,占16.42%。最后,以第237条第3款"裁决违背社会公共利益"为由的案件较少,为13件,占比9.70%,详见表4。

表4 网络仲裁司法审查消极结果的事由分布情况

消极司法审查结果分布事由		件数/件	比例/% [a]
仲裁庭的组成或者仲裁程序违反法定程序	原则概括性	43	32.09
	开庭	28	20.90
	送达	26	19.40
	时间	21	15.67
	约定指定仲裁员	1	0.75
网络仲裁缺失正当法律依据		28	20.90
未达成网络仲裁合意		22	16.42
违背社会公共利益		13	9.70

a 比例为事由占样本中网络仲裁司法审查消极结果的裁定总数,而一个裁定中会涉及多个事由,因此各个事由比例相加不等于1。

本文对事由的分析与归类,并无法直接判断不予执行的原因系仲裁庭自身原因、司法审查有误,抑或是网络仲裁本身发展仍然存在一定问题。因为收集裁定的渠道有限,信息资源必然受到客观上的限制。更重要的是,网络仲裁与司法审查均属于争议解决领域,仲裁庭和法院自身都享有一定的自由裁量权,因此不能仅凭裁定文本或者在司法审查结束后进行挑错性质的复核,从而否定网络仲裁或者司法审查。鉴于这种来自源头的困境,本文把研究获得的事由建立在一种偏向可能性的基础上,而不是肯定明确的基础上。

基于这样的维度考虑,可将本文检索获得的172份样本中得到不予执行网络仲裁的事由主要分为以下类别:程序的事由、网络仲裁缺失正当法律依据的事由、未达成网络仲裁合意的事由、违背社会公共利益的事由。

(一)有关不予执行网络仲裁裁决的程序事由

在本文的172份样本中,由于程序因素引起的不予执行网络仲裁的情形较多，按照占不予执行裁定总数的比例从高到低，可细分为概括性的程序事由、否定不进行网络开庭审理的程序事由、电子送达制度设计缺陷的程序事由、违反时间规则的程序事由、当事人约定违反仲裁程序事由。

1. 概括性的程序事由

就概括性的程序事由而言，其占样本中网络仲裁司法审查消极结果的裁定总数比例最高，达到32.09%，但各法院裁定中说理部分均较简单。例如，一份由四川省某基层人民法院作出的不予执行裁定："该裁决书仲裁的程序违反法定程序。依照《中华人民共和国民事诉讼法》第2条第2款第3项的规定，裁定驳回执行申请。"该裁定书并未提及违反的程序是何程序，也并未结合法律条文进行论证，缺少必要的说理。

此类概括性事由的另一个特征是直接引用最高人民法院《关于仲裁机构"先予仲裁"裁决或者调解书立案、执行等法律适用问题的批复》(以下简称《批复》)。先予仲裁属于湛江仲裁委员会的创新制度，其又称无争议同时仲裁，是指合同双方为避免纠纷，节省争议解决成本，在合同中约定就合同所涉及的权利义务提前仲裁的一种形式。其最本质特点是在未发生纠纷时提前仲裁。对此，理论界和实务界均有支持者与反对者，但2018年6月5日，《批复》打开了司法实践的新局面——认为先予仲裁属于"仲裁庭的组成或者仲裁程序违反程序"的情形。

实际上，先予仲裁并不等同于网络仲裁，甚至不可称为仲裁。笔者认为，先予仲裁在纠纷尚未发生之前确认债权的强制执行力，实际发挥债权文书公证的职能，即先予仲裁的过程如同审查合同一般，没有需要查明的纠纷事实，必然会使另一方当事人失去实质上的申请回避、提供证据、答辩等基本程序权利。这也是先予仲裁与网络仲裁最大的区别，前者的仲裁流程仅仅是一种形式，后者进行的是实质的仲裁流程，只不过形式从线下转换为线上。

网络仲裁中之所以常常出现先予仲裁的情形，是因为先予仲裁的案件大多为涉及网贷平台的案件，而先予仲裁和网络仲裁的结合具有高效的特性，恰好符合网贷平台处置"坏债"的速度需求，因此两者常常会如影随形。

综上所述,先予仲裁并不是网络仲裁获得消极司法审查结果的原因,最高人民法院对于先予仲裁的否定,并不意味对网络仲裁的否定,合法合规的网络仲裁,依然可稳健发展与完善。

2. 否定不进行网络开庭审理的程序事由

审理作为仲裁的必经程序,系仲裁的核心环节之一。对于网络仲裁的审理方式,现已建立的仲裁委员会大多以书面审理为原则,以开庭审理为例外,①通常只有仲裁庭认为有必要或当事人共同申请时才会开庭审理。在此需要注意的是,网络仲裁中采取书面审理为原则,并不影响其为网络仲裁。笔者已在上文对网络仲裁进行定义,网络仲裁是以传统仲裁原理为基础,核心环节需要依托网络进行的争议解决办法,其中核心环节是指仲裁证据的提交、仲裁当事人之间信息的处理和交换、仲裁中的质证与辩论、裁决的作出。因此,虽然网络仲裁采取书面审理的规则,但网络仲裁的其他核心环节仍然依托网络进行,网络仲裁本质并未受到影响。

对此,有法院认为,②网络仲裁庭以不开庭的方式作出裁决,此过程缺乏正当的法律依据,同时也未对被执行人的程序权利给予应有保护。笔者认为,网络仲裁庭的审理规则与法院的审理规则存在一定的矛盾与冲突。网络仲裁以书面审理为原则,开庭审理为例外;而法院则以开庭审理为原则,不开庭审理(或书面审理)为例外。因此,法院在审查网络仲裁裁决作出的程序时,必然会考虑书面审理所带来的对当事人质证、辩论等权利的削弱,同时由于审理的非当场性、书面案情的查阅、回应的滞后性更容易使仲裁员对当事人所表达的意思产生不可避免的误解,造成程序与实体的不公正。

3. 电子送达制度设计缺陷的程序事由

电子送达与通知事由导致的网络仲裁不予执行的情形主要体现在以下两个方面:

---

① 例如,《中国广州仲裁委员会网络仲裁规则》第24条第1款规定:"仲裁庭对网络仲裁案件进行书面审理。仲裁庭可以通过本会网络仲裁平台向当事人发出问题单,当事人应当自收到该问题单之日起五日内通过本会网络仲裁平台作出说明,逾期未说明的,视为放弃说明的权利。"

② 参见湛江市中级人民法院民事裁定书,(2018)粤08执380号。

一是电子送达本身性质的影响，即电子送达方式由于其虚拟性往往无法确认已送达，法院会认定仲裁委员会未能充分证明其将相关文书确已送达当事人。例如，一份广西壮族自治区某中级人民法院作出的裁定：本院认为……本案中衢州仲裁委员会在未有充分证据证实相关文书送达被执行人的情形下缺席仲裁，被执行人未能出庭、未能提供证据、申请回避和提交答辩等，故衢州仲裁委员会未能保障被执行人的基本程序权利，存在仲裁庭仲裁违反法定程序，可能出现权利人利用其强势地位强迫义务人放弃其仲裁程序的抗辩利益、损害义务人权利问题的发生……故本院依法驳回该仲裁裁决执行申请。

该问题源于网络仲裁庭的送达程序要求与法院不同，前者更宽松。由于依托于互联网，网络仲裁庭的送达方式一般为电子送达，送达地址为仲裁协议中约定的电子邮箱及移动通信号码（包括但不限于手机号码、微信账号、QQ 账号）。实际上，法院也有采取电子送达方式的规定——《民事诉讼法》第 87 条。[①] 二者均有采取电子送达的方式，为何法院认为网络仲裁庭的电子送达无效？笔者认为，原因在于二者对电子送达地址的确认程度要求不同。对于网络仲裁庭来说，电子送达地址一般源于合同载明内容，出于效率的角度考虑，其实际送达前并不会与被送达人确认，完成送达行为后也不会与被送达人核实。但是对于法院来说，电子送达方式仅仅是传统送达方式的辅助工具，法院若采取电子送达方式，必须对电子送达地址进行严格的确认收悉。故法院对于电子送达方式要求较高，态度也更加审慎。

二是大多数的网络仲裁送达规则与法院送达规则产生冲突，即网络仲裁裁决书通常采取电子送达方式，但法院认为网络仲裁裁决书不得通过电子送达方式送达："仲裁裁决书的送达应依照民事诉讼法关于送达的相关规定，本案仲裁裁决书是通过手机短信及电子邮箱送达的，违背《民事诉讼法》和《仲裁法》的规定。"[②]

---

① 《民事诉讼法》第 87 条规定："经受送达人同意，人民法院可以采用传真、电子邮件等能够确认其收悉的方式送达诉讼文书，但判决书、裁定书、调解书除外。采用前款方式送达的，以传真、电子邮件等到达受送达人特定系统的日期为送达日期。"

② 参见韶关市中级人民法院民事裁定书，(2018)粤 02 执 183 号。

笔者认为,该问题源于网络仲裁庭的送达范围与法院的不同。网络仲裁裁决书通常采取电子送达方式,但对于法院送达来说,《民事诉讼法》第87条严格限制了电子送达的范围,排除判决书、裁定书、调解书适用电子送达的可能。网络仲裁裁决书与法院出具的裁定书相比,网络仲裁裁决书与人民法院出具的生效判决书、裁定书、调解书具有相似的法律效力,均可确认法律事实并具有强制执行力。因此,大部分人民法院往往认为《民事诉讼法》第87条实际从法律意义上否定了裁决书电子送达的可能,从而否定网络仲裁的电子送达是有效送达。

4. 违反时间规则的程序事由

违反时间规则的程序事由,是指仲裁庭未严格遵守有关仲裁的时间规则审理纠纷或者主持调解。有关该程序事由的案件均由广东省某中级人民法院作出:"根据进行网络仲裁的仲裁委员会有关网络仲裁的规则规定当事人于五日内选定仲裁员,逾期未能选定的,由委员会主任指定。其中根据《民法总则》第201条与《民事诉讼法》第82条,五日应当从下一日开始计算,而该仲裁委员会从当日开始计算,属程序违法,因而不能成为人民法院的执行依据,裁定驳回执行申请。"①违反时间规则的程序事由的出现说明仲裁委员会对时间规则存在认知误差,仲裁委员会应当认真研究和改进。此外,对于该事项还有另外一种解释,即法院对网络仲裁本身的司法审查难以把握,通过其他"无关紧要事由"否定网络仲裁,反映了司法对于网络仲裁的不确定性态度。

5. 当事人约定事项违反仲裁程序的事由

在本文样本中,当事人约定事项违反仲裁程序的事由,是指双方约定放弃选定仲裁员的权利,由仲裁委员会主任进行指定,这种约定违反仲裁程序。例如,广西壮族自治区某中级人民法院作出一份不予执行裁定:《借款合同》中约定双方同意由仲裁委员会主任指定一名独任仲裁员通过网络书面审理与该合

---

① 参见肇庆市中级人民法院民事裁定书,(2018)粤12执310号。

同相关的一切争议,该格式条款剥夺了当事人选择仲裁规则、出庭、提供证据、申请回避和提交答辩等权利。

(二)网络仲裁缺失正当法律依据的事由

网络仲裁作为一种新兴事物,必然会出现网络仲裁是否存在正当法律依据的问题。例如,广东省某中级人民法院在一申请执行网络仲裁的案件中认为,根据《仲裁法》第15条和第75条的规定,中国仲裁协会是仲裁规则的制定者,仲裁委员会也可以依照《仲裁法》或《民事诉讼法》的有关规定制定仲裁暂行规则。目前中国仲裁协会并没有制定相应的网络仲裁规则,《民事诉讼法》和《仲裁法》也未作出规定,在此情况下,仲裁机构以独任仲裁的方式不开庭进行网络仲裁并作出裁决,其裁决过程对被执行人的权利缺乏《仲裁法》规定的应有保护,它不属于《仲裁法》和《民事诉讼法》意义上的仲裁。因此,申请执行人以这种网络仲裁裁决作为依据,向法院申请强制执行不符合法律规定,对其申请予以驳回。

笔者认为,网络仲裁是否缺失正当法律依据,取决于网络仲裁是否系一种全新的仲裁形式?探究网络仲裁与传统仲裁的异同,实际可参照互联网法院裁判与传统法院裁判的异同。互联网法院是将互联网技术与传统物理法院全面糅合的一种审理模式,具有效率等优势。但其争议解决机制及作出裁判的法律依据与传统法院并无迥异之处。其与传统法院最大区别为其依托互联网,将起诉、调解、立案、举证、质证、开庭、判决到执行等进行网上一体化。相比之下,网络仲裁与传统仲裁也与此类似,网络仲裁源于传统仲裁,其建立于传统仲裁的架构之上,将仲裁流程管理在线化,实际并未创设新的仲裁模式。因此,它并不是一种全新的争议解决方式,可将它纳入现行仲裁制度框架内。

因此,网络仲裁审理及其裁决所依据的法律,包括实体事项和程序事项的法律依据基本上与传统仲裁相同。故即使没有《民事诉讼法》《仲裁法》关于网络仲裁的规定,也可适用传统仲裁的一般规定。

(三)未达成网络仲裁合意——电子证据效力问题

对网络仲裁合意的质疑源于网络仲裁中不可避免出现的电子签名问题。

在样本中第一份有关电子签名的裁定中，法院否认“点击协议”的合意效力，认为该协议无电子签名。作出该裁定的湖南省某中级人民法院认为：“《消费金融服务协议》，没有协议三方的签名或盖章，也没有电子数据生成时公证机构的公证、或经依法设立的电子认证服务提供者的认证，或其他能够保证自形成时起，内容保持完整、未被更改的电子数据等证据材料，不能确定该协议系协议三方的真实意思表示，故协议中的仲裁条款不能认定。”

点击协议，是指协议一方将协议内容载于互联网上发出要约，另一方以鼠标点击的方式表示承诺，从而达成合意的协议。[①] 点击协议由于其依托于互联网，无须电子签名，只需点击同意即可表示承诺。这当然也是达成合意的一种方式，但由于电子证据一定的空间虚拟性与法律结果的真实性需求具有一定的距离，其真实性、合法性和关联性需要进一步确认。该法院在此处对电子证据的真实有效性提出质疑，从而质疑仲裁合意，具有一定合理性。

第二份对电子签名的质疑系由重庆市某中级人民法院作出的，其直接否定一方当事人的某一种电子签名的效力：“涉案《借款服务合同》中一方当事人陈×照沪的签名为打印体，且《借款服务合同补充协议》的签订时间不明确，仅凭该证据不足以证明双方签订协议。”

笔者认为，打印体的电子签名所签订的协议并不能证明双方达成仲裁合意。这是因为电子签名本质为签名，其需要满足与传统签名相同的功能，即表明文件来源、同意文件所载内容的意思表示、表明签名者对文件完整性和正确性负责。单纯的打印体签字可以随意篡改、复制，无法保障打印体签字与签字人意志具有联系，更无法达成以上签名所需要的专有功能。

(四)违背公共利益

违背公共利益作为《民事诉讼法》第237条第3款规定的不予执行仲裁裁决的事由之一，在网络仲裁案件中的适用频率并不高，其出现的原因与网络仲裁受理的争议类别有关。

---

① 参见刘颖、骆文怡：《论点击合同》，载《武汉大学学报(社会科学版)》2003年第3期。

首先,网络仲裁时常适用于涉网贷平台的纠纷,而网贷平台有陷入经营范围与实际经营不符的风险。例如,贵州省某中级人民法院在一案件中认为:"×公司通过互联网平台,向不特定主体从事贷款业务,此经营行为涉及金融借贷业务,与其经营范围不符。由于衢州仲裁委员会在出具仲裁裁决书时未对《借款合同》的合法性予以确认,该裁决书的执行,将损害借款人的权益,违背社会公共利益。"

其次,网贷平台所涉及的过高的借款利率也可能被裁定违背公共利益。一份由广西壮族自治区某中级人民法院作出的裁定:"被申请人应偿还的借款利息、借款服务费、逾期还款违约金总额超出了年利率24%,该裁决违反了《最高人民法院关于审理民间借贷案件适用法律若干问题的规定》第二十六条、第三十条的规定,亦违背社会公共利益。"

五、网络仲裁机制之困境与解决路径

网络仲裁若想获得进一步发展,甚至超越和代替传统的仲裁方式,其必须在遵循现有法律框架与执行机制的前提下发挥其效率优势。因为网络仲裁若只是空有其方便快捷的特点,但其裁决却无法得到法院的承认与执行,那么,网络仲裁本身便失去了意义。因此,对于以上网络仲裁司法审查的消极结果,本文从法律制度、仲裁规则、实体问题方面进行分析,并提出以下针对性建议:

(一)构建网络仲裁法律制度

网络仲裁机制若想获得进一步发展,需要与之相契合的法律环境。其中最大的问题在于,中国没有专门的网络仲裁法律制度,网络仲裁能否直接适用《仲裁法》也存在争议。由前文已知,在不予执行网络仲裁裁决的事由中,概括性的程序事由占样本中网络仲裁司法审查消极结果的裁定总数比例最高,达到32.09%,法院以"先予仲裁"为由不予执行。从表面看,这类案件多为网贷平台案件,而某些网贷平台确实更容易出现"先予仲裁"情形,但并非所有网贷平台案件均存在"先予仲裁"情形。法院通过否定"先予仲裁"全面否定网络仲裁,此现象的深层原因是在未有明确立法前,法院需要谨慎对待网络仲裁裁决的执行。

为避免各地仲裁委员会制定迥异的网络仲裁规则,从而限制网络仲裁的应用,笔者建议:第一,在《仲裁法》中引入网络仲裁的概念,赋予网络仲裁明确的法律地位;第二,在《仲裁法》中明确在网络进行的申请仲裁、提交证据、送达、开庭、作出裁决,在未有其他证据证明违反相关程序的情况下,与传统程序具有相同的法律效力;第三,在以保障当事人程序权利为原则的基础上,放宽对于网络仲裁审理、送达形式的要求。

至于网络仲裁的仲裁地问题,由于目前中国仲裁机构受理的网络仲裁案件主要是国内案件,本文的实证分析部分并未显露出这一困境。但未来随着网络仲裁的发展,该问题必然会逐渐显露。因此,中国在进行网络仲裁立法时,需要考虑网络仲裁的仲裁地的合理归属。目前存在"仲裁本座说""仲裁员所在地说""仲裁作出地说""网络服务器说"。为实务界普遍接受的理论为"仲裁本座说",①即先由当事人约定网上仲裁的仲裁地;当事人无约定时,以仲裁委员会所在地为仲裁地,仲裁裁决视为在仲裁地作出。

(二)构建网络仲裁规则

为了实现良性、长足的发展,网络仲裁需要法律赋予其合法地位,也需要仲裁机构制定完善的网络仲裁规则。而网络仲裁作为一种争议解决方式,程序正义是在构建网络仲裁规则时需要着重强调的。前文所提的审理方式、通知与送达问题,是构建网络仲裁规则需要重点关注的程序问题。

1. 有关通知与送达的网络仲裁规则

若要保障当事人充分的程序权利,有效的通知与送达是必不可少的。前文已经提及,网络仲裁的通知与送达中存在两大问题:一是电子送达本身性质的问题,即电子送达方式由于其虚拟性往往无法确认已送达;二是大多数网络仲裁送达规则与法院送达规则的冲突问题,即网络仲裁裁决书通常采取电子送达

---

① 参见《中国国际经济贸易仲裁委员会仲裁规则》(2015年版)第31条,载中国国际经济贸易仲裁委员会网,http://www.cietac.org.cn/index.php?m=Page&a=index&id=14。

方式,而《民事诉讼法》禁止裁决书电子送达。

对于第一个问题,可以采取多种方式解决:第一,采取电子邮件与短信或其他可获得回执的电子送达方式结合送达。由于在约定网络仲裁协议时,当事人双方往往约定多种电子通信方式,但在实践中电子邮箱的使用率受到是否为当事人专有、工作邮箱较少查看等因素的限制。而其他单一的电子送达方式要么无法传送法律文件,要么使用频率更低。但两者甚至三者以上的电子送达方式相结合,既克服了法律文件难以传送的障碍,又利用多渠道减弱网络的虚拟性,与法律所要求的真实性有所靠近。第二,在采取电子邮件与短信送达相结合的基础上,增设自动回执。现今,早已有阅后留痕的技术。就电子邮件而言,目前大型邮箱服务商(如163邮箱、126邮箱)均有阅读后发送回执的功能,但在实践操作中,需要收件人同意后才可发送回执。对此,仲裁机构应与邮箱服务商展开合作,对于仲裁文书的发送可无须收件人同意即可在其阅读后自动发送回执,具体操作方式可通过收件人注册邮箱时通过邮箱服务协议、注册邮箱后通过补充协议约定。就短信而言,可采取"弹屏短信"方式获取送达回证。弹屏短信,是指仲裁机构发送的短信以对话框的方式在收信人的手机屏幕上显示,其要求收信人必须阅读,并且需要点击对话框中的"关闭"后才可继续进行其他手机应用的操作。一旦收信人点击"关闭",通信服务商会发送阅读回执,由此起到阅后留痕的作用①。第三,可补充适用网络仲裁的电子仲裁平台获取送达回执,即收件人或收信人使用电子邮件抑或短信方式获得的关联码登录电子仲裁平台查看有关案件信息时,仲裁机构系统也可获取送达回执。

此外,为确保电子送达地址的准确性、增强电子送达的合意,可建议一方当事人在签订仲裁协议时,以加粗黑体或者其他方式提请另一方注意有关电子送达条款。

对于第二个问题,其本质上是根源性的法律问题。网络仲裁裁决书通常采取电子送达方式;而《民事诉讼法》第87条却从合意要件(受送达人同意)、送

① 李铁柱:《北京互联网法院试用弹屏短信 当事人收到短信手机屏幕被锁定》,载人民网,http://bj.people.com.cn/n2/2018/1028/c82840-32210764.html。

达媒介(采用传真、电子邮件等能够确认收悉的方式)、司法文书范围(判决书、裁定书、调解书除外)、与其他送达方式(传统送达优先于电子送达)的顺序等方面严格限制电子送达。为探究协调方案,应分析为何《民事诉讼法》作出如此限制。实际上,作此限制主要出于两个原因:一是判决书、裁定书、调解书属于诉讼结果文书,其对当事人的实体权利义务会能产生直接影响,难以通过其他程序方式补救,而电子送达方式存在一定的被篡改、拦截的安全风险,因此二者风险与利益并不匹配。二是电子送达的文件往往以复印件的形式体现,在申请执行中会遇到非原件的法律效力困境。

对此,笔者建议:首先,电子送达的安全性风险是由技术引起的,则其也应当由技术手段解决。就电子邮件而言,目前实现安全邮箱系统的优势技术主要有"数据加密"。数据加密,是指采取一定的变换方式对信息进行保密;[①]变换方式,是指对邮件内容进行公共与个人的对称加密,个人用户利用个人密钥签发信息或解密收到的信息,而其他用户则使用对应公共密钥收发信息,由此可降低邮件内容篡改或拦截的风险阈值。其次,原件的法律效力问题可通过其他平行方式解决,如仲裁委员会出具效力证明书,论证送达过程。

综上所述,由于科技高速发展,法律的规定相对滞后,传统守旧的送达形式仍然被立法者与司法者坚守。为了使仲裁实践跟上科技发展的步伐,现代仲裁机构应当利用先进的技术进行仲裁法律文书的送达,将仲裁从不合时宜的送达方式中解放出来。

2. 有关审理的网络仲裁规则

目前,大部分的网络仲裁规则均规定以"书面审理为原则,开庭审理为例外"。而法院一般以开庭审理为原则,不开庭审理(或书面审理)为例外。二者存在的冲突与对立,实际上是效率价值与公正价值的博弈。就二者价值位阶而言,公正应当是所有合法化争议解决方式的生命,也是程序背后的价值目标与底线。无论构建网络仲裁程序是否倾向追求效率,我们都应该以"公平"为标

① 参见郑倩:《基于PKI技术的安全邮件系统的研究与实现》,北京邮电大学2014年硕士学位论文,第6页。

准,在公平的射程范围之内追求效率。正如罗尔斯所言,“某些法律制度,不管它们如何有效率和安排有序,只要它们不正义,就必须加以改造或废除”。[①] 回到网络仲裁与法院在审理方式上的冲突,不开庭实际会使仲裁员感官上无法直接地获取当事人的神态与语气的变化,也使当事人的质证与辩论具有延迟性或者削弱质证与辩论的效果,进而极大影响了仲裁的公正性。因此,网络仲裁不应当为追求效率价值而忽视公正价值。笔者建议,网络仲裁应当以在线开庭为原则,当事人申请书面审查或者仲裁庭认为确有必要为例外,即原则上利用网络视频会议系统实现网上同步交流,从而使网络仲裁当事人和代理人均参与到案件中;例外情况下,由当事人双方协议选择审理方式或未协议时由仲裁庭依据具体情况作出决定。

以上属于网络仲裁规则的建构建议,仍需要得到法律的允许与肯定,否则其将因违反法律而无法得以适用。

(三)改善网络仲裁的合意达成问题

网络仲裁法律制度与网络仲裁规则的构建系网络仲裁有效发挥其作用的最核心的两个部分,但一份网络仲裁裁决若想得到执行,不得不考虑网络仲裁的前提,即网络仲裁合意的达成。网络仲裁合意的达成中存在的问题,具体可体现为前文所分析的点击协议的事后易篡改性,打印电子签名的非可靠性。

就点击协议而言,当今法律实际已不对仲裁合意的形式过于苛求,但点击后的协议取证较困难,难以保证仲裁协议具有一致性与完整性。对此,笔者建议在达成网络仲裁合意时,在当事人双方处均自动生成附有电子签名的仲裁协议,以防日后法院质疑其一致性与完整性。在条件允许的情况下,仍可申请国家机关对其公证,增强该份协议的可信度。

就电子签名而言,法律虽然对其规定了一些基本可靠的条件,但其在法律层面仅是以概念、理论形式呈现,这就意味着只要满足法律规定的基本要求,电子签名可以自身的方式去具体实现。而实际上已有成熟的电子签名技术——

① 参见[美]罗尔斯:《正义论》(修订版),何怀宏等译,中国社会科学出版社 2009 年版,第 3 页。

数字签名。数字签名,是指附着在身份认证背后的一系列数据电文,数字签名的任何变动都会影响电子签名,从而影响身份认证。数字签名的流程大致为:发送数据电文时,发送方生成数据电文标志,然后用自己的私钥对这个标志进行加密,接收方收到的将是带有加密性质的数据标志和数据电文,然后接受方也可对数据电文进行计算,用发送方的公钥对加密的这个数据电文标志进行解密,如果发送方的数据电文和数据电文标志在进行计算和解密以后与发送方本来的一致,那就可以完全确认,这个数据电文和标志就是来自发送方的。①

综上所述,尽管具有可靠性的电子签名与传统签章具有相同的法律效力,但电子签名具有一定虚拟性,其也使电子签名所同意的协议内容具有一定的虚拟性,其仍然需要实务界在实践中达成统一认识。

六、结语

网络仲裁正经受严峻的司法考验。虽然不能武断地认为,需要对网络仲裁进行新的立法,但对于法律的修改或者适当的法律解释是必要的。同时,网络仲裁规则的构建与网络仲裁合意的达成问题也是网络仲裁发展中的关键。总之,对于网络仲裁的实证研究也应从司法审查扩大至其他方面,从而使有关网络仲裁的研究与完善更具有实证基础。

① 参见万以娴:《电子签章法律问题研究》,人民法院出版社2001年版,第101页。

ICSID 仲裁裁决的执行困境与中国国际投资仲裁裁决的承认与执行机制研究

黄宋劼*

摘要：解决投资争端国际中心(International Centre for the Settlement of Investment Disputes,ICSID)仲裁裁决借由《华盛顿公约》所构建的承认与执行机制被评价为是一套“自足的”制度,其仲裁裁决的执行依靠的是败诉东道国政府的自觉履行,《华盛顿公约》并未规定任何强制执行程序;对于败诉东道国拒不执行 ICSID 仲裁裁决的情况,《华盛顿公约》也未规定十分行之有效的惩罚机制。ICSID 仲裁中的败诉东道国完全可以利用《华盛顿公约》第 55 条规定的国家主权豁免制度逃避责任。因此,ICSID 仲裁裁决的执行受制于国家主权豁免制度而面临现实和潜在的困境。中国在“一带一路”建设稳步推进的背景下,中国国际投资仲裁裁决的承认与执行机制却不尽完善,具体表现为中国现有的仲裁司法审查制度将有可能阻却涉华国际投资仲裁裁决的承认与执行。为保障涉华国际投资仲裁裁决在中国获得承认与执行,应完善中国的国际投资仲裁裁决的承认与执行机制。一方面,中国应当在不违反《华盛顿公约》精神的基础上建立适合中国的 ICSID 仲裁裁决承认与执行机制、制定相关国家主权豁免立法;另一方面,中国可以借鉴司法互惠关系探索与他国建立更多的国际

* 上海对外经贸大学 2016 级国际法学硕士研究生。

投资仲裁互惠关系，以保障通过其他非ICSID仲裁方式解决的国际投资争议解决结果（如判决）获得承认与执行。

关键词：ICSID仲裁裁决执行困境　国际投资仲裁裁决的承认与执行机制　涉华国际投资仲裁　“一带一路”

一、引言

传统的“投资者—国家”争端解决机制（Investor-State Dispute Settlement，ISDS）多为政治协商、外交保护和诉诸武力等，但在第二次世界大战后，人们意识到传统方式不能满足国际社会和平共同发展的需求。在20世纪60年代，资本主义世界相对繁荣，发达资本主义国家大量资本需向外寻找市场，一些发展中国家在独立后努力发展经济，急需资金。在这一国际投资大发展的背景下，为了能够弥补传统的解决国际投资争端的方法与双边条约出现的技术上与程序上的“缺陷”，建立一种有效的机制，在世界银行的积极倡导和主持下，发达国家与发展中国家于1965年共同制订和缔结了《解决国家与他国国民之间投资争议公约》（Convention on the Settlement of Investment Disputes Between States and Nationals of Other States，以下简称《华盛顿公约》），并据此设立了ICSID。由《华盛顿公约》创立的ICSID仲裁机制，一方面，反对将国际投资争议政治化，反对以外交保护和武力索债作为解决投资者与东道国之间投资争议的方式；另一方面，也不赞成由东道国排他性地管辖此类争议，而是主张运用中立的国际仲裁方式解决争议。① ICSID作为目前最“权威”的国际投资争端解决机构，在国际投资大发展时期以寻求国家和个人投资者之间平衡点的姿态解决了许多国际投资争议。但随着世界经济政治的进一步发展，ICSID机制的实践面临越来越多的困境，其权威性越发受到挑战。

从裁决既判力和执行力的角度来看，ICSID裁决的承认与执行问题是ICSID巩固其权威性最重要的一环。现代国际投资仲裁大多根据双边投资协

---

① 刘笋：《国际投资仲裁引发的若干危机及应对之策述评》，载《法学研究》2008年第6期。

定(Bilateral Investment Treaty,BIT)发起,而 ICSID 所作出的国际投资仲裁裁决的承认与执行制度则规定于《华盛顿公约》之中,非 ICSID 作出的国际投资仲裁裁决则一般通过争议双方事前约定或通过 1958 年《承认及执行外国仲裁裁决公约》(以下简称《纽约公约》)进行,但由于 ICSID 仲裁机制是 ISDS 机制中被广泛运用的,故本文将主要讨论 ICSID 以及《华盛顿公约》所共同构建的国际投资仲裁裁决承认与执行机制问题。伴随而来的问题主要包括:现有 ICSID 仲裁裁决的承认与执行机制为何? ICSID 仲裁裁决的实际执行状况如何以及是否存在障碍? 而从中国实际出发,涉华国际投资仲裁裁决在中国的承认与执行问题则更应受到重视。因此,本文将从 ICSID 现有机制出发,分析 ICSID 仲裁裁决的承认与执行机制及其现状,并探讨导致其执行困难的原因,并结合中国实际讨论涉华国际投资仲裁裁决在中国承认与执行的相关问题及制度构想。

二、ICSID 仲裁裁决的执行困境概述

ICSID 作为全球最大的国际投资争端解决机构,其仲裁裁决的承认与执行问题日益受到关注。《华盛顿公约》所构建的 ICSID 仲裁裁决承认与执行机制虽然被评价为是一套"自足的"制度,但受制于国家主权豁免制度,其承认与执行机制面临现实和潜在的困境。

(一)ICSID 仲裁裁决的承认与执行机制

ICSID 仲裁机制的承认与执行制度规定在《华盛顿公约》第 53 条至第 55 条中,形成了一套简单、自动且自足的体系。简言之,《华盛顿公约》第 53 条规定了缔约国不得逾越公约内机制推翻 ICSID 仲裁裁决的效力;第 54 条要求缔约方负有无条件承认 ICSID 仲裁裁决并予以执行的义务;第 55 条则留下国家主权豁免制度在 ICSID 仲裁裁决承认与执行机制中的适用空间。上述 3 条规定构成一套完整的 ICSID 承认与执行制度,主要体现在这 3 条款之间以及与《华盛顿公约》其他条款的相互作用之中。

1. ICSID 仲裁裁决的承认机制

《华盛顿公约》第 53 条直接、明确地规定了 ICSID 仲裁裁决的承认机制。同时,《华盛顿公约》第 53 条与第 25 条和第 54 条共同构成了一套完整的仲裁裁决承认机制。

首先,《华盛顿公约》第 53 条规定:“裁决对双方有约束力。不得进行任何上诉或采取任何其他除本公约规定外的补救办法。除依照本公约有关规定予以停止执行的情况外,每一方应遵守和履行裁决的规定。”第 53 条明确规定 ICSID 仲裁裁决对争议双方具有约束力,且不得通过逾越《华盛顿公约》所规定的机制进行上诉或者采取其他补救手段,这样的规定进一步排除了其他非和平、非良性 ISDS 机制的适用空间。与第 53 条配套的是《华盛顿公约》第 25 条规定的 ICSID 管辖权条款,该条规定,中心的管辖适用于缔约方(或缔约方指派到中心的该国的任何组成部分或机构)和另一缔约方国民之间直接因投资而产生的任何法律争端,而该项争端经双方书面同意提交给中心。当双方表示同意后,任何一方不得单方面撤销其同意。换言之,当缔约方同意将投资者与国家间争议提交 ICSID 解决时,就已明示放弃了主权国家享有的管辖豁免,至于争议过程中的管辖权异议往往是针对案件事实本身是否属于 ICSID 仲裁制度中的可仲裁事由而进行的讨论。而当 ICISD 仲裁庭作出裁判后,借由第 53 条的规定,其裁判即原始地取得了对双方的约束力。两相作用下,ICSID 仲裁裁决获得了既判力,也为进一步的承认机制打下基础。

其次,《华盛顿公约》第 54 条第 1 款规定,每一缔约方应承认本公约作出的裁决具有约束力,并在其领土内履行该裁决所加的财政义务,正如该裁决是该国法院的最后判决一样。具有联邦宪法的缔约方可以在联邦法院或通过该法院执行该裁决,并可规定联邦法院应把该裁决视为其组成的一邦的法院作出的最后判决。第 54 条第 1 款明确要求所有缔约方承认 ICSID 所作出的裁决具有约束力,将其裁判的效力与缔约方国内法院终审裁判的约束力画等号,并要求所有缔约方在其领土范围内履行 ICSID 仲裁裁决所附加的财政义务,这使加入《华盛顿公约》的主权国家不得不承认 ICSID 所作裁判具有权威性。而第 54

条第 2 款规定，要求在一缔约方领土内予以承认或执行的一方，应向该缔约方为此目的而指定的主管法院或其他机构提供经秘书长核证无误的该裁决的副本一份。每一缔约方应将为此目的而指定的主管法院或其他机构以及随后关于此项指定的任何变动通知秘书长。在《华盛顿公约》第 54 条内部规定的相互作用下，强制赋予了缔约方无条件承认 ICSID 仲裁裁决的义务以及告知 ICSID 秘书长有关裁决承认与执行情况的义务，使通过第 53 条获得的既判力得以强化。

综上，ICSID 仲裁裁决的承认机制通过《华盛顿公约》第 53 条和第 25 条的相互作用以及第 54 条规定的作用下，使缔约方负有无条件承认 ICSID 仲裁裁决既判力的义务，并同时排除了缔约方管辖豁免和国内司法干预的适用空间，一方面，体现了 ICSID 仲裁这一特殊形式的国际商事仲裁在其裁决承认阶段也仍具备国际商事仲裁的内核，即契约性；另一方面，满足并体现了 ICSID 机制创设的目的和宗旨，是一套完整的承认机制。

2. ICSID 仲裁裁决的执行机制

如前文所述，《华盛顿公约》使缔约方负有无条件承认其裁决的义务，为 ICSID 仲裁裁决的执行打下基础。但《华盛顿公约》第 53 条至第 55 条所规定的执行机制却缺乏执行力的保证，主要体现在下述三个方面。

首先，《华盛顿公约》并未规定完整的强制执行程序，第 54 条所规定的执行义务仅限于金钱义务，如支付赔偿金及利息，而对于非金钱义务则仍要求缔约方自觉履行。

其次，《华盛顿公约》第 55 条规定，第 54 条的规定不得解释为背离任何缔约方现行的关于免除该国或任何外国予以执行的法律。因为国家主权豁免制度仍可适用于 ICSID 仲裁裁决的执行阶段，所以可能导致 ICSID 仲裁裁决的执行申请人还需再进行一轮争议，甚至有可能使有利于自身的裁决最终无法得到执行。

最后，《华盛顿公约》第 27 条所规定的不遵守或不执行 ICSID 裁决的法律后果的适用空间和可能性过窄,[①]加大了败诉东道国拖延执行或不执行ICSID仲裁裁决的可能性。在上述条款的综合作用下,胜诉投资者仅能通过第54条的规定获得金钱赔偿,但这一获赔还可能受到国家主权豁免制度的阻碍。

可见,ICISD仲裁裁决的执行机制虽看似健全,但实际上是缺乏执行力保证的。从投资者与东道国的关系来看,二者本就实力悬殊,投资者在通过ICSID机制获得了与东道国平等对话解决争议的渠道并获得了有利于自身的裁决结果后,却还需要通过东道国国内相关司法途径实现自身利益,这本身就不能体现仲裁的契约性。所以《华盛顿公约》要求缔约国自觉履行裁判,并且排除了公共秩序保留,不允许缔约方对承认和执行ICSID仲裁裁决作出任何保留,这么做确实在一定程度上保障了执行力。但《华盛顿公约》仅赋予了投资者申请强制执行裁决中金钱义务的权利,使ICSID仲裁裁决的执行申请人可申请强制执行的范围大大缩小,而投资利益本身就是一个大命题,有时非金钱义务所带给投资者的效益是远远大于金钱义务的。[②] 与此同时,《华盛顿公约》又留下了国家主权豁免制度在执行阶段的适用空间,使东道国完全有可能通过国内有关国家豁免的司法制度加以规避自身所负的执行义务,甚至借此制度报复胜诉的投资者。此外,当东道国拒不遵守和执行裁决后,《华盛顿公约》又赋予投资者母国恢复并适用外交保护途径以保护母国投资者的非良性ISDS机制,这本质上违背了《华盛顿公约》"序言"部分所确立的和平解决国际投资争议的精神,原本所搭建的平等对话桥梁因此失去最后一块制度保障。在ICSID仲裁裁决的执行阶段,任何现有的承认和执行ICSID裁决的国际制度都没有为执行申请人提供任何简单有效的方法。

综上所述,将ICSID仲裁的承认与执行机制区分来看,其承认机制是一套

---

① 《华盛顿公约》第27条第1款规定:"缔约国对于其国民和另一缔约国根据本公约已同意交付或已交付仲裁的争端,不得给予外交保护或提出国际要求,除非该另一缔约国未能遵守和履行对此项争端所作出的裁决。"该条第2款规定:"在第一款中,外交保护不应包括纯粹为了促进争端的解决而进行的非正式的外交上的交往。"

② 例如,ICSID仲裁庭裁定投资者与东道国之间订立的投资合同有效、不构成征收或裁定东道国遵照投资合同继续签发许可证等非金钱义务对于投资者来说可能更有利。

完整的、符合《华盛顿公约》精神且彰显商事仲裁契约性的制度,但其执行制度缺乏有力的执行保障。ICSID 仲裁裁决已形成了“自足的”承认机制,但执行机制却受到了国家主权豁免制度的挑战和阻碍。

(二)国家主权豁免制度导致的执行困境

如前文所述,在 ICSID 仲裁中败诉的东道国往往会自觉履行执行的义务,但国家主权豁免制度是胜诉投资者申请执行 ICSID 仲裁裁决的障碍,特别是如何寻获不享有执行豁免的东道国财产。本文将引用“AIG 私募股权有限公司诉哈萨克斯坦”(AIG Capital Partners, Inc., CJSC Tema Real Estate Company v. Kazakhstan, ICSID Case No. ARB/01/6,以下简称“AIG 诉哈萨克斯坦案”)以及“利比里亚东部木材公司诉利比里亚”(Liberian Eastern Timber Corporation v. Republic of Liberia, ICSID Case No. ARB/83/2,以下简称“LETCO 诉利比里亚案”)两案阐述实践中国家主权豁免制度对 ICSID 裁决执行造成的阻碍,即在实践中投资者难以定位并证明申请执行的财产属于东道国的财产。

1. 难以寻获东道国可被执行财产

在“LETCO 诉利比里亚案”中,[①]法国 LETCO 公司在 1986 年 3 月 31 日获得有利于自己的 ICSID 仲裁裁决后,由于利比里亚未自觉执行相关裁决,LETCO 公司遂在美国纽约南部地区法院请求强制执行利比里亚在美国的资产。[②]

首先,LETCO 公司获得了美国纽约南部地区法院承认并执行相关裁决的裁定,但利比里亚很快提出了国家主权豁免请求。美国纽约南部地区法院遂根据美国《1976 年外国主权豁免法》的相关规定进行审查,并通过《1976 年外国主权豁免法》第 1610 条认定 LETCO 公司申请执行的利比里亚在美国的资产不可执行,因其是用于利比里亚主权职能的税收收入,而不是用于商业职能的

① 参见余劲松:《国际投资法》,法律出版社 2018 年版,第 342 页。

② Lucy Reed, Jan Paulsson, Nigel Blackaby, *Guide to ICSID Arbitration* (Second Edition), Kluwer Law International, 2010, p. 188.

财产,于是美国纽约南部地区法院撤销了对相关财产的执行命令。其次,LETCO公司又在美国哥伦比亚特区法院请求执行利比里亚位于华盛顿的大使馆的银行账户中的资产,但最终美国哥伦比亚特区法院又撤销了相关查封命令,理由是根据《维也纳外交关系公约》和美国《1976年外国主权豁免法》的规定,上述相关账户中的资金具有公共性质且大使馆银行账户因享有外交豁免权是免予查封扣押的。[①]

由"LETCO诉利比里亚案"的执行过程可以看出,美国在其国内有关国家主权豁免的法律中都注重对国家资产是否用于"商业活动"(Commercial Activity)[②]进行审查,但因证明执行财产用于"商业活动"的举证责任在执行申请人一方,故导致的后果是ICSID裁决的执行申请人在有相关国家主权豁免制度立法的国家难以找到合适且合格的被申请执行的东道国资产。ICSID仲裁裁决的执行申请人只能像LETCO公司一样不断寻找相关资产,再予以证明其是否属于可被执行的财产,徒增执行申请人的司法成本,而在缺乏相关国家主权豁免制度立法的国家则更加难以实际执行败诉东道国的资产以填补遭受的损失。美国《1976年外国主权豁免法》对豁免的例外并未有明晰界定,更未对"商业活动"进行认定,但如下述"AIG诉哈萨克斯坦案"一样,即使申请执行地有相关的立法或司法对"商业活动"进行了规定,执行申请人也难以寻获符合标准的东道国财产。

2. 难以界定东道国财产的属性

在"AIG诉哈萨克斯坦案"中[③],美国AIG公司实际控股的CJSC Tema房地产公司,于1999年12月13日与哈萨克斯坦投资局签订房地产建设合同。在完成大部分建设后,哈萨克斯坦发布停止施工的命令。CJSC Tema房地产公

---

① Anastasiia Filipiuk, *Enforcement of ICSID Arbitration Awards and Sovereign Immunity*, http://www.etd.ceu.hu/2016/filipiuk_anastasiia.pdf, July 20, 2020.

② 有学者将其翻译为"商业行为"、"商业目的"、"商业活动"或"商业资产",均意为用于商业的国家资产,为方便表述,本文统一表述为"商业活动"。

③ "AIG Capital Partners, Inc., CJSC Tema Real Estate Company v. Kazakhstan (ICSID Case No. ARB/01/6)", https://www.italaw.com/sites/default/files/case-documents/italaw3077.pdf, July 20, 2020.

司遂于2000年6月16日以不可抗力为由,解除其与下游建筑承包商的施工合同并支付了违约金。为解决争议,AIG公司于2001年6月4日向ICSID发起针对哈萨克斯坦的国际投资仲裁。该案经仲裁庭审议后,裁定哈萨克斯坦政府部门的行为构成对投资者在哈萨克斯坦境内投资的征收,哈萨克斯坦政府应当向投资者支付非法征收赔偿金以及预期利益损失。随后AIG公司试图在英国执行ICSID裁决,并成功在英国登记了该裁决的执行请求。但AIG公司试图将第三方银行以哈萨克斯坦国家银行的名义在英国持有的,且利益归属于哈萨克斯坦国家银行的现金和证券作为执行标的。AIG公司认为,上述资产是哈萨克斯坦的资产因而获得了这些账户的临时扣押命令,但哈萨克斯坦和哈萨克斯坦国家银行随即提出适用国家主权豁免制度。①

英国法院在其分析过程中认为,如果被认定为是用于"商业活动"的财产则不属于豁免的例外,是可以被执行的国家财产。因此,英国法院在对主权国家财产进行强制执行时需要"确定一国中央银行或货币当局所持有的某一特定资产,在相关的时间内,是否正在使用或打算用于商业活动"。② 法院在分析后确定,对于第三方银行以哈萨克斯坦国家银行的名义在英国持有的,且利益归属于哈萨克斯坦国家银行的现金和证券,哈萨克斯坦国家银行对其享有相关的专属合同权利。因此,"在所有情况下,哈萨克斯坦国家银行的财产不应被视为正在使用或打算用于商业活动"。③ 故法院作出裁定认为,上述哈萨克斯

---

① "AIG Capital Partners Inc. and Another v. Republic of Kazakhstan (National Bank of Kazakhstan Intervening), Queen's Bench Division of the High Court of England and Wales, October 20, 2005, [2005] E. W. H. C. Comm. 2239, 129 I. L. R. 589, 589 – 628 (2007)", https://www.italaw.com/sites/default/files/case-documents/ita0022.pdf, July 20, 2020. R. Doak Bishop, James Crawford, et al., *Foreign Investment Disputes: Cases, Materials and Commentary* (*Second Edition*), Kluwer Law International, 2014, p. 1264 – 1271.

② "AIG Capital Partners Inc. and Another v. Republic of Kazakhstan (National Bank of Kazakhstan Intervening), Queen's Bench Division of the High Court of England and Wales, October 20, 2005, [2005] E. W. H. C. Comm. 2239, 129 I. L. R. 589, 589 – 628, para. 58 (2007)", https://www.italaw.com/sites/default/files/case-documents/ita0022.pdf, July 20, 2020.

③ "AIG Capital Partners, Inc., CJSC Tema Real Estate Company v. Kazakhstan (ICSID Case No. ARB/01/6)", https://www.italaw.com/sites/default/files/case-documents/italaw3077.pdf, July 20, 2020.

坦国家银行的财产受到英国法院完全执行豁免的保护，法院随即解除了临时扣押令。

在上述案例中，英国法院根据其《1978年国家豁免法》以及国家主权豁免制度的一般规则的规定，审查最重要的标准是申请执行的标的是否属于国家资产以及是否正在用于或打算用于"商业活动"。正因如此，证明申请执行的财产是否用于"商业活动"则成为投资者所负担的举证责任，而投资者难以举证证明申请执行的财产属于东道国用于"商业活动"的财产。并且由于一国法院并不愿意侵犯外国主权，故申请执行地法院也不愿在实际的案件中清晰界定相关判断标准以供投资者参考辅证。

综上，在申请执行ICISD仲裁裁决的过程中，一旦东道国运用国家主权豁免制度阻碍执行，随即产生的就是申请执行财产的属性问题。一方面，申请执行地法院不愿干涉他国主权，故不愿作出相关属性判断的标准；另一方面，申请执行人承担了相关举证责任，却没有相关依据予以辅证。在此情况下，ICSID仲裁裁决的执行因难以界定东道国财产的属性而受阻。

总体而言，在国际法层面，有关国家主权豁免最重要的两个条约是2004年《联合国豁免公约》和1972年《欧洲国家豁免公约》，但《联合国豁免公约》至今仍未生效，而《欧洲国家豁免公约》缔约方数量有限，所以两大公约的实际影响力非常有限。而在国内法层面，国家豁免立法在英美法系的英国、美国等国表现为成文立法，而大陆法系的主要国家均没有国家豁免的专门立法，需要从案例中梳理该国的国家主权豁免规则。在国内立法中，美国《1976年外国主权豁免法》和英国《1978年国家豁免法》有关仲裁与国家豁免的规定最全面。[①] 但从上述两个案例可以看出，两部国内立法的实际操作空间十分有限，且有关法院对于"商业活动"的解释较狭窄且严格，故在实践中往往不能保障ICSID裁决得到实际执行。并且国内立法相较一般国际法规则的不稳定性更大，主权国家完全可以通过国内司法程序修改相关国家主权豁免的立法，从而加大ICSID

① 杨玲：《论条约仲裁裁决执行中的国家豁免——以ICSID裁决执行为中心》，载《法学评论》2012年第6期。

裁决实际执行的难度。

三、涉华国际投资仲裁裁决在中国承认与执行的障碍

"一带一路"倡议自2013年提出至今,已在国际贸易和国际投资领域产生巨大影响,尤其在国际投资领域。根据《2020年世界投资报告》统计,中国自2016年起引入外国直接投资(Foreign Direct Investment,FDI)流量以平均每年2.525%的比率增长,引出FDI流量以平均每年2.9%的比率增长。[①] 随之而来的,是中国为"一带一路"建设所提供的司法服务也渐趋完善。2015年7月,最高人民法院发布《关于人民法院为"一带一路"建设提供司法服务和保障的若干意见》,规定人民法院应当加强承认与执行涉"一带一路"仲裁的司法审查,保障仲裁机制能够为加强"一带一路"司法保障、化解投资纠纷发挥积极作用。2017年7月,在最高人民法院发布的《涉"一带一路"建设典型案例》(第二批)中,中国认定与新加坡之间的互惠关系,首次承认和执行了新加坡法院商事判决,这体现了人民法院为"一带一路"沿线国投资提供有力司法服务的决心,也打开了人民法院执行涉"一带一路"生效裁判文书的新局面。此外,2017年9月19日,中国国际经济贸易仲裁委员(以下简称贸仲)召开新闻发布会,发布了《中国国际经济贸易仲裁委员会国际投资争端仲裁规则》(以下简称《投资仲裁规则》)。《投资仲裁规则》的出台,填补了中国国际投资仲裁领域的空白,丰富和发展了中国投资仲裁实践,为中国企业提供解决与东道国投资争端的制度化保障,为营造中国更加国际化、法治化、便利化的营商环境迈出了坚实一步。[②] 由此可见,中国司法机关和仲裁机构为提高"一带一路"建设中的争议解决服务水平不断地作出尝试,其重点是推动国际投资仲裁制度在中国的完善,而其中最重要的一环仍然是仲裁裁决的承认与执行制度。

---

① 《2020年世界投资报告——国别报告:中国》(World Investment Report 2020 - Country Fact Sheet: China),载联合国贸易和发展会议(United Nations Conference on Trade and Development, UNCTAD)网,https://unctad.org/sections/dite_dir/docs/wir2020/wir20_fs_cn_en.pdf。

② 《贸仲〈投资仲裁规则〉新闻发布会通信稿》,载贸仲网站2017年9月19日,http://www.cietac.org.cn/index.php?m=Article&a=show&id=14450。

在上述“一带一路”建设相关配套司法服务中,我们应当重视涉华国际投资仲裁裁决在中国承认与执行的相关问题。但不可否认的是,无论是ICSID还是非ICSID国际商事仲裁机构作出的涉华国际投资仲裁裁决,其在中国的承认与执行存在制度阻碍。

(一)涉华ICSID仲裁裁决在中国的承认与执行可能遭到中国仲裁司法审查制度的阻碍

涉华国际投资争议在ICSID仲裁机制项下止步于管辖权争议阶段,自然也就没有涉华ICSID仲裁裁决在中国承认与执行的实践案例。虽然在实践中没有涉华ICSID仲裁裁决在中国法院进入承认与执行程序,但结合《仲裁法》和《民事诉讼法》等相关法律规定可以推知,将来涉华ICSID仲裁裁决在中国法院进行承认和执行时可能遭遇中国仲裁司法审查制度的障碍。

2017年12月26日,最高人民法院颁布《关于审理仲裁司法审查案件若干问题的规定》(法释〔2017〕22号)以及《关于仲裁司法审查案件报核问题的有关规定》(法释〔2017〕21号)(以下合称《最高院仲裁司法审查规定》),两部司法解释都已生效。此次颁布的《最高院仲裁司法审查规定》是继《民事诉讼法》《仲裁法》以及相关司法解释颁布并修订后,再一次以规范性文件形式重述中国《仲裁法》的适用及中国仲裁司法审查制度。《最高院仲裁司法审查规定》最大的亮点是其列明了仲裁司法审查案件的6种类型,[①]并且人民法院在进行仲裁司法审查时不再区分涉外仲裁机构与非涉外仲裁机构所作出的裁决,统一适用《民事诉讼法》的相关规定。[②]

---

① 最高人民法院《关于审理仲裁司法审查案件若干问题的规定》以及《关于仲裁司法审查案件报核问题的有关规定》第1条作出了相同的规定:“本规定所称仲裁司法审查案件,包括下列案件:(一)申请确认仲裁协议效力案件;(二)申请撤销我国内地仲裁机构的仲裁裁决案件;(三)申请执行我国内地仲裁机构的仲裁裁决案件;(四)申请认可和执行香港特别行政区、澳门特别行政区、台湾地区仲裁裁决案件;(五)申请承认和执行外国仲裁裁决案件;(六)其他仲裁司法审查案件。”

② 最高人民法院《关于审理仲裁司法审查案件若干问题的规定》第17条规定:“人民法院对申请执行我国内地仲裁机构作出的非涉外仲裁裁决案件的审查,适用《中华人民共和国民事诉讼法》第二百三十七条的规定。人民法院对申请执行我国内地仲裁机构作出的涉外仲裁裁决案件的审查,适用《中华人民共和国民事诉讼法》第二百七十四条的规定。”

虽然此次颁布的《最高院仲裁司法审查规定》加强了仲裁司法审查的统一归口管理，并系统完善了仲裁司法审查的实务操作规程，具有支持仲裁发展的积极意义，但它们共同构成的仲裁司法审查制度在实践中可能不符合《华盛顿公约》所确立的 ICSID 仲裁裁决承认与执行机制，不适应涉华国际投资仲裁裁决在中国法院承认和执行的要求。具体而言，根据《华盛顿公约》第 53 条的规定，该公约的缔约方在 ICSID 仲裁庭发布最终裁决后被禁止采取其他非《华盛顿公约》机制（如执行地国的国内机制）进行救济。而《最高院仲裁司法审查规定》列明的 6 种不予执行仲裁裁决的情况尽管被认为主要针对的是普通商事仲裁案件，并且迄今为止在中国的司法实践中也并未见到涉及对 ICSID 仲裁裁决进行司法审查的案例，但至少从条文规定上并没有明确将 ICSID 仲裁案件排除在外。同时，《民事诉讼法》第 237 条规定的人民法院不予执行仲裁机构裁决制度中，①也同样未明确排除该制度适用于 ICSID 仲裁案件的可能性。因此，ICSID 仲裁裁决是有可能在中国的仲裁司法审查制度下被撤销或不予承认和执行的。这也意味着，中国法院若根据前述《最高院仲裁司法审查规定》和《民事诉讼法》的规定，拒绝承认和执行 ICSID 仲裁裁决，就是采取了《华盛顿公约》以外的机制进行救济，而这是被《华盛顿公约》所禁止的。

（二）涉华非 ICSID 的国际投资争议仲裁裁决无法通过《纽约公约》在中国获得承认与执行

ICSID 作为全球最大的解决国际投资争议的机构，其仲裁庭作出的仲裁裁决可借由《华盛顿公约》的规定进入裁决后的承认与执行阶段。但其他非

① 《民事诉讼法》第 237 条规定："对依法设立的仲裁机构的裁决，一方当事人不履行的，对方当事人可以向有管辖权的人民法院申请执行。受申请的人民法院应当执行。被申请人提出证据证明仲裁裁决有下列情形之一的，经人民法院组成合议庭审查核实，裁定不予执行：（一）当事人在合同中没有订有仲裁条款或者事后没有达成书面仲裁协议的；（二）裁决的事项不属于仲裁协议的范围或者仲裁机构无权仲裁的；（三）仲裁庭的组成或者仲裁的程序违反法定程序的；（四）裁决所根据的证据是伪造的；（五）对方当事人向仲裁机构隐瞒了足以影响公正裁决的证据的；（六）仲裁员在仲裁该案时有贪污受贿，徇私舞弊，枉法裁决行为的。人民法院认定执行该裁决违背社会公共利益的，裁定不予执行。裁定书应当送达双方当事人和仲裁机构。仲裁裁决被人民法院裁定不予执行的，当事人可以根据双方达成的书面仲裁协议重新申请仲裁，也可以向人民法院起诉。"

ICSID 仲裁机构，如常设仲裁法院（Permanent Court of Arbitration，PCA）、国际商会仲裁院（International Chamber of Commerce，ICC）、斯德哥尔摩商会仲裁院（The Arbitration Institute of the Stockholm Chamber of Commerce，AISCC）等国际商事仲裁机构也受理国际投资仲裁案件。这些非 ICSID 国际商事仲裁机构所作出的国际投资仲裁裁决，其承认与执行通常而言需要依靠东道国自觉履行，或根据东道国以及申请承认与执行裁决地的国内相关立法进行申请。虽然《纽约公约》本身并没有排除国际投资仲裁裁决适用的空间，但根据《纽约公约》的相关规定，适用《纽约公约》的裁决开启承认与执行程序仍然需要依靠国内法的规定。因此，一国法院如依照《纽约公约》开启对国际投资仲裁裁决的司法审查程序，其结果将难以预见。①

但根据中国加入《纽约公约》时所作的保留，②涉华非 ICSID 的国际投资仲裁裁决无法通过《纽约公约》在中国申请承认与执行的。例如，一个中国投资者与日本政府发生了国际投资争议并将争议提交 PCA 进行仲裁，那么中国投资者就 PCA 所作出的国际投资仲裁裁决无法通过《纽约公约》在中国申请承认并执行日本在中国的财产，从而加大了中国投资者的维权成本。

综上所述，《最高院仲裁司法审查规定》，一方面，有意扩大仲裁司法审查制度的覆盖范围，完善中国仲裁裁决承认与执行制度的公信力；另一方面，加强了《纽约公约》在中国仲裁司法审查制度中的作用。但从中国现行仲裁司法审查制度以及《纽约公约》目前在中国的适用空间来看，中国现行的仲裁承认与执行机制以及仲裁司法审查制度，可能不适应涉华国际投资仲裁裁决（包括 ICSID 与非 ICSID 仲裁机构作出的裁决）在中国顺利地获得承认与执行。

① 池漫郊：《国际仲裁体制的若干问题及完善》，法律出版社2014年版，第317页。

② 根据中国加入该公约时所作的商事保留声明，中国仅对按照我国法律属于契约性和非契约性商事法律关系所引起的争议适用《纽约公约》。所谓“契约性和非契约性商事法律关系”，具体是指由于合同、侵权或者根据有关法律规定而产生的经济上的权利义务关系，如货物买卖、财产租赁、工程承包、加工承揽、技术转让、合资经营、合作经营、勘探开发自然资源、保险、信贷、劳务、代理、咨询服务和海上、民用航空、铁路、公路的客货运输以及产品责任、环境污染、海上事故和所有权争议等，但不包括外国投资者与东道国政府之间的争端。

四、完善涉华国际投资仲裁裁决在中国承认与执行制度的构想

随着“一带一路”建设的推进,涉华国际投资(尤其是“一带一路”沿线国家间的国际投资)获得了更大发展。在此背景下,为了给涉华国际投资提供司法保障,进一步促进涉华国际投资的发展,有必要完善涉华国际投资仲裁裁决在中国承认与执行的制度。针对ICSID作出的涉华国际投资仲裁裁决,中国应当探索建立与《华盛顿公约》相匹配的承认与执行机制以及国家主权豁免制度;而针对其他非ICSID的仲裁机构作出的涉华国际投资仲裁裁决以及通过非国际投资仲裁解决的涉华国际投资争议,中国可以借鉴司法互惠关系探索建立仲裁互惠关系并审慎评估《纽约公约》的适用空间。

(一)探索建立ICSID仲裁裁决承认执行机制与国家主权豁免制度

在“一带一路”建设的背景下,针对涉华ICSID仲裁裁决,中国需要有与《华盛顿公约》规定的承认与执行机制相配套的仲裁承认与执行机制,此外,还需要有国家主权豁免制度的相关立法。

首先,如前文所述,考虑到中国目前的仲裁裁决承认与执行制度中的司法审查程序有可能不符合ICSID仲裁审议的案件在中国获得承认与执行的要求。为了改变这一局面,笔者认为,中国当前的仲裁司法审查制度在明确不适用于ICSID作出的国际投资仲裁裁决的大前提下,应当重新评估和完善相关仲裁裁决司法审查制度,并加以立法化、确定化。

其次,考虑到中国目前并没有相关国家主权豁免的立法,笔者认为,应当将国家主权豁免制度的立法工作提上议程,并审慎考虑中国的国家主权豁免制度是应当继续主张完全豁免还是限制豁免。针对ICSID仲裁裁决的承认与执行,中国相关国家主权豁免制度应主张限制豁免。一方面,中国目前所主张的国家主权绝对豁免立场,使中国赴外投资的投资者在海外投资受到投资地东道国的侵害时既无法在中国发起国际投资仲裁,也无法在获得有利裁决后在中国执行外国国家的财产;另一方面,在国家主权绝对豁免的立场下,势必动摇外国投资者来中国进行投资的信心。因此,在“一带一路”建设的背景下,中国目前采用

的国家主权绝对豁免立场难以有效保护中国赴外国投资的投资者，也无法更多、更好地吸引外国投资者来中国进行投资，故国家主权完全豁免制度与中国国际投资的发展不相适应。可喜的是，虽然中国目前坚持的是完全国家主权豁免，这在中国立法、司法和外交活动中都有所体现，但中国早在2005年就参与了《联合国国家及其财产管辖豁免公约》的谈判，近年出台的相关法律文件也不断强调仲裁制度在解决国际投资争端中的作用。①

（二）借鉴司法互惠关系探索并完善通过非ICSID仲裁方式解决的涉华国际投资争议的承认与执行机制

在最高人民法院于2017年5月发布的《第二批涉"一带一路"建设典型案例》中的第五个案例，即在"高尔集团股份有限公司申请承认和执行新加坡高等法院民事判决案"中，②江苏省南京市中级人民法院通过认定中国与新加坡的司法互惠关系，首次承认与执行了新加坡法院商事判决，这为推动"一带一路"背景下ISDS机制的承认与执行提供了可资借鉴的思路。

一方面，针对其他非ICSID的国际商事仲裁机构作出的涉华国际投资仲裁裁决，可参考司法互惠关系探索建立仲裁互惠关系也是完善国际投资争议在中国承认与执行制度的构想，并可能推动ISDS机制的进一步发展。但这种尝试需要审慎评估《纽约公约》在其中的适用空间，中国的仲裁机构也应当为这种尝试加强对国际投资仲裁的学习。另一方面，国际投资争议除通过国际投资仲裁外，还可以通过如协商、调解、东道国国内司法救济等多种途径解决。如上文所述，像新加坡法院作出的商事判决，其本质上属于法院判决，亦可以通过国家间司法互惠关系进行承认和执行。但是中国仅与37个国家签订了民商事领域

---

① 全小莲、刘步蟾：《"一带一路"司法服务中的ISDS裁决承认与执行问题研究》，载《人民法治》2018年第2期。

② 最高人民法院：《第二批涉"一带一路"建设典型案例》，载最高人民法院网站2017年5月15日，http://www.court.gov.cn/zixun-xiangqing-44722.html。

的司法协助条约,其中有 32 个国家为“一带一路”沿线国,[①]而截至 2020 年 1 月,已有 138 个国家与中国签订了“一带一路”合作文件。[②] 因此,笔者认为,中国应当积极与他国在民商事领域签订司法协助条约,尤其是“一带一路”倡议的沿线国。此外,中国已签署了于 2019 年 7 月 2 日达成的《承认与执行外国民商事判决公约》(Convention on the Recognition and Enforcement of Foreign Judgments in Civil or Commercial Matters),[③]该公约的批准和实施将有利于完善涉华国际投资判决的承认与执行机制。

五、结语

总结全文,《华盛顿公约》“自足的”仲裁裁决承认和执行制度中,仅仲裁裁决承认机制保障了 ICSID 仲裁裁决的权威性和既判力,但在《华盛顿公约》制度本身和国家主权豁免制度的作用下,其执行机制缺乏执行力导致了 ICSID 仲裁裁决面临难以执行的困境。

在“一带一路”建设的背景下,中国应当注重预防与解决潜在的涉华国际投资争议,而当涉华国际投资争议得到解决后则更应注重相关结果的最终实现。从目前情况看,涉华国际投资仲裁在中国的承认与执行机制和制度并不完备,无法很好地承担《华盛顿公约》规定的国际条约义务。因此,为确保涉华国际投资仲裁可以在中国获得良好的承认与执行,中国首先应当探索建立符合《华盛顿公约》的 ICSID 仲裁裁决承认与执行机制并开启国家主权豁免的制度设计,其次可以尝试建立国际投资仲裁互惠关系以保障其他非 ICSID 的国际仲

---

① 中国目前在民商事领域仅与 37 个国家签订了司法协助条约,分别为阿尔及利亚、阿根廷、阿联酋、埃及、埃塞俄比亚、巴西、白俄罗斯、保加利亚、波黑、波兰、朝鲜、俄罗斯、法国、古巴、哈萨克斯坦、韩国、吉尔吉斯斯坦、科威特、老挝、立陶宛、罗马尼亚、蒙古、秘鲁、摩洛哥、塞浦路斯、塔吉克斯坦、泰国、突尼斯、土耳其、乌克兰、乌兹别克斯坦、西班牙、希腊、新加坡、匈牙利、意大利、越南。除阿根廷、巴西、朝鲜、法国与西班牙外均为“一带一路”沿线国。

② 刘梦:《已同中国签订共建“一带一路”合作文件的国家一览》,载中国一带一路网 2021 年 3 月 12 日,https://www.yidaiyilu.gov.cn/gbjg/gbgk/77073.htm。

③ 《海牙国际私法会议第22届外交大会通过〈承认与执行外国民商事判决公约〉》,载最高人民法院国际商事法庭官网 2019 年 7 月 13 日,http://cicc.court.gov.cn/html/1/218/149/156/1271.html。

裁机构作出的涉华国际投资仲裁裁决获得承认与执行,并积极与他国(尤其是“一带一路”沿线国)达成在民商事领域的司法互惠协定,从而完善通过其他非国际投资仲裁方式解决的涉华国际投资争议的承认与执行机制。

国际商事仲裁透明度与保密性的平衡发展及对中国的启示

唐 峰*

摘要：与其他国际商事纠纷解决机制相比，保密性一直是国际商事仲裁的重要特征和竞争优势之一。近年来，透明度在国际仲裁界中备受热议，特别是随着国际投资仲裁迅速发展，国际上有关增加国际仲裁程序的公开性和透明度的呼声越来越高。增加国际商事仲裁程序的透明度要求与商事仲裁自身保密性要求相悖，但随着仲裁实践进一步发展，对两者出现了一种平衡的需求。比较和分析不同法域及国际仲裁机构处理保密性与透明度的方式，不难发现，平衡两者的核心在于划定保密义务的范围以及增加透明度规则的比例。这对中国商事仲裁立法和实践具有重要启发意义。较长一段时间里，中国《仲裁法》和仲裁规则所确立的保密性制度并不完善，以致在仲裁实践中适用保密性制度时存在理解上的偏差。以国外立法和实践经验为鉴，以中国本土商事仲裁制度为本，建议中国《仲裁法》和仲裁规则应完善其保密性制度，重视透明度规则对商事仲裁发展的积极影响，引导争端当事方订立保密协议、建立仲裁信息分类和公开制度、重点公开仲裁裁决、提高中国仲裁规则国际化水平。

关键词：国际商事仲裁　透明度　保密性

---

* 武汉大学法学院经济法学硕士研究生。

一、引言

2013年,习近平主席提出建设"一带一路"的倡议,得到了国际社会的广泛关注,各国积极响应和参与。在"一带一路"建设过程中,中国对外商业贸易和投资活动数量大幅增加,与此同时也产生了大量国际商事纠纷。国际商事仲裁在解决这些国际商事纠纷上相对其他国际商事纠纷解决方式具有效率高、成本低和国际执行保障强等优势,因此它是各方争议解决的重要选择之一。2015年4月,国务院发布了《进一步深化中国(上海)自由贸易试验区改革开放方案的通知》,宣布支持国际商事争端解决机构进驻中国。如我国香港特别行政区国际仲裁中心、新加坡国际仲裁中心和国际商会仲裁院等国际知名仲裁机构都在上海自由贸易试验区设立了各自的办事处,给中外当事人解决国际商事纠纷提供了更多选择。中国国际经济贸易仲裁委员会主编的《中国国际商事仲裁年度报告(2018~2019)》指出,2018年,全国255家仲裁委员会共受理案件544,536件,同比增加305,176件,增长率为127%;案件标的总额6950亿元,比2017年增加1612亿元,增长率为30%。其中,中国国际经济贸易仲裁委员会(以下简称贸仲)受理仲裁案件2962件,涉案标的额人民币1015.9亿元,创历史新高。[①] 未来,随着"一带一路"持续深入推进、中国对外开放步伐不断加快,中外当事人对国际商事争端解决法律服务的需求也会不断增加,特别是非诉讼纠纷解决法律服务,如国际商事仲裁。

国际商事仲裁在学术理论上是国际经济法中一种非常重要的国际商事纠纷解决机制。而国际商事仲裁透明度与保密性的平衡问题又是该纠纷解决制度中的一个重要问题。透明度能够保障仲裁案件的公平处理,保密性则激励争议双方发挥其主观能动性、降低案件对后续争议方商事活动的不良影响。但上述国际商事仲裁的两种价值在一定程度上处于对立状态。为促进国际商事仲裁机制进一步完善和发展,需在制度设计上平衡两者之间的冲突。为了更好地

① 中国国际经济贸易仲裁委员会主编:《中国国际商事仲裁年度报告(2018~2019)》,法律出版社2019年版,第1页。

解决国际商事纠纷,服务"一带一路"和自贸区建设,有必要通过对国际商事仲裁透明度与保密性平衡问题的研究,使中国商事仲裁制度的相关立法更加合理,从而为处理国际商事纠纷提供更优化的制度保障。

国内关于国际商事仲裁透明度与保密性平衡发展的研究较少。关于国际商事仲裁保密性的研究,最早且较完整的是杨良宜先生的著作《仲裁法:从1996年英国仲裁法到国际商务仲裁》。该书第十三章介绍了仲裁的机密性①及其适用范围、有关国家的制度和相关案例节选,以及案例中由于仲裁机密性可能出现的问题,但并没有详细讨论这些问题。在中国知网上,无论是关于仲裁保密性的论文,还是关于国际商事仲裁透明度的研究,都不多见。其中,林其敏女士的《国际商事仲裁的透明度问题研究》一文对该问题的研究较深入。涉及国际商事仲裁透明度和保密性平衡问题的期刊论文大多是通过论述保密性及其例外来体现,而并不直接对保密性和透明度平衡问题进行研究。对于这种研究现状,笔者认为原因有二:一是中国商事仲裁发展虽然迅速,但立法和实践深度有限,因此"保密性是原则,公开是例外"的观念深入人心,而透明度的概念是随着联合国国际贸易法委员会关于投资仲裁的透明度规则②的传播才不断进入中国学者的视野。二是在选题时,实践的不足也阻碍了对相关问题研究的开展。近年来,随着中国进一步走向国际舞台,国际商事仲裁在中国日益受到重视,研究此问题的国内学者和研究成果也越来越多。

国外关于该问题的研究则较为丰富和深入。比如,艾米·施密特(Amy J. Schmitz)在《破解仲裁私密难题》③一文中讨论了仲裁私密性④的迷思,建议起草关于透明度的条款。在《仲裁保密假定》⑤一文中,其分析了保密性的优势和劣势,建议综合平衡各方利益,决定仲裁是否保密。辛迪·柏斯(Cindy G.

---

① 依笔者理解,"机密性"与本文所述"保密性"内涵基本相同。

② "UNCITRAL Rules on Transparency in Treaty-Based Arbitration Between Investors and States",中国学者一般译为《贸易法委员会投资人与国家间基于条约仲裁透明度规则》(以下简称《透明度规则》)。

③ See Amy J. Schmitz, *Untangling the Privacy Paradox in Arbitration*, University of Kansas Law Review 54, 2011, p. 1211.

④ "私密性"与"保密性"含义并非完全相同,具体区别详见下文。

⑤ See Amy J. Schmitz, *Assuming Silence in Arbitration*, New Jersey Lawyer 269, 2011, p. 16.

Buys)在《国际仲裁中保密性与透明度的紧张关系》[①]一文中,讨论了国际仲裁保密性和透明度之间的紧张关系,并倾向弱化仲裁的保密性。凯瑟琳·罗杰斯(Catherine A. Rogers)在《国际商事仲裁之透明度》[②]一文中,探索了透明度的概念界定和国际商事仲裁一些重要的透明度改革措施,并认为强制性的透明度改革要在国际水平上进行,并且最终要从根本上重构国际商事仲裁制度。克里斯多夫·亨克尔(Christoph Henkel)在《国际商事仲裁保密义务的司法执行方法:工作成果原则》[③]一文中,讨论了工作成果主义(Work-Product Doctrine)这一美国民事诉讼法理论如何运用于国际商事仲裁中作为判断是否需要保密的工具,以便平衡各方利益。马修·卡莫迪(Matthew Carmody)在《推翻保密性假定:国际贸易法委员会应否应用于国际商事仲裁》[④]一文中,讨论了受到国际投资仲裁《透明度规则》影响的国际商事仲裁,并认为《透明度规则》的影响力应该扩展到国际商事仲裁领域并得以适用。董雪莲(Sherlin Hsie-lien Tung)和布莱恩·林(Brian Lin)在《国际商事仲裁是否需要更多透明度》[⑤]中讨论了众多国际仲裁机构进行透明度改革的举措,认为在保密性与透明度中间,后者应获得更多关注。总体来说,国外关于上述问题的研究有以下特点:一是注重利益平衡;二是强调尊重当事人的意愿和公共利益。

在上述研究的基础上,笔者通过总结国内外有关国际商事仲裁透明度与保密性平衡问题的研究,着重分析研究各国以及各国际商事仲裁机构在平衡保密性和透明度上的立法和实践,指出中国仲裁法和中国仲裁规则在该问题上的不

---

① See Cindy G. Buys, *The Tensions between Confidentiality and Transparency in International Arbitration*, The American Review of International Arbitration 14, 2003, p. 121.

② See Catherine A. Rogers, *Transparency in International Commercial Arbitration*, University of Kansas Law Review 54, 2006, p. 1301.

③ See Christoph Henkel, *The Work Product Doctrine as a Means toward a Judicially Enforceable Duty of Confidentiality in International Commercial Arbitration*, North Carolina Journal of International Law and Commercial Regulation 37, 2012, p. 1059.

④ See Matthew Carmody, *Overturning the Presumption of Confidentiality: Should the UNCITRAL Rules on Transparency Be Applied to International Commercial Arbitration*, International Trade & Business Law Review 19, 2016, p. 96.

⑤ See Sherlin Hsie-lien Tung & Brian Lin, *More Transparency in International Commercial Arbitration: To Have or Not to Have*, Contemporary Asia Arbitration Journal 11, 2018, p. 21.

足之处,并试图提出完善中国立法的建议。

二、国际商事仲裁保密性弱化和透明度增加概述

随着跨国企业腐败丑闻的影响不断扩散,国际社会普遍要求对影响人们生活众多方面的商业组织和机构进行更多监督,尤其是当其处于某种争议中时。在国际商事仲裁领域这一需求也逐渐凸显,体现为各国仲裁法律制度、仲裁规则在制度设计上的转向,即在对待仲裁的保密性上,弱化严格的保密义务、增加透明度规则的比例。了解国际商事仲裁保密性与透明度内涵、厘清上述两个概念的边界,有助于理解国际商事仲裁透明度需求增加的逻辑。

(一)相关概念的区分

区分保密性与私密性两者之间的差异,厘清透明度与披露、公众参与 3 个术语的关系,是正确认识保密性与透明度两种价值在国际商事仲裁中重要地位的基础,也是深入分析和探讨不同法域和国际仲裁机构在平衡保密性和透明度上的立法和实践的前提。因此,有必要对上述两组相关概念的内涵进行深入挖掘。

1. 保密性与私密性

保密性是仲裁最显著的特征之一,且一直都是争端当事方选择其作为纠纷解决方式的重要原因。在国际商事仲裁领域,尽管近些年来仲裁的保密性受到一定程度的冲击并逐渐被弱化,①但它仍被视为仲裁优势和吸引力的一个重要方面。对于国际商事仲裁保密性的概念,国际上并无一致性意见,但依不公开审理的原则以及学界相关论文印证,可认为保密性大致指的是国际商事仲裁参与方不得将与仲裁案件有关的资料文件信息,包括当事人、证据、非证据材料、仲裁裁决等向第三方扩散传播。传统观念认为,保密性在仲裁程序中具有重大优势,可以提高仲裁程序的效率,不仅给争端当事方提供一个自由协商的平台,同时也减少了媒体和商业竞争者以及其他非当事方获取重要商业信息的可能。

---

① 对透明度的要求起源于国际投资仲裁,但近年来国际商事仲裁的保密性也逐渐弱化,透明度逐渐增加。参见毛樑:《国际商事仲裁保密性的弱化》,载《北京仲裁》2016 年第 4 期。

由于它使当事方在仲裁中不受其客户或是市场的监督，从而有更多机会达成在受到此类监督时可能无法达成的协议。另外，由于当事方一般不愿因自己不履行达成的协议而使对方当事人向法院申请执行仲裁裁决，从而造成仲裁裁决的公开，争端当事方履行仲裁裁决和相关协议的意愿会更强。[①]

理解国际商事仲裁的保密性并不难，但想要轻易将它与仲裁私密性区分却并不容易。仲裁私密性意指仲裁仅与争端当事方有关，任何与仲裁案件无关的第三方无事实或法律上的原因不应参与仲裁程序中来。保密性和私密性之间的微妙差异使争端当事方错误地认为他们的纠纷会因为仲裁程序的私密性而自动保密。[②] 但实际上，仲裁的私密性，是指在没有争端当事方或是仲裁员同意的情况下，第三方不能参与仲裁程序。而保密性则更倾向减少信息的传播，包括仲裁的内容、所提供的证据和所产生的文件、仲裁庭的裁决、仲裁庭的记录和仲裁裁决等。私密性可看作一种实现保密性的手段，但在何种程度上私密性会导致保密义务的产生并没有定论。一方面，可以说两者同时在仲裁中发挥作用，互为补充，仲裁私密性保障仲裁保密性的实现；另一方面，两者又各司其职，仲裁私密性管谁该不该参加仲裁程序，而保密性则管谁有义务不扩散与仲裁相关的文件和信息。

商事仲裁私密性与国内法院的信息公开透明是相对立的。[③] 这种私密性源于国际条约或协议。1958 年的《承认及执行外国仲裁裁决公约》(以下简称《纽约公约》)是关于国际商事仲裁的重要条约，但其并未涉及仲裁程序中的保密条款，而是强调仲裁裁决的承认与执行。1976 年《联合国国际贸易法委员会仲裁规则》(以下简称《贸法会仲裁规则》)则包含了有限的保密规定，如第 25

---

① See Sherlin Hsie-lien Tung & Brian Lin, *More Transparency in International Commercial Arbitration: To Have or Not to Have*, Contemporary Asia Arbitration Journal 11, 2018, p. 25.

② See Alexis C. Brown, *Presumption Meets Reality: An Exploration of the Confidentiality Obligation in International Commercial Arbitration*, American University International Law Review 16, 2001, p. 989 – 996.

③ See Florentino P. Feiciano, *The Order Public Dimensions of Confidentiality and Transparency in International Arbitration: Examining Confidentiality in the Light of Governance Requirements in International Investment and Trade Arbitration*, PHIL. L. J. 87, 2012, p. 4.

条第 4 款和第 32 条第 5 款规定,仲裁程序中使用的仲裁裁决和其他材料或文件几乎不能被公开。然而,2010 年《贸法会仲裁规则》在 1976 年颁布的基础上进行了修改,将 1976 年颁布的《贸法会仲裁规则》第 32 条第 5 款替换成了 2010 年《贸法会仲裁规则》的第 34 条第 5 款,规定在所有当事方同意或是因法律义务为保护或是获取法律上的权利或与法律程序相关可以向法院或是其他机构披露。这些修改增强了仲裁程序的效率,同时也反映了仲裁实践向更透明的方向发展。

实际上,早在 1996 年,联合国国际贸易法委员会就注意到各国在处理仲裁保密性问题上存在差异。由于这些差异,争端当事方不能因为达成的仲裁协议或是仲裁条款中没有明确涉及保密性问题就认为所有的国家都承认默示保密义务。[①] 例如,澳大利亚最高法院(High Court of Australia)认为仲裁程序完全保密是做不到的。[②] 因此,即使存在详细的保密协议也不能保证完全实现保密性,而要根据每个案件的事实分别确保保密义务的实现。[③] 修改《贸法会仲裁规则》正是为了尽量消除这些差异。

2. 透明度与披露、公众参与

透明度在国际法中并没有准确的定义,它的同义词通常是"公开性"(openness)。在《布莱克法律词典》中,透明度用在财务信息披露、组织机构与公众存在利害关系的情形中,虽然被经常引用但很少被定义。透明度实际上是一个以信息为中心的概念,它依赖公开性和信息获取,被视为一种与更负责、更民主和更合法的国际治理模式相关联的需求,在仲裁领域中,它包含了文件和其他材料的披露、公开听证、第三方参与仲裁和公众参与。[④]

---

① 1996 年联合国国际贸易法会议第二十九次会议文件结论。

② Esso Australia Resources Ltd. v. Plowman (1995) 128 ALR 391 (Austl.).

③ See Alexis C. Brown, *Presumption Meets Reality: An Exploration of the Confidentiality Obligation in International Commercial Arbitration*, American University International Law Review 16, 2001, p. 974 – 996.

④ See Matthew Carmody, *Overturning the Presumption of Confidentiality: Should the UNCITRAL Rules on Transparency Be Applied to International Commercial Arbitration*, International Trade & Business Law Review 19, 2016, p. 150 – 157.

公众参与,是指公民有独立参与争议解决程序的权利。区分透明度和公众参与有助于理解呼吁增加国际商事仲裁透明度背后的逻辑。公众参与和透明度都有助于保障公众对仲裁程序的知情权并监督仲裁员的工作。但两者仍然有不同内涵,即公众参与只是个人独立的权利而透明度则与整个仲裁体系有关。① 在国际商事仲裁的语境下,对整个仲裁制度来说透明度是必要的,但有时公众参与在特定情况下则可以被牺牲掉。原因在于公众参与主要源自对国内个人独立权利保障需要的考量,但国际商事仲裁中,在不涉及事实或法律上的利害关系时,坚持让一个巴西公民有权参与一个涉及德国法规范、争端当事方为中国人和俄罗斯人的国际商事仲裁案件程序显然是没有意义的。而在实践中,一些国际仲裁庭赞成通过公众参与的方式保证仲裁的透明度实际上是将公众参与作为实现透明度的必要工具。国内公众参与和国际公众参与的根本区别在于,国内立法者要考虑到不能侵犯公民参与程序、了解案情的基本权利,而无论案件是否与特定人有利害关系,从而实现司法的教育、指引等功能,但在国际纠纷中这样的考虑则是多余的。②

"披露"重点关注的是公开某种特定的、可辨认的信息,一般是为了满足某种特定的管理或规制目的,但透明度要求还包括大量与这类信息不相关的活动。③ 和公众参与一样,披露也可以作为一种实现透明度的工具。例如,仲裁员需要披露自己的利益冲突,让自己以一种透明的方式获任,否则其所在仲裁庭作出的裁决很可能因存在利益偏见而被申请撤销。披露的主要目的是保护公共利益,任何不涉及公共利益的披露都应该受到限制。由于国际商事仲裁的当事方通常都是私主体,且是为了解决商事纠纷,因而披露申请很少会获得批准。

---

① See Catherine A. Rogers, *Transparency in International Commercial Arbitration*, University of Kansas Law Review 54, 2006, p. 1306.

② See Avinash Poorooye & Ronan Feehily, *Confidentiality and Transparency in International Commercial Arbitration: Finding the Right Balance*, Harvard Negotiation Law Review 22, 2017, p. 284.

③ See Catherine A. Rogers, *Transparency in International Commercial Arbitration*, University of Kansas Law Review 54, 2006, p. 1306 – 1320.

（二）保密性弱化和透明度增强的原因

1. 保密性弱化的原因

仲裁保密性弱化的其中一个原因是保密性受制于公共利益等因素。尽管保密性是仲裁的一个重要特征且在解决纠纷上具有相当的优势——促进仲裁效率的提高，但它并非全然没有缺点。国际商事仲裁通常是在私主体之间进行，但有时当事方也可能是某个政府或是由政府拥有和控制的实体或组织。在这类案件中，有可能涉及公共利益，公众就有权利知道仲裁庭如何作出裁决以及该裁决对他们的影响。国际商事仲裁也可能涉及非法行为，如腐败、贿赂、洗钱和欺诈等案件，这类案件有时不只涉及私主体，还可能涉及政府官员或是跨国公司工作人员，由于这类案件的裁决往往会引起相关产业政策和人员的调整，甚至会影响消费者选择等公众利益，难以保密。此外，保密性还可能受限于政府职责等。

保密性之所以弱化，还因为严格保密不利于仲裁的发展。从国际仲裁法律秩序整体来看，保密性还可能会对国际仲裁的发展带来障碍。从仲裁质量看，保密性可能会让仲裁员缺乏监督，进而导致低质量甚至不公正的仲裁裁决。由于仲裁裁决是保密的，仅有相关当事方和仲裁庭知晓，无论仲裁裁决的质量是好是坏，对仲裁裁决提出质疑会极为困难。最坏的情况是，仲裁员作出不公正的仲裁裁决也不会受到监督和处罚，仲裁的质量可能会下滑，这并非不可能发生。从仲裁裁决的一致性看，保密性可能会导致相似或相同案件在适用相同的规则和法律条款时产生不一致的裁决，导致不公平的仲裁结果。从国际仲裁的发展看，保密的仲裁裁决难以成为学者们研究国际仲裁的一手资料，不利于国际仲裁理论研究的进一步发展。

由于仲裁保密性的要求时常与为公共利益而披露的要求相冲突，即使在争端当事方之间关于这些材料和文件存在明确的保密协议，许多法院也开始要求在司法审查案件中披露在仲裁程序中形成的材料和文件。[①] 从仲裁程序本身

① See Alexis C. Brown, *Presumption Meets Reality: An Exploration of the Confidentiality Obligation in International Commercial Arbitration*, American University International Law Review 16, 2001, p. 974 – 975.

看,不同参与主体的责任并不相同,如仲裁员有普遍的保密义务,而争端当事方的保密义务则常常取决于是否存在相关保密协议。从一国仲裁法律和实践看,不同国家对保密性采取的做法也不相同。有的国家承认默示保密义务(如英国),有的国家不承认默示保密义务,只看当事方之间是否存在保密协议或是制定法的规定。但即使是在承认默示保密义务的国家,这种保密义务也不是绝对的,而是存在各种各样的限制和例外。在具体个案中,仲裁的保密性可能会被推翻,而当事方可能被要求进行强制披露,特别是在涉及腐败、贿赂、洗钱和诈骗等犯罪问题的案件中。实际上,保密义务在各种限制中被弱化的情况在一定程度上也意味着透明度的增强。

2. 透明度增强的原因

仲裁透明度的增强存在如下原因:

一是竞争因素。透明度能提高仲裁的可信度和可接受程度,因为它增大了对仲裁员、律师和争端当事方追责的可能性,也使仲裁的裁决更加准确。仲裁员知道,在透明度规则下,任何仲裁裁决都有可能被学者研究或是公众监督,因此在作出裁决时仲裁员会倾向对案件进行充分地研究和调查后再作出决定。这其实也就保证了公民获取信息权利的实现,也保证了公平、法治、平等和正当程序的实现,因此争端当事方多会选择透明度较高的仲裁规则和仲裁机构。于是,为吸引商事纠纷当事人以获取竞争优势,成为仲裁机构实施增加仲裁透明度举措的动力。

二是有条件地公开仲裁裁决有利于裁决之间的协调,增强对裁决结果的预判。目前,多家国际仲裁机构都规定在当事人同意的情形下,可以公开仲裁裁决书。[①] 这些公开的仲裁裁决为创造客观标准以评价仲裁员,以及评估仲裁程序中的公共利益提供了实践基础。尽管仲裁员并不受仲裁先例的法律约束,但为了保持一种推理上和存续上的意义,[②]仲裁员们会参考过去的仲裁裁决。这

① 具体仲裁机构和规定可见下文。

② See Catherine A. Rogers, *Transparency in International Commercial Arbitration*, University of Kansas Law Review 54, 2006, p. 1306 – 1320.

表明在争端当事方不反对的情况下，仲裁机构是支持推动仲裁裁决的编撰活动公开的。虽然仲裁裁决没有判例的约束力，但在国际商事仲裁中却具有很高的参考价值。[①] 仲裁先例[②]的存在增加了仲裁的可预测性和选择仲裁解决纠纷的信心，同时，仲裁裁决的公开也让争端当事方有机会预测己方的赢面和监督仲裁员是否裁决公正，这对希望利用仲裁解决国际商事纠纷的当事人来说显然是非常重要的。在不破坏仲裁保密性的前提下，争端当事方就可以借此获得由仲裁裁决透明公开带来的帮助，虽然仅仅是根据仲裁先例作出的结果预测。

增强透明度的好处还包括可以防止发生不必要的讼累、促进仲裁法制发展以及提高仲裁员在进行专业裁量时的工作效率等。正是因为增强透明度更有助于促进仲裁的整体发展，所以国际上要求增强仲裁透明度的呼声才会越来越高。

三、国外商事仲裁保密规则和平衡实践

保密性和透明度两者的平衡并非一句口号，它体现在各国法院关于保密性问题的判决意见中，也反映在各国仲裁法、国际仲裁机构的仲裁规则变迁中。

（一）各国商事仲裁保密制度与平衡实践

为了找到一个实现平衡仲裁保密性和透明度的最佳方式，有必要深入分析和探讨各个国家所采取的不同处理方式。

1. 默示保密模式及其发展

早些年时，英国和法国在商事仲裁领域采用了默示保密模式，但随着仲裁实践发展，两国不再固守僵化的严格保密做法，而是转向限缩模式的保密乃至明示保密。[③] 承认默示保密义务，即在争端当事方之间没有保密协议，且在仲裁协议或是仲裁条款中也没有涉及保密义务时，仲裁仍然需要保密。英国、法

① See Catherine A. Rogers, *Transparency in International Commercial Arbitration*, University of Kansas Law Review 54, 2006, p. 1306 – 1320.

② 有必要强调“仲裁先例”并非有约束力的先例，而仅是被公开的先前存在的案例。

③ 下文英国仲裁保密性限制扩张、法国仲裁保密义务存在证明要求等法院实践做法体现出这一点。

国的法院都认为仲裁程序的私密性是确保仲裁保密的重要内容,而仲裁的保密事实反过来也是达成仲裁协议时承认默示保密义务的重要证明,因此保密性不仅是仲裁的必要特征,而且是仲裁私密性的一个隐含的必然结果。[①]

英国商事仲裁中对保密性的规定和实践来自3个重要案例:“多林贝克(Dolling-Baker)案”、[②]“海森(Hassneh)案”[③]和“艾力运输(Ali Shipping)案”。[④] 在“多林贝克案”中,法官开始认识到了保密性的法律性质,认定其是从仲裁的私密性中产生的一种默示保密义务。仲裁程序中产生的或是直接用于仲裁的证据或文件都应保密,而且这种保密性存在例外。随后,在“海森案”中,法官扩大了保密性义务的范围,由于默示保密义务从仲裁庭审的私密性中衍生出来,这种义务范围应扩大至仲裁过程中产生的所有资料。法官还认为,私密性是仲裁本身的属性,仲裁需要保密不是因为仲裁中的文件需要保密,而是私密性要求第三方不得进入仲裁,除非经过同意,否则都应当保密。同时,该案明确了具体的保密性例外,即出于保护一方当事人的合理需求时,保密性可以被突破。在“艾力运输案”中,法官进一步认定,保密义务来自法律的默示,而不仅是出于习惯或是商业效用上的考虑,这种义务在争端当事方订立仲裁协议或是仲裁条款时就已经隐含在其中,成为一种必备条款。同时,该案也增加了法院指令和公共利益两种例外。

从3个案件发展来看,尽管英国法院认为,这种保密义务是法律默示的、是隐含在仲裁协议或是仲裁条款中的,但它的例外仍然呈现一种扩大趋势。而且,这种趋势在进入21世纪后进一步发展。在2003年的“艾吉斯(Agies)案”中[⑤],英国枢密院司法委员会不再引用“艾力运输案”的观点,转而批判该案中

---

① See Christoph Henkel, *The Work Product Doctrine as a Means toward a Judicially Enforceable Duty of Confidentiality in International Commercial Arbitration*, North Carolina Journal of International Law and Commercial Regulation 37, 2012, p. 1067.

② Dolling-Baker v. Merrett (1990) 1 WLR 1205 (K. B.).

③ Hassneh Ins. v. Steuart J. Mew (1993) 2 Lloyd's Rep. 243 (K. B.).

④ Ali Shipping Corp. v. Shipyard Trogir (1998) 2 All ER 136 (K. B.).

⑤ Associated Electric and Gas Insurance Services Ltd. v. European Reinsurance Co. of Zurich ("Agies").

不考虑当事方意志和公共利益的统一保密观点,认为它不应该笼统地将仲裁裁决和仲裁过程中产生的文件都纳入保密范围。而在 2004 年的“莫斯科城(City of Moscow)案”①中,法院认为在当事方有正当理由披露仲裁的开始、存在和结果时,并不违反保密义务。换言之,只要当事方有正当理由、具有事实上或法律上的原因,例如,为行使一项法定权利或请求权或者遵循国际交易惯例的要求,披露一般不会被视为违反保密义务。可见,这种保密性的例外已经扩展到了较广泛的程度。英国法院虽未明确表示放弃仲裁默示保密的做法,但默示保密义务的范围逐渐被限缩,其例外呈现不断扩张的趋势,这冲击了默示保密的传统并体现出关注仲裁透明度的倾向。

法国关于保密性的立法最早可追溯至 1981 年法国《民事诉讼法典》(以下简称法国《民诉法》)。在保密性问题上,法国《民诉法》规定仲裁员审议需遵循保密义务。法国仲裁实践从“埃塔(Aita v. Ojjeh)案”开始关注仲裁的保密性,该案中法官对保密性的态度是,保密义务是伴随仲裁协议存在的默示义务,即使当事方没有签订保密协议,它也应该被遵守。法国对仲裁保密性一直保持上述态度,直到 2004 年的“那飞科(Nafimco v. Foster Wheeler Trading Company)案”。在该案中,原告请求被告赔偿因其违反保密义务披露资产负债表而导致原告产生的损失,但巴黎上诉法院拒绝了这一主张。理由是原告没有证明法国国际商事仲裁法上保密义务的存在,也没有证明双方是否有放弃保密义务的协议。可见,这时法国法院通过增加对保密义务、保密协议的证明要求,事实上确认了保密义务不再是一种默示义务,而是一种需要明确约定的义务。

2. 明示保密模式

和英国、法国法院不同,美国、澳大利亚和瑞典法院并不承认默示保密义务。也即后者只承认明确约定的保密义务,在当事方没有明确的保密协议,或者达成的仲裁协议或仲裁条款中没有涉及保密问题时,法院认为不需要对仲裁保密。虽然这 3 个国家的法院都承认仲裁的私密性,仲裁程序在没有当事方同

---

① Dept. of Econ. Policy & City of Moscow v. Bankers Tr. (2004) EWCA (Civ.) 314 (K. B.).

意时也排除第三方的介入,但不认为这种私密性要求会延伸至仲裁中的文件和仲裁裁决。

美国法院在保密性实践中多次拒绝了当事方请求保全仲裁中的文件以防止其被披露的要求,理由是当事方之间没有签订明确的保密协议,也就不存在保密义务。[①] 同时,美国法院还说明,仲裁的私密性并不等同于保密性,私密性只是不允许第三人未经同意进入仲裁,而并非不允许当事方合理地披露仲裁文件。保密协议只约束争端当事方,他人对仲裁文件有合理需要而当事方进行披露并不违反保密性。

澳大利亚法院在保密性实践中认为,只有当事方之间有明确约定,才会产生切实的保密义务,否则法院不承认保密义务的存在。[②] 同时法院还强调了公共利益的优先性,认为当案件涉及公共利益时,仲裁的保密性并不是绝对的,由于公共利益优先于当事方的商业利益,仲裁庭有权将仲裁中的文件披露给政府,否则就会妨碍政府对公共事务的监督管理。当然,政府在获取仲裁中的文件后也应该遵守保密义务,在未经同意的情况下不得披露给他人。

瑞典法院认为,如果当事方没有签订保密协议,那么仲裁的保密性就不能被当然接受。想要确保存在保密义务,只有订立明确的合同或是选择明确的仲裁规则。只要当事方没有约定,瑞典法院就不认为当事方达成的仲裁协议或是仲裁条款中存在默示的保密条款。

3. 制定法模式

一般来说,除上述两种由法院来裁决仲裁是否需要保密的情况外,国际上还存在一种由制定法来规范仲裁保密性的实践。新加坡和新西兰就是这种做法的两个典型例证。新加坡采取了一种公开仲裁裁决的独特方式,被认为是亚洲仲裁的先驱。而新西兰则规定了一种全面编撰仲裁保密性案件的做法。

新加坡《仲裁法》第75条第3款规定,[③]只有当事方同意或是满足法院公

---

① United States v. Panhandle Eastern Corporation and Contship Containerlines v. PPG Industries.

② 许佩琰:《商事仲裁保密性的弱化趋势研究》,上海师范大学2018年硕士学位论文,第23页。

③ Singapore Arbitration Act, § 75(3) (July 31, 2002).

开信息的要求时,则不会公开包括当事方在仲裁中的身份信息在内的当事方有理由希望保密的任何信息,才能对保密信息进行披露。该法第 57 条第 4 款还规定,[①]法院给出了裁决理由并认为在裁决关系主要的法律利益的情况下,应该指令该裁决可以在法律报告或是专业刊物上发表。上述法条表明,新加坡立法机构希望将裁决予以编撰并传播以促进仲裁法律的发展,同时也希望通过允许当事方隐藏特定的事项以示对仲裁的私密性和保密性本质的尊重。这种立法者实现的平衡提醒我们,保密性和透明度可以共存而不一定会被视为两种相互对立的价值或是利益。

同时新加坡《仲裁法》第 57 条第 4 款还规定,当当事方有理由希望在公开报告中隐藏任何事项时,法院应该指令在报告中予以隐藏。当这些事项实在无法隐藏时,法院应该指令报告在合理期限内不得公开,合理期限一般不超过 10 年。目前只有新加坡规定了这项内容。

1996 年新西兰《仲裁法》规定,当事方和仲裁庭不得披露仲裁协议中的保密信息。[②] 其中该法第 2 条定义了保密信息的范围包括但不限于任何有关于仲裁程序或是在仲裁程序中产生的信息、裁决书、案件陈述、申请书、证据、笔录和翻译本。该法第 14 条第 3 款[③]规定了大量的保密性例外,以示仲裁保密义务的非绝对性,例如,允许向当事方的专业人员或是其他建议人员披露保密信息。

(二)各国际仲裁机构商事仲裁规则的平衡安排

各国际仲裁机构仲裁规则在保密性问题上的制度安排也体现了增强透明度的实践需求。

1. 香港国际仲裁中心(Hong Kong International Arbitration Centre,HKIAC)的平衡安排

2013 年《香港国际仲裁中心机构仲裁规则》[④]第 42 条规定了保密性条款,

---

① Singapore Arbitration Act, § 57(4) (July 31, 2002).

② New Zealand Arbitration Act, § 14B (Sept. 2, 1996).

③ Ibid., § 14C (Sept. 2, 1996).

④ 2013 年《香港国际仲裁中心机构仲裁规则》,保密性规定载香港国际仲裁中心网,https://www.hkiac.org/zh-hans/arbitration/rules-practice-notes/administered-arbitration-rules/hkiac-administered-2013-2。

禁止当事方公开、披露或是传播任何与具体仲裁程序或是仲裁裁决书有关的信息。仲裁庭的合议也应保密的规定进一步强调了对仲裁庭的专业法律裁量意见的保密。然而,一方面,它既规定了在特定情况下仲裁中心不阻止仲裁有关信息的扩散,如依法定义务向任何政府机关、监管机关、法院或仲裁庭公布、披露或传送信息;另一方面,在满足一定条件的前提下,如同时满足已向仲裁中心申请公开、公开时隐去当事人名称且当事人不反对3个条件,就可以公开仲裁裁决。目前,HKIAC 2018年新仲裁规则已经“出炉”,关于保密性问题增加了对第三方资助的披露要求。

2. 国际商会仲裁院(The International Chamber of Commerce,ICC)的平衡安排

《880－4 CHI 国际商会2017年仲裁规则－2014年调解规则》(以下简称《国际商会仲裁规则》)[①]并没有明确指出所有的国际商会仲裁都是保密的。在没有当事方协议时,国际商会仲裁庭在当事方的请求下可以作出对关于仲裁程序或是任何与仲裁相关的事项进行保密的指令。同时,国际商会仲裁庭也采取措施保护商业秘密和保密信息。另外,《国际商会仲裁规则》附录1规定,仲裁院的工作属保密性质,参与这些工作的任何人,无论其以何等身份参与,都必须尊重这一工作性质;附录2规定,提交仲裁院的文件或在仲裁院程序进行过程中由仲裁院或秘书处拟制的文件仅向仲裁院委员、秘书处及仲裁院院长决定准许参加会议的人员提供,不能披露给任何国际商会的外部人员,包括当事方。在个别情况下,仲裁院院长或秘书长还可以允许学术研究人员查阅裁决书及其他的一般性文件,但备忘录、笔记、意见陈述及当事人寄送的仲裁程序范围内的文件除外。《秘书人员工作指南》(Secretariat's Guide)还规定,国际商会在当事方同意时可公开裁决书,而在当事方不同意公开时国际商会只能公开经过删减编撰的裁决书。

---

① 《880－4 CHI 国际商会2017年仲裁规则－2014年调解规则》,ICC－2017－Arbitration-and－2014－Mediation-Rules-chinese-version. pdf。

3. 伦敦国际仲裁院（The London Court of International Arbitration，LCIA）的平衡安排

2014年《伦敦国际仲裁院仲裁规则》[①]第30条规定了仲裁程序的保密性，除非法律要求、为保护或是追求某项法律权利或者在法律程序中申请执行或是质疑某个仲裁裁决书的情形，禁止当事方公开任何文件或是信息。它也规定仲裁庭的专业法律裁量意见应当保密，且只有当事方的预先书面同意，仲裁裁决书才能公开。

4. 新加坡国际仲裁中心（Singapore International Arbitration Centre，SIAC）的平衡安排

2016年《新加坡国际仲裁中心仲裁规则》[②]第39条规定仲裁程序中包括仲裁庭的专业法律裁量意见和仲裁裁决书在内的所有关于仲裁程序的事项都要保密。但它随后也规定了一系列保密性例外，如依据有管辖权法院的命令或是传票，行使或是执行一项法定权利或请求权，可以不遵守保密义务；并且该规则授权仲裁庭可以在当事方违反保密协议时向其发布支付成本的命令或是裁决。此外，2016年《新加坡国际仲裁中心仲裁规则》第32条第12款也授权新加坡国际仲裁中心在取得当事方同意的情况下可以公布仲裁裁决。

5. 斯德哥尔摩商会仲裁院（Stockholm Chamber of Commerce，SCC）的平衡安排

2017年《斯德哥尔摩商会仲裁院仲裁规则》[③]第3条规定，除非当事方之间另有协议，当事方、SCC和仲裁庭需要对仲裁和仲裁裁决进行保密。《斯德哥尔摩商会仲裁院仲裁规则》附录1第9条进一步规定机构也需要对仲裁保密。

上述仲裁机构除国际商会仲裁院外，都明确规定了仲裁的保密性。国际商会仲裁院并不将保密义务施加于当事方或是仲裁庭，而是让它的仲裁院和秘书人员履行保密义务，把是否希望仲裁保密的决定权交给当事方。其他具体保密

---

① 《伦敦国际仲裁院仲裁规则》，LCIA Arbitration Rules effective 1 October 2014 - website. pdf。

② 《新加坡国际仲裁中心仲裁规则》，SIAC Rules 2016_Chinese_Final. pdf。

③ See Sherlin Hsie-lien Tung & Brian Lin, *More Transparency in International Commercial Arbitration: To Have or Not to Have*, Contemporary Asia Arbitration Journal 11, 2018, p. 33.

事项的对比,可参见表1。

表1 各仲裁机构保密事项对比

保密事项	HKIAC	ICC	LCIA	SIAC	SCC
有无概括性保密条款	有	没有明确规定,但普遍认为有[a]	有	有	有
是否明确允许公开仲裁裁决	是	未规定	是	是	未规定
是否明确要求仲裁庭的专业法律裁量意见保密	是	未规定	是	是	未规定
是否明确紧急仲裁员和专家证人有保密义务	是	未规定	未规定	是	未规定
是否明确秘书人员有保密义务	是	没有明确规定,但普遍认为有[b]	未规定	未规定	未规定

a. ICC对于其工作的保密性质在《国际商会仲裁规则》中进行了确认。

b. 详见《国际商会仲裁规则》。

从表1中可以看出,虽然各国际仲裁机构都明确表示允许公开仲裁裁决,但在概括性保密条款下,仲裁庭的专业法律裁量意见仍然不能公开。但为了回应国际上增加仲裁透明度的要求,各国际仲裁机构都放宽对保密性的要求,通过公布更多的仲裁程序细节以提高仲裁程序、仲裁庭裁决的透明度。ICC为了增加其仲裁的透明度开始公开关于更换仲裁员、启动替换程序、合并仲裁程序和预先裁决的裁决理由。[①] 同时,ICC也开始在其官方网站上公布最近仲裁案件的仲裁员的姓名、国籍以及是不是独任仲裁员、边席仲裁员和首席仲裁员等

① Rajinder Bassi & Jon Newman, *Increased Transparency in International Commercial Arbitration* (August 2016), https://www.financierworldwide.com/increased-transparency-in-international-commercial-arbitration/#.WvvqWoiFPIW.

信息。[①] LCIA 从 2014 年开始就在当事方质疑仲裁员时向其提供审议决定的理由。HKIAC 也发布了《仲裁员质疑实务指引》,保证裁决受到质疑时,当事方、被质疑的仲裁员和其他仲裁庭人员能够知晓审议决定理由,尽管 HKIAC 声称其没有义务公布上述理由。[②] SCC 虽然没有公布仲裁员质疑审议决定理由,但它也会定期发布上述关于质疑仲裁员的决定的摘要。[③] LCIA 和 SCC 还公布了平均仲裁费用和仲裁员任期的具体数据,SCC 甚至还公布了关于争议规模大小和仲裁庭如何分配仲裁费用的细节。[④]

从目前来看,各国际仲裁机构倾向在本身仲裁规则之外增加自身仲裁实践的透明度,虽举措各有重叠且稍显凌乱,但也能从上述措施中获取一些启示。首先,国际仲裁机构重视对仲裁员及选任信息的透明化,向申请仲裁的当事人公布其与仲裁有关的教育、工作信息,让潜在当事人充分了解某一仲裁员。其次,国际仲裁机构关注仲裁庭与争议双方在仲裁程序中的互动,尽可能为当事人提供合理、有效的程序争议处理服务,如给出审议仲裁员质疑并作出决定的理由。最后,国际仲裁机构从公布争议双方关注的细节出发,如公开关于仲裁费用的安排,以建立整个仲裁机构的透明度标准,打造良好透明度形象、形成竞争优势。在国内商事仲裁层面,可以说,仲裁的保密义务已不再遵循严格的默示保密原则,并且逐渐走向明示保密乃至直接的制定法保密。让一国法院或立法者改变立场的政策考量有很多,如保障公共利益、公民民主权利、促进仲裁发展等,但无论是明示保密还是法律确定的保密义务,都表现了对仲裁这一争议解决机制保密性的限制,即保密义务有其边界,增加透明度更有其不可被忽视

---

① ICC, *ICC Begins Publishing Arbitrator Information in Drive for Improved Transparency* (Jun. 27, 2016), https://iccwbo.org/media-wall/news-speeches/icc-begins-publishing-arbitrator-information-in-drive-for-improved-transparency.

② 《仲裁员质疑实务指引》,载香港国际仲裁中心网,https://www.hkiac.org/sites/default/files/ck_filebrowser/PDF/arbitration/4_Practice%20Note_2014_SC.pdf。

③ Rajinder Bassi & Jon Newman, *Increased Transparency in International Commercial Arbitration* (Aug. 2016), https://www.financierworldwide.com/increased-transparency-in-international-commercial-arbitration/#.WvvqWoiFPIW.

④ LCIA, *LCIA Releases Costs and Duration Data* (3 November 2015), https://www.lcia.org/News/lcia-releases-costs-and-duration-data.aspx#_ftn1.

的正当性。在国际商事仲裁层面,保密性在一定程度上阻碍了国际商事仲裁的发展,不利于高效解决国际商事纠纷,因此在仲裁规则设计上弱化保密性、提升透明度成为主流意见。但在平衡保密性、透明度二者的制度供给时,一些保密性制度底线不能突破,一般应尊重当事人的意思自治(如保密协议要求),以保障争议双方的合法权益;但对于仲裁的程序性争议处理意见、仲裁裁决案情部分和裁决要旨等都应在不损害当事方利益的前提下予以公开,以透明度规则保障各方利益得以实现。

四、中国商事仲裁保密性制度立法和实践现状及不足

前文对商事仲裁保密性和透明度平衡问题的探究为分析中国商事仲裁保密性制度问题提供了一条基本思路,即首先应承认保密性是仲裁解决商事纠纷的优势,其次应厘清仲裁保密义务的边界,最后通过弱化保密性和增加透明度来平衡两者的力量。同时应注意,由于该问题与每一个仲裁案件息息相关,因此需注重讨论制度实效。

中国商事仲裁制度虽然起步较晚,但发展迅速。截至2018年,中国已有国内仲裁机构255家,涉外仲裁机构除贸仲及其分会和中国海事仲裁委员会外,北京、上海、深圳和香港特别行政区也设有独立的国际商事仲裁机构。随着中国自贸试验区工作的持续推进,必将会有更多的国内仲裁机构和涉外仲裁机构乃至知名国际仲裁机构的办事处进驻中国自贸试验区,中国仲裁的发展前景可期。但中国仲裁发展过程中出现的问题却不能被忽视,只有深入分析这些问题并找出相对应的解决方案,中国仲裁才会得以可持续发展。下文将主要从商事仲裁制度的角度对中国仲裁立法和仲裁规则在保密性和透明度问题的规定进行分析探讨,试图发现其中不足之处,并为后文的完善建议奠定基础。

(一)《仲裁法》第40条立法和实践现状及不足

1. 仲裁立法现状及不足

《仲裁法》在1994年制定并于1995年正式施行,距今已有20多年。近几年来,最高人民法院连续推出了指导仲裁司法审查和仲裁裁决执行的一系列重

要司法文件,包括最高人民法院《关于审理仲裁司法审查案件若干问题的规定》《关于人民法院办理仲裁裁决执行案件若干问题的规定》等,为中国商事仲裁实践的发展创造了新的契机。《仲裁法》虽已统领中国仲裁实践迅速发展了20多年,但本身并未有过任何修改且其司法解释也屈指可数,因此一些最新的国际仲裁理念还未及时得以植入,存在一定的滞后性。

关于仲裁保密性和透明度问题,中国仲裁立法和实践相对前文中一些发达国家的立法和实践还是相对滞后的。《仲裁法》第40条规定:"仲裁不公开进行。当事人协议公开的,可以公开进行,但涉及国家秘密的除外。"可见,中国仲裁对于仲裁保密性的态度是原则上不公开进行,当事人协议公开是例外情形。但与其说这是关于保密性的规定,还不如说是对仲裁审理方式的规定。显然,立法者考虑到审理方式的公开与保密就决定了第三方未经过当事方或是仲裁庭的同意便不得参与仲裁程序,体现的是仲裁的私密性。但立法者并没有明确仲裁中保密义务的存在。因为立法者并没有明确当事方、仲裁员、仲裁秘书人员以及参与仲裁程序人员的保密义务,立法者也没有明确上述仲裁保密义务的具体范围,即是否包括对仲裁事实本身、仲裁程序抑或是仲裁程序中产生和使用的文件以及仲裁裁决的保密,更没有明确在何种情形下上述人员不需要遵守该保密义务,更遑论对相关人员违反保密义务的认定和救济措施了。

毋庸置疑,仲裁保密性的存在具有重要的价值和现实意义。① 仲裁的保密性应当是当事人有权期待的一种利益,在仲裁中,保密应当是常态,而公开应当是例外。② 另外,仲裁的透明度对争议的公正处理也具有重大价值。一直以来,中国国内仲裁的两大问题就是仲裁司法审查内外有别和仲裁机构的独立性问题。这两大问题成为中国仲裁机构国际化进程中需要解决的问题。坚持推进透明度改革能在很大程度上缓解上述问题,助力中国仲裁的发展。因此,随着国际商事仲裁的发展,中国《仲裁法》的不足之处已经不只局限在保密性问题,在仲裁透明度与保密性不再被视为相互对立的两种价值的语境下,中国

① 辛柏春:《国际商事仲裁保密性问题探析》,载《当代法学》2016年第2期。
② 郭玉军、梅秋玲:《仲裁的保密性问题研究》,载《法学评论》2004年第2期。

《仲裁法》缺乏透明度要求开始成为一个值得关注的问题。

2.《仲裁法》实践现状及不足

从《仲裁法》的实践层面来看，中国仲裁立法相对仲裁实践是滞后的。一个重要的问题是仲裁法与其他法律之间的冲突。理论上，商事仲裁保密性与其他部门法所要求的信息公开规定相冲突。例如，为保护众多投资者的利益，《证券法》要求上市公司定期披露合规信息，当上市公司涉仲裁案件时，仲裁程序中产生的文件若符合《证券法》的要求则本应予以公布，但当事人若依据保密义务或保密协议主张不得将相关信息予以泄露，就可能产生以仲裁保密性制度规避监管的问题。例如，上市公司涉仲裁案件，当年利润可能严重下滑甚至发生亏损，实际控制人及控股股东筹划股权转让。为保持股价稳定和市场信心，上市公司及其控股股东、实际控制人可能以保密义务为由封锁消息而不履行《证券法》(2019 年修订)第 80 条、第 81 条，《上市公司信息披露管理办法》第 30 条关于重大事件的报告义务。同样的法律冲突问题还发生在物权公示案件中，物权权属证明文件因参与仲裁程序被一方当事人以保密义务要求不得公示，从而给后续其他关联案件的处理带来障碍。另一个问题是，常常有当事方利用仲裁的不公开审理原则虚构仲裁案件，掩盖其非法目的，侵犯案外人的合法权益，同时也造成了司法资源的巨大浪费。

实务界对适用《仲裁法》第 40 条裁判案件的说理，往往也存在差距。在“祁门县人民法院、黄山市方圆建工有限公司等申请撤销仲裁裁决案”中，被告代理人方某的妻子郑某在仲裁过程中一直坐在申请人的席位上，双方当事人未对郑某申请回避并且郑某在仲裁过程中没有发表任何意见，也没有妨碍和干扰案件的审理。最后，某中级人民法院认为，县人民法院对郑某旁听没有提出任何异议，郑某也没有实施任何干扰仲裁开庭的行为，不足以影响裁决，故仲裁裁决不违反法定程序。显然，在该案中，郑某是案外第三人，需要经过双方当事人同意才能进入仲裁程序，而不是仅仅需要满足双方当事人不申请回避的条件，不公开审理与不干扰审理显然是不同的。同时，从该中级人民法院的裁定中也可以看出法院对《仲裁法》第 40 条理解上的问题，即将程序的违法性与仲裁的保密性相混淆,认为不干扰审理就不违反不公开审理。

在“谢某诉长沙某公司仲裁裁决案”中,谢某认为在仲裁委员会组织的调解会上,仲裁委员会副秘书长属于案外人,违反了仲裁不公开审理的原则。但某市中级人民法院认为,副秘书长虽然参与了调解会,但其目的是帮助双方当事人和平解决纠纷,对仲裁庭认定案件事实和适用法律没有任何影响,因此不属于违反不公开审理原则。显然,在该案中法院认为调解会不需要受仲裁保密性的约束,关于这是否缩小了保密义务的范围,值得进一步商榷。[①]

(二)中国仲裁规则之不足

中国仲裁规则在保密性问题的处理上也存在不足,主要体现在中国仲裁机构的仲裁规则上。下面,笔者将以《中国国际经济贸易仲裁委员会仲裁规则》(以下简称《贸仲规则》)为例,分析其关于保密性制度存在的问题,以期为中国仲裁规则保密性制度的完善提供参考。

贸仲是中国仲裁最具代表性的仲裁机构之一,其近几年的发展极为引人注目,受案量逐年上升,国际声誉也有了显著的提高。2014 年修订的《贸仲规则》第 38 条也对保密性作出了规定:“(一)仲裁庭审理案件不公开进行。双方当事人要求公开审理的,由仲裁庭决定是否公开审理。(二)不公开审理的案件,双方当事人及其仲裁代理人、仲裁员、证人、翻译、仲裁庭咨询的专家和指定的鉴定人,以及其他有关人员,均不得对外界透露案件实体和程序的有关情况。”《贸仲规则》在确认不公开审理原则的基础上,进一步规定了仲裁保密义务的主体和仲裁保密义务的范围。

但美中不足的是,该保密义务的范围规定得过于模糊。对于“案件实体和程序的有关情况”的理解需要进一步具体化,比如,如何认定一个案件事实或法律争议属于仲裁实体事项,又如何认定相应的仲裁程序事项,只有具体化才具有可操作性,才能在仲裁实践中得到有效适用,过于宽泛的规定有时还可能给仲裁实践带来困扰。另外,由于仲裁遵循意思自治原则,争端当事方可能会

---

① 许佩琰:《商事仲裁保密性的弱化趋势研究》,上海师范大学 2018 年硕士学位论文,第 35 页。

在保密协议中约定双方保密义务的范围,对当事方也规定如此宽泛的保密义务可能有悖当事人的意思自治。《贸仲规则》也没有明确规定仲裁保密性的例外、违反仲裁保密义务的救济措施。

另外,《贸仲规则》没有规定透明度要求。仲裁透明度不仅对中国国内仲裁的发展具有重要意义,它的价值和作用在国际商事仲裁中更重要。在各国联系日益紧密,跨国公司国际商事交易日益频繁的背景下,仲裁机构之间、仲裁员之间和律师之间,都存在激烈竞争。为了吸引更多的商业当事人和获取更多的市场份额,仲裁机构一直在不断提高仲裁的公信力。为了实现程序公正和透明度,仅仅让仲裁员来确保公正是不够的,公正的实现还要让当事方和公众能够看到。过去10年,国际商事仲裁中透明度得到了显著增强,仲裁机构逐渐采取了更详尽和明确的行为规范以及更透明的程序规则。这些规则显然比只引用抽象的法律原则和模糊的公平正义概念更实用和具有说服力。争端当事方显然也更希望自己无所不包的商业合同得到更专业和精准的把控,从而选择仲裁规则更详尽明确、仲裁程序更透明的仲裁机构。

五、国际商事仲裁规则及完善中国商事仲裁制度

在仲裁实践中,处理保密性与透明度的平衡问题应当以仲裁法和仲裁规则为基本遵循。国际商事仲裁保密性弱化、透明度增强的趋势在各国仲裁法、仲裁规则以及国际仲裁机构的仲裁规则中得以体现,这为完善中国商事仲裁制度关于保密性和透明度的规定提供了借鉴。当前,中国商事仲裁制度应当致力于划清仲裁保密义务的边界、提高透明度规则的比例。

(一)完善中国《仲裁法》和中国仲裁规则关于保密性的规定

英国皇家玛丽大学2015年关于仲裁保密性的调查报告中显示,仲裁的保密性和私密性的重要性在所有仲裁追求的价值中排名第二,[①]可见保密性在商

---

① 2015 *International Arbitration Survey*: *Improvements and Innovations in International Arbitration*, Queen Mary University of London, http://www. arbitration. qmul. ac. uk/media/arbitration/docs/2015_International_Arbitration_Survey. pdf.

事仲裁使用者们心中的地位。明确确认仲裁保密义务的存在有利于进一步扩大仲裁的吸引力、提高仲裁的使用率、促进仲裁事业的发展。因此,完善中国《仲裁法》、仲裁规则中关于保密制度的规定具有重要意义。

对中国《仲裁法》关于保密义务规定(主要是该法第40条)的完善要立足中国仲裁实践,有针对性地解决当下中国仲裁法在实施过程中遇到的问题、预防将来可能出现的问题。同时,还需要对中国各个仲裁机构的仲裁规则中关于保密性的规定进行完善。

1. 对中国仲裁保密义务主体的完善

完善《仲裁法》关于保密义务的规定,先要在坚持仲裁不公开审理原则的基础上确立保密义务的存在,并给出保密义务的定义。在此基础上,《仲裁法》可进一步明确保密义务的主体。一般而言,仲裁保密义务的主体包括仲裁庭、仲裁员和相关的秘书人员、争端当事方及其仲裁代理人、证人、翻译人员、仲裁庭咨询的专家和指定的鉴定人员以及参与仲裁的其他相关人员。上述保密义务的主体还可进一步分为当事方、仲裁庭和第三人三大类别。当事方包括双方当事人及他们的仲裁代理人。当事人的保密义务因商事仲裁的私密性而默认其当然负有保密义务,但仲裁代理人的保密义务可以选择类似美国律师与仲裁庭之间签订的共同防止和分享信息协议(Joint Defense and Sharing Agreements)以及律师的工作成果保护原则(work-product doctrine),即仲裁代理人与仲裁庭签署保密协议,以防止在后续仲裁程序中披露本仲裁程序中的信息和法律规定仲裁代理人的工作成果,也可以根据当事人与仲裁代理人之间的保密协议来确保其保密义务。

仲裁庭的保密义务是被广泛认可的,即仲裁庭应当受到保密义务的约束,所有仲裁员、仲裁机构、仲裁程序中的工作人员都应当遵守保密义务。其中,最值得关注的一点就是,对于仲裁庭审议的专业法律裁量意见的保密性。关于这一点,与仲裁审理方式一样,保密应当是原则,公开应当是例外。有国外仲裁实践指出,在涉及公共利益时,仲裁庭有权向政府披露仲裁程序中的信息和文件,以避免对政府管理公共事务职能构成妨碍,同时政府也应当遵守相应的保密义务。[①]

证人、翻译、咨询专家、鉴定人等为证明各方观点、还原案件事实和帮助仲裁庭作出判断的非案件当事方的人员统称为第三方。证人如果有需要,可以接触保密的仲裁材料,但应当对该信息保密。申请证人作证的当事人对证人的保密义务承担责任。对于专家证人,《世界知识产权组织仲裁中心仲裁规则》第40条第1款规定,经与各方当事人协商,仲裁庭可指定一名或数名专家就特定事项提出专家报告,专家证人应根据仲裁庭提出的条件签署保密协议。其他第三方人员的保密义务主要由当事人与第三方人员之间的委托协议规范,若当事人申请,则仲裁机构也可要求签署一般保密协议。

完善《仲裁法》第40条中关于保密义务主体的部分,可在该条明确规定以下仲裁程序参与者,负有不得向与仲裁案件无关第三方扩散有关信息的保密义务:(1)申请人、被申请人、仲裁代理人;(2)仲裁员、秘书、其他仲裁庭工作人员;(3)证人;(4)翻译人、鉴定人;(5)仲裁庭咨询专家;(6)其他仲裁程序参与人员、仲裁案件信息知情人员。

2. 对中国仲裁保密义务范围的完善

对仲裁保密义务的范围,中国《仲裁法》、仲裁规则存在一些不足。《仲裁法》没有对这一问题进行规定。而根据《贸仲规则》第38条的规定,仲裁保密义务的范围是"案件实体和程序的有关情况",但在仲裁实践中根据这一模糊的保密义务范围认定具体保密事项存在障碍。这些情况可能包括仲裁事实本身、仲裁程序中为仲裁准备的仲裁申请书、证据文件等,以及仲裁程序中产生的仲裁裁决书、调解书等。关于仲裁事实本身的保密性,仲裁规则很少会作出专门的规定。原因在于,要对仲裁程序保密就要求争端当事方不能够透露仲裁程序的启动、仲裁当事方的姓名或名称及任何与仲裁有关的实质性内容,而在大多数情况下,仲裁当事方会自愿或非自愿地向利益相关方透露仲裁事实的存在。因此,只有少数国际仲裁机构在仲裁规则中提到了对仲裁事实本身的保密

---

① High Court of Australia, Esso Australia Resources Ltd. and Others V. Plowman (Minister for Energy and Minerals) and Others, Australian Law Reports.

要求,如 SIAC 和 HKIAC。

对仲裁程序中为仲裁准备和在仲裁程序中产生的文件材料的保密,是仲裁保密义务的重要对象。《新加坡国际仲裁中心仲裁规则》规定,仲裁程序中任何相关信息都是保密的,包括仲裁存在的事实、仲裁请求、证据文件、仲裁裁决以及为仲裁准备的其他文件。该规则还解释,其他文件包括事实陈述、答辩书、仲裁代理人的答辩意见、证人证言、专家报告和法律备忘录等。对仲裁的审议过程应当保密。仲裁庭有义务保证仲裁员的专业法律裁量意见、观点和立场等信息的保密性。但对仲裁审议过程的保密也不是绝对的,在仲裁庭和当事人同意的情况下,也可以允许仲裁庭披露其审议文件。

对于仲裁裁决,可以将是否保密的决定权完全交给争端当事方。在仲裁裁决作出后仲裁庭应及时询问双方当事人是否愿意将案件仲裁裁决在隐去重要个人信息后公开。对当事人不同意公开的仲裁裁决,由相关工作人员仅摘录裁判要旨,汇编成书予以公开。

完善《仲裁法》第 40 条中关于保密义务范围的部分,可在该条增加第 3 款规定有关信息,这些信息包括但不限于仲裁准备和仲裁程序过程中产生的仲裁请求、证据文件、仲裁裁决及其他与案件事实和程序相关的文件。对于仲裁规则来说,以《贸仲规则》第 38 条为例,可对"案件实体和程序的有关"的信息作出更具体的规定。但在强化透明度方面,需对保密义务范围有所限定,如对于仲裁裁决,可规定特殊保密条件,以促进仲裁裁决公开;对程序处理事项,则应尽量公开审议处理结果的理由。

3. 对违反保密义务的认定和救济措施的完善

中国《仲裁法》、仲裁规则对保密义务违反的认定和救济措施的完善尚未明确。笔者认为,对保密义务的违反主要可以分为两类:一是因签署保密协议而负有保密义务的当事方和部分第三人违反保密义务;二是因法律或仲裁规则有规定,而仲裁庭、当事方以及部分第三人违反法律或仲裁规则规定的保密义务。因保密协议产生的保密义务实际上是一种合同义务,可以按照合同责任来认定处理。因法律规定产生的保密义务,可以由法律直接对此类情况应当承担何种责任作出规定。此外,若违反的保密义务来自仲裁规则,义务违反者如何承担责任则相对复杂。其一,若仲裁规则所含保密义务内容范围与国内法保密义务有所重合,对重合部分保密义务的违反可由仲裁庭根据国内法规范给出类似的问责方案;其二,对仲裁规则所规定的仲裁机构所在地国法定保密义务以外的保密义务的违反(主要考虑争端双方),其虽并非"法定义务",强制当事方履行保密义务仍具备正当性,即争端双方在选择仲裁机构或仲裁规则时具备自治合意。因而,一方当事人违反此类保密义务的责任仍可先由争端双方协商、仲裁庭确认,若争端双方难以达成共识,则可由仲裁庭依据仲裁规则或规则应用指引等裁决参考文件给出恰当问责方案。但违反义务一方当事人应当承担何种责任?由于此时保密义务来源并非保密协议,而是源自仲裁规则,因而可参照侵权责任予以认定,对故意违反保密义务的行为实施惩戒。对于违反保密义务的救济措施,笔者认为,至少可以包括以下3种:一是停止继续泄露保密信息的行为;二是损害赔偿;三是停止泄露行为和损害赔偿。仲裁庭可以发布禁止令以停止披露保密信息。

(二)积极引导争端当事方订立保密协议

尽管中国《仲裁法》和仲裁规则都对保密性问题有概括性规定,但若争端当事方仅仅把仲裁保密性的概括性规定纳入仲裁协议或是仲裁条款中,而没有就仲裁的保密事项达成任何具体协议,这可能会在适用过程中造成困难。例如,一方当事人若是违反保密义务,是否需要重新申请仲裁、是否需要更改保密协议或保密条款、如何对因违反保密义务遭受损害一方进行救济,这些都是可能产生的问题,若没有进一步详细的约定,这些情况发生时就会严重影响仲裁的效率。因此,仲裁协议中关于仲裁保密问题的部分应尽可能明确和详细,对仲裁保密义务的主体、范围、救济措施等都尽可能作出约定,使保密义务更加明确。

仲裁机构应积极引导争议各方订立保密协议。仲裁机构可以通过制定相关的引导性文件,告知争端当事方仲裁保密性存在的必要性和违反保密义务的危害性,提供保密性义务示范条款或是模板,对部分仲裁规则还可以采取"不反对即同意”的订立方式，充分使争端当事方知晓并引导其在律师的协助下订立相关保密协议。同时，若是在仲裁过程中，争端当事方想要通过申请订立保密性的补充协议保护自己的利益，仲裁庭应当允许。目前，LCIA 就允许当事人在仲裁过程中向仲裁庭申请保密令，在仲裁开庭时向仲裁庭提交新的保密条款，作为一种补救手段，仲裁庭将根据新的仲裁条款发布保密令。

（三）建立仲裁信息分类和公开制度，重点公开仲裁裁决

仲裁信息应当予以分类，针对不同信息的不同保密要求分类处理。根据中国仲裁的立法和实践情况，笔者将仲裁信息按不同维度进行分类：

第一个维度是按照仲裁程序发展的时间顺序，从争端当事方申请仲裁开始到仲裁庭作出仲裁裁决，分为仲裁程序开始前的信息、仲裁程序中的信息和仲裁裁决。仲裁程序开始前的信息主要是仲裁员的信息。争端当事方选择仲裁作为争议解决手段的一个重要原因是，他们可以选择自己的仲裁员，仲裁机构对可供选择的仲裁员可以在其官方网站上公布每个仲裁员的履历和收费标准，方便当事方选择，同时也可以提高仲裁机构的独立性，接受更广泛的监督，以保证仲裁的质量。仲裁程序中的信息除案件事实和法律争议有关的证据材料、案情陈述、分析论证等外，还包括翻译文件、法律检索记录等。

对仲裁程序中的信息还可以从第二个维度展开分类，即根据有无保密性要求和是否存在保密性例外来进行分类，分为有保密要求且无保密性例外的信息、有保密要求但有保密性例外的信息以及无保密要求的信息。有保密要求且无保密性例外的信息包括争端当事方的姓名、名称、身份等具体事实信息和部分与案件实体和程序有关的信息。有保密要求且有保密性例外的信息包括中国《公司法》和《证券法》等法律要求强制披露的信息，请求从国内法院获取证据、临时救济和执行裁决时的有关仲裁信息，接受司法监督和其他监督时披露的信息和其他可以突破保密性的仲裁信息。

值得重点关注的是仲裁裁决的保密与公开问题。无论是当事人自愿披露仲裁裁决还是仲裁机构主动公开仲裁裁决，都将有助于仲裁的立法和实践以及学者的研究。笔者认为，在今后的透明度改革中可以考虑规定仲裁裁决公开的

减损规则。由法律规定公开仲裁裁决的普遍性义务,但可以由争端当事方约定是否对该要求进行减损甚至排除。在仲裁裁决作出时,仲裁庭应当向当事人询问是否减损或是排除公开仲裁裁决的规定义务,即当事人可以根据商业秘密、个人隐私等理由,在一定程度上排除该规则的适用。对当事人要求减损或是排除仲裁裁决公开规则的仲裁裁决,仲裁庭应告知当事人仲裁庭将仅摘录裁决要旨并经编撰后公开。

(四)增强中国仲裁规则国际化水平

随着国际商事仲裁在全世界范围内的发展,国际商事仲裁的透明度改革也在如火如荼地进行,新的仲裁规则不断回应着国际社会对提高国际仲裁透明度的要求。中国国际仲裁规则要积极适应国际环境,不断实践和摸索适合中国社会和中国商业的改革模式,增加中国国际商事仲裁的透明度。例如,在保密制度和实践中,《贸仲规则》可借鉴国际仲裁机构仲裁规则,建立完备的仲裁员信息公示制度、构建商事仲裁透明度标准体系,提高《贸仲规则》的国际化水平。

六、结语

随着全球经济、信息互联的深入发展,国际商事活动日益频繁,国际商事纠纷随之增加,国际商事仲裁也不断发展,产生了值得借鉴和学习的新经验,透明度改革就是其中一个重要方面。近年来,中国国际商事仲裁业发展迅猛,日益成为国际商事主体关注的对象。但应当看到,中国《仲裁法》和仲裁机构仲裁规则在保密制度规定上还存在较大可完善的空间。结合中国仲裁立法和实践,完善中国商事仲裁制度,促进仲裁发展,乃当务之急。为此,一项重要工作就是进一步修改完善《仲裁法》和仲裁规则关于保密制度的规定,同时增加透明度规则,提升中国仲裁的公信力和影响力。

A Theoretical Framework for the Legitimacy of International Commercial Arbitration

—Fuller's Interactionism and Its Implications on the Concept of International Arbitration

Dan Xie *

Abstract: This article examines and critically assesses current legal theories of international commercial arbitration — the territorialism, pluralism and autonomous arbitral legal order. International arbitration, in either theory or practice, has gone through three stages of development successively — localised, delocalised (or pluralistic) and transnational arbitral legal order. However, the current scholarships of territorialism, pluralism and autonomous arbitral legal order cannot provide a sound theoretical framework to explain the creation of normative rights and obligations, the operation of diversified normative systems (party autonomy, rules of arbitral institutions, soft law, domestic legal

---

* Dan Xie is a Ph. D. Candidate at University of New South Wales, Australia. She was also the visiting scholar at Max Planck Institute Luxembourg for Procedural Law (1 August 2019 – 30 December 2019). She holds an L. L. M. in International Commercial Arbitration (Magna Cum Laude) from Stockholm University and an L. L. M. in Civil and Commercial Law (Summa Cum Laude) and an L. L. B. (Summa Cum Laude) from China University of Political Science and Law. Her current research is in the areas of international commercial arbitration law, private international law, company law and contract law.

order, international conventions) and their interaction with another. This article aims to fill this gap with Lon L. Fuller's theory. Based on Fuller's interactionism thesis, the authority of international commercial arbitration derives from the general societal acceptance arising from the dynamic interactions of actors in the community of international arbitration. The stabilisation of interactional expectancies can arise from parties' agreement, activities of arbitrators or arbitral institutions, decisions of courts and international conventions. Thus, party autonomy, rules and codes of arbitral institutions, international commercial arbitration practice, national arbitration laws and international conventions can together create normative rights and obligations for actors and generate ordering effects in the domain of international commercial arbitration simultaneously.

Ⅰ. Introduction

Issues regarding the source of arbitrators' power, and the legal nature of the process and its objective are related to the "legitimacy" of international arbitration.① There are three theories of international arbitration accounting for the entire phenomenon including its sources, its objectives and its structure. The first is the territorial theory according to which the effectiveness of arbitration stems from the legal order of the State where the arbitration takes place. This proposition relegates international arbitration to a component of a single national legal order, i. e., the legal order of the arbitral seat.② The second, pluralism theory, anchors international arbitration in a plurality of national legal orders — all legal orders that are willing, under certain conditions, to recognise the effectiveness of an

① Emmanuel Gaillard, *Legal Theory of International Arbitration*, Martinus Nijhoff Publishers, 2010, p. 2. Gaillard used the term legitimacy to explain the legal source of international commercial arbitration on which the international commercial arbitration is considered legitimate.

② See section Ⅱ.

international arbitration award. [①]

Last, the autonomous arbitration theory recognises the autonomy of international arbitration that generates an authentic arbitral legal order. [②] Among the international commercial arbitration community, the idea of autonomous international arbitration against localised perspective (*lexarbitri* or *lexfori*) remains important and popular in some quarters. [③]It probably reached its apogee a couple of decades ago and has been on the wane since figures like Berthold Goldman and Philippe Fouchard passed from the scene. Emmanuel Gaillard continues to vigorously wave the flag for this contingent, but it has fewer adherents than in the past. Also, the idea of an autonomous (or delocalised) international commercial arbitration lacks an adequate theoretical foundation, which makes this theory inadequate and less convincing.

Specifically, some leading proponents of autonomous international arbitration

---

① See section Ⅲ.

② See section Ⅳ.

③ Regarding the proponents of autonomous international arbitration, see Emmanuel Gaillard, *The Emerging System of International Arbitration: Defining System*, American Society of International Law Proceedings of Annual Meetings 106(1), 2012; Emmanuel Gaillard, *Sociology of International Arbitration*, Arbitration International 31 (1), 2015; Emmanuel Gaillard, *Legal Theory of International Arbitration*, Martinus Nijhoff Publishers, 2010; Jan Paulsson, *Delocalisation of International Commercial Arbitration: When and Why it Matters*, International and Comparative Law Quarterly 32 (1), 1983; Jan Paulsson, *Arbitration in Three Dimensions*, International and Comparative Law Quarterly 60(2), 2011; Jan Paulsson, *The Idea of Arbitration*, Oxford University Press, 2013; Gabrielle Kaufmann-Kohler, *Globalization of Arbitral Procedure*, Vanderbilt Journal of Transnational Law 36, 2003; Gabrielle Kaufmann-Kohler, *Soft Law in International Arbitration: Codification and Normativity*, Journal of International Dispute Settlement 1 (2), 2010; Julian D. M. Lew, *Achieving the Dream: Autonomous Arbitration*, Arbitration International 22, 2006; Julian D. M. Lew, *Is There a Global Free-Standing Body of Substantive Arbitration Law*, in Albert Jan van den Berg, ed., International Arbitration: The Coming of a New Age?, Kluwer Law International, 2013.

legal order equated the delocalised arbitration with a dream① or faith,② which seems to depend mainly on the will to believe.③ Although the international arbitration scholars tried to justify the autonomy of international commercial arbitration based on globalisation,④ soft law,⑤ international arbitration community,⑥ international arbitration culture⑦ or constitutional analysis,⑧ most of them have tended to gloss over the difficulties regarding the legitimacy of arbitration which only the philosophy of law can address.

Still, several brilliant scholars have faced the most challenging part of international commercial arbitration law.⑨ Albeit in different ways, Gaillard and Paulsson sought to demonstrate that arbitration may be effective under

① See Julian D. M. Lew, *Achieving the Dream: Autonomous Arbitration*, Arbitration International 22, 2006, p.179.

② See Gabrielle Kaufmann-Kohler, *Globalization of Arbitral Procedure*, Vanderbilt Journal of Transnational Law 36, 2003; Gabrielle Kaufmann-Kohler, *Arbitral Precedent: Dream, Necessity or Excuse?*, Arbitration International 23(3), 2007; Gabrielle Kaufmann-Kohler, *Soft Law in International Arbitration: Codification and Normativity*, Journal of International Dispute Settlement 1(2), 2010.

③ See Ralf Michaels, *Dreaming Law without a State: Scholarship on Autonomous International Arbitration as Utopian Literature*, London Review of International Law 1(1), 2013, p.39.

④ See Gabrielle Kaufmann-Kohler, *Globalization of Arbitral Procedure*, Vanderbilt Journal of Transnational Law 36, 2003.

⑤ See Gabrielle Kaufmann-Kohler, *Soft Law in International Arbitration: Codification and Normativity*, Journal of International Dispute Settlement 1(2), 2010.

⑥ Ibid., p.295.

⑦ See Joshua Karton, *International Arbitration Culture and Global Governance*, in Walter Mattli and Thomas Dietz, eds., International Arbitration and Global Governance: Contending Theories and Evidence, Oxford University Press, 2014, p. 74 – 116; see also Joshua Karton, *The Culture of International Arbitration and the Evolution of Contract Law*, Oxford University Press, 2013, p.17 – 39.

⑧ Stephan W. Schill, *Developing a Framework for the Legitimacy of International Arbitration*, in Albert Jan van den Berg, ed., Legitimacy: Myths, Realities, Challenges, Wolters Kluwer Law & Business, 2015, p.789; Stephan W Schill, *Conceptions of Legitimacy of International Arbitration*, in David D Caron et al., eds., Practising Virtue: Inside International Arbitration, Oxford University Press, 2015, p.106.

⑨ Emmanuel Gaillard, *Legal Theory of International Arbitration*, Martinus Nijhoff Publishers, 2010; Jan Paulsson, *The Idea of Arbitration*, Oxford University Press, 2013; Joshua Karton, *The Structure of International Arbitration Law and the Exercise of Arbitral Authority*, Contemporary Asia Arbitration Journal 8(2), 2015.

arrangements that do not depend at all on national law or judges. However, from the analysis below, neither Gaillard's nor Paulsson's propositions are tenable. The current theories of international commercial arbitration cannot provide a sound foundation for an autonomous international arbitration legal order. They do not provide a sufficient and concrete legal structure to explain the legitimacy of international commercial arbitration and the way that international arbitration rules① are created and interact with one another.

This paper is intended to address this gap through Lon L. Fuller's theories. It introduces Fuller's "eunomics" and interactionism theories to explain the creation and operation of the normative systems, including party autonomy, rules of arbitral institutions, soft law, domestic legal order, international conventions, and their interactions with one another within an autonomous arbitral legal order. Fuller's concept of law and interactionism theory strengthen the basis for an autonomous arbitration legal order. First, Fuller's broad notion of law makes possible an autonomous international commercial arbitration legal order.② In his influential work *Human Interaction and the Law*, Fuller categorised the law into three types: customary law (or "implicit law" as he called it),③ contract law and enacted law.④ He did not tie the concept of law to the State sovereignty and

---

① The term "international arbitration rules" here refers not to rules of arbitral institutions, but to the "normal rules" of international arbitration legal order, including but not limited to institutional rules, guidelines, statutes, conventions.

② See section Ⅴ.

③ Lon L. Fuller, *Anatomy of the Law*, Frederick A Praeger, 1968, p.43.

④ The term "contract law" here refers not to the law of or about contracts, but to the "law" a contract itself brings into existence. See Lon L. Fuller, *Human Interaction and the Law*, American Journal of Jurisprudence 14, 1969.

provided more fertile sources for international arbitration. ①

Further, Fuller's interactionism theory② suggests a dynamic interplay between law and its subjects, offering us a way to see the creation and development of party autonomy, institutional rules, international arbitral practice, national statutes and international conventions and their interplay with relevant actors. The social actors of international commercial arbitration include parties, counsel, arbitrators, arbitral institutions, courts, national legislators, international convention drafters. These actors interact with one another through parties' agreement, activities of arbitrators and arbitral institutions, decisions of courts and international conventions, which generate stabilised interactional expectancies. Thus, the authoritative sources of international commercial arbitration are not exclusive to State laws. Instead, party autonomy, rules and codes of arbitral institutions, international commercial arbitration practice and soft law, together with State laws, decisions of courts concerning arbitration and international conventions, can create normative rights and obligations on actors and generate ordering effects simultaneously.

Accordingly, this paper proceeds as follows. Section Ⅱ discusses the role of *lexarbitri* in the validity of arbitration agreement and arbitral procedure and the impacts of the decisions of the court of arbitral seat on the forum courts. Section Ⅲ evaluates delocalisation trend and the jurisdictions in favour of it. Section Ⅳ critically reviews the proposition of automomous arbitration legal order with Gaillard and Paulsson's theories. Section Ⅴ introduces Fuller's interactionism

① Fuller considered that a lawmaker is not a necessary element of the notion of law. Accordingly, this broad concept of law makes possible the independent international arbitral legal order. Additionally, Fuller explicitly attributed the force of customary law to the fact that it has found direct expression in the conduct of men toward one another, as opposed to "made" law which is enacted or authoritatively declared. See Lon L. Fuller, *Human Interaction and the Law*, American Journal of Jurisprudence 14, 1969, p. 1.

② Fuller reviewed laws, whatever forms they are, as arising out of human interaction and serving to order and facilitate interaction. See subsection Ⅴ (A).

theory and its implications on the sources of international commercial arbitration. Section Ⅵ concludes this paper and argues that party autonomy, rules and codes of arbitral institutions, international commercial arbitration practice, together with state laws and international conventions, can create normative rights and obligations on actors and generate ordering effects.

Ⅱ. The Territorialism Theory

The territorialism theory posits that the legitimacy of international commercial arbitration arises from the arbitral seat. This section analyses the role of *lexarbitri* in the arbitral procedure and the validity of an arbitration agreement and the impacts of the procedural decisions of the supervisory jurisdiction of the arbitral seat on enforcing courts. From the discussion below, it is reasonable to conclude that the legitimacy of international commercial arbitration does not arise from the *lexarbitri*, and the decisions of the courts in the arbitral seat should not have an impact on the enforcing courts.

A. The Role of *Lexarbitri* in Validity of Arbitration Agreement and Arbitral Procedure

Francis Mann is the leading proponent of the territorialism theory. In his *Lex Facit Arbitrum*(the law makes the arbitrator) published in 1967, he wrote:

Just as, notwithstanding its notoriously misleading name, every system of private international law is a system of national law, every arbitration is a national arbitration, that is to say, subject to a specific system of national law. ①

The *lexarbitri* cannot be the law of any country other than that of the arbitration tribunal's seat. No act of the parties can have any legal effect except as

① F. A. Mann, *Lex Facit Arbitrum*, in Pieter Sanders, ed. , International Arbitration Liber Amicorum for Martin Domke, Martinus Nijhoff, 1967, p. 159.

the result of the sanction given to it by a legal system. ①

There is a pronounced similarity between the national judge and the arbitrator in that both of them are subject to the local sovereign. If, in contrast to the national judge, the arbitrator is in many respects, but by no means with uniformity, allowed and even ordered by municipal legislators to accept the commands of the parties, this is because, and to the extent that, the local sovereign so provides. ②

This conception assumes that the legitimacy of arbitration arises out of the *lexarbitri*— the seat of arbitration. It attributes the power of the arbitrators and the normative effect of parties' actions to the local sovereign rather than parties' agreement. Francis Mann is not the only proponent of the territorialism view. Jean-François Poudret and Sébastien Besson in their remarkable study, *Comparative Law of International Arbitration*, stated:

Without entering into a philosophical debate, we consider that the parties' will is necessarily based on a legal system from which it derives its validity. The *lexarbitri* builds the foundation (Grundnorm) for the effectiveness for the arbitration agreement. Together with the public international law, it constitutes one of the two potential bases for arbitration. ③

Poudret and Besson perceived that the validity of parties' agreement would arise from the *lexarbitri*. According to their theory, given that the arbitration agreement is the foundation stone of international arbitration, reasonably, it can be concluded that the authority of international arbitration stems from the sovereign of the arbitral seat.

---

① F. A. Mann, *Lex Facit Arbitrum*, in Pieter Sanders, ed., International Arbitration Liber Amicorum for Martin Domke, Martinus Nijhoff, 1967, p. 161.

② Ibid.

③ Jean-François Poudret and Sébastien Besson, *Comparative Law of International Arbitration*, Sweet & Maxwell, 2nd ed., 2007, p. 83.

Moreover, Poudret and Bessone emphasised that it was the *lexarbitri* and the public international law (the international conventions, especially the New York Convention) that recognised and enforced arbitration agreements and foreign arbitral awards. Admittedly, only the national court possesses the coercive power to rescue the arbitration when it is in danger of foundering. However, it is the party autonomy, with some limits under the domestic law and public international law, that constitutes the basis for international arbitration. The arbitration agreement derives its validity from the party autonomy, which is why most parties honour their arbitration agreement and arbitral award voluntarily.

This territorialism is based on positive law theory. Legal positivism generally attributes the property of law only to those rules that are derived from a lawmaking authority existing as a political or social fact.① However, under the theories of natural law② and contract law, it is not necessary for the contract to acquire validity through sovereign recognition. Parties may freely forego all their private rights. Only when this disposition may affect the public interest, can the national court limit it. In other words, the amount of government intervention should be confined to a minimum. In international commercial arbitration, the foundation stone of modern international arbitration is an agreement by the parties to submit any disputes to arbitration.③ This doctrine has been recognised by domestic law as well.

For instance, Article 2059 of the French Civil Code provides that "all persons

---

① Suri Ratnapala, *Jurisprudence*, Cambridge, Cambridge University Press, 3rd ed., 2017, p. 27.

② Ibid., p. 141 – 142. An examination of all the strands of natural law would take up a large volume. Briefly, the common element in all strands of natural law is that it is a kind of universal law that is not humanly created. Although natural law theories vary in aims and content but they share one central idea: that there is a kind of higher non-human "law", based on morality, against which the moral or legal force of human law can be measured.

③ Nigel Blackaby et al., *Redfern and Hunter on International Arbitration*, Oxford University Press, 6th ed., 2015, p. 12.

may enter into a *compromise arbitration* on rights of which they have the free disposal". ① Although Article 2060 further provides that parties may not agree to arbitrate disputes in a series of particular fields (such as family law) and "more generally in all matters concerning public order",② this limitation has been construed in a very restrictive way by French courts. Similarly, § 1030 (1) of the German Code of Civil Procedure provides that any claim under property law may be the subject of arbitration. Moreover, the claims involving a non-economic interest that the parties are entitled to dispose of freely may be the subject matter of an arbitration agreement as well. ③

From the aforementioned provisions of statutes, it is evident that it is not the national law that confers the validity to the arbitration agreement. Instead, it is the party autonomy itself that brings the arbitration agreement into being. The primary function of national law is to enforce an arbitration agreement when the parties do not comply voluntarily with such agreement.

Admittedly, the courts play important roles in the whole process of international arbitration — pre-arbitration (e.g., the court refers parties to arbitration), during arbitration (e.g., the court of the arbitral seat provides interim measures) and post-arbitration (the enforcing courts' recognition and enforcement of foreign awards). However, national courts do not provide the legitimacy of international arbitration. Instead, they support and supervise the proceedings of international arbitration and function only when the international arbitration cannot go well under the discretion of a tribunal or without obtaining voluntary performance by parties. After all, most international arbitral proceedings progress smoothly under

---

① *Code civil* [Civil Code] (France) art 2059.

② *Code civil* [Civil Code] (France) art 2060.

③ *Code of Civil Procedure* (Germany) § 1030(1) [Samson-Übersetzungen GmbH and Carmen von Schöning trans, *Code of Civil Procedure* (https://www.gesetze-im-internet.de/englisch_zpo/englisch_zpo.html)].

the control of arbitrators complying with the arbitral rules, and secure the voluntary performance by the parties without the assistance of the national courts either in the seat or the enforcement fora.

The arbitration procedure is dependent more on party autonomy and the tribunal's discretion than on the court of the seat and the *lexarbitri*. Meanwhile, the courts of the seat usually defer to arbitrators' procedural discretion in the conduct of arbitral proceedings. This deference to party autonomy and the tribunals' discretion in procedural matters ensures the flexibility of international arbitration.

Additionally, the New York Convention has adopted this first-second sequential approach to the arbitral procedure as well. One of the grounds on which the opposing party may apply for non-recognition or non-enforcement of international arbitration awards under the New York Convention — Article Ⅴ (1) (d) provides:

The composition of the arbitral authority or the arbitral procedure was not in accordance with the agreement of the parties, or, failing such agreement, was not in accordance with the law of the country where the arbitration took place. ①

Article Ⅴ (1)(d) provides that an enforcement court must first see whether parties had agreed on the composition of the arbitral tribunal or the arbitration procedure and whether such agreement was violated. The court applies the law of the country where the arbitration took place only if there was no agreement between the parties on the constitution of the arbitral tribunal.

The 1961 European Convention on International Commercial Arbitration extended this further. According to Article Ⅳ (1) of this convention, in the absence of an agreement between the parties, the arbitrators determine the arbitral

---

① *Convention on the Recognition and Enforcement of Foreign Arbitral Awards*, open for signature 10 June 1958, 330 UNTS 3 (entered into force 7 June 1959) art Ⅴ(1)(d).

proceedings without any reference to the law of the seat.① Unlike the previous attitude regarding the validity of the arbitral agreement, Poudret and Besson considered that the law of civil procedure in force at the place of the seat of the arbitration was not binding on the arbitrators in the absence of procedural agreements of the parties.②

In summary, the *lexarbitri* plays a significant role in arbitral proceedings, including but not limited to, setting aside an award, appointing arbitrators when parties cannot conclude an agreement, and providing interim measures. However, the arbitration agreement is the foundation of international commercial arbitration, and the validity of the arbitration agreement arises from the parties' will rather than from the *lexarbitri*.

B. The Decisions of the Supervisory Jurisdiction of Arbitral Seat

Another strong argument for the choice of territoralismis that the recognition and enforcement of the set-aside award would be meaningless as the set-aside award ceases to exist.③ Thus, it is necessary to explore the impacts of the supervisory court's decision at the arbitral seat on the forum enforcement jurisdictions. There are two types of decisions made by the court of the seat in the setting aside proceedings: the upholding decisions and the set-aside decisions. From the detailed discussion below, it is clear that the decision of the court of the arbitral seat should not have any impact on the enforcing courts.

---

① *European Convention on International Commercial Arbitration*, opened for signature 21 April 1961, 484 UNTS 349 (entered into force 18 October 1965) art Ⅳ (1).

② Jean-François Poudret and Sébastien Besson, *Comparative Law of International Arbitration*, Sweet & Maxwell, 2nd ed., 2007, p. 463.

③ Albert Jan van den Berg, *The* 1958 *New York Arbitration Convention Revisited*, Swiss Arbitration Association Special Series 15, 2001, p. 125; Hamid G. Gharavi, *The International Effectiveness of The Annulment of An Arbitral Award*, Kluwer Arbitration International, 2002, p. 114; Georgios Petrochilos, *Procedural Law in International Arbitration*, Oxford University Press, 2004, p. 336.

(i) The Effects of Upholding Decisions

The first circumstance concerns the case in which the court of the seat denies the request of annulment by the opposing party. Enforcing courts take different stances on the decision upholding the arbitral award by the court of the arbitral seat.

The English High Court of Justice held that the party who complained that the award was defective or that the arbitration was defectively conducted must in the first place invoke the supervisory jurisdiction of the seat of the arbitration. ① The English High Court further considered that it was discouraging for the English courts to re-investigate the procedural defects in the conduct of arbitration that had already been determined by the supervisory court. This approach was intended to give weight to the policy of sustaining the finality of international awards. ② The English High Court held that if the remedy was applied for but was refused by the court of the seat of arbitration, it was usually to be a strong policy of the English court to sustain the finality of the determination of the supervisory jurisdiction, except in exceptional cases where the supervisory court could not intervene even where there had been obvious and serious breaches of basic principles of justice. This was because the English High Court held that parties who agreed to arbitrate in a particular jurisdiction were bound by the arbitration procedure and the supervisory jurisdiction of the arbitral seat. ③

Another argument of the approach deferring to the decisions of the arbitral seat is based on the doctrines of *res judicata* or claim/issue estoppel. For instance, the Court of Appeal of Munich confirmed the preclusive effects to a

---

① Minmetals Germany GmbH v. Ferco Steel Ltd. [1999] CLC 647, 661.

② Ibid. See also IPOC International Growth Fund Limited v. L. V. Finance Group Limited (Unreported, British Virgin Islands Court of Appeal, 18 June 2007) [34].

③ Minmetals Germany GmbH v. Ferco Steel Ltd. [1999] CLC 647, 661; IPOC International Growth Fund Limited v. L. V. Finance Group Limited (Unreported, British Virgin Islands Court of Appeal, 18 June 2007) [34].

Spanish decision refusing to set aside an award. After confirming that the Spanish judgement met the requirements of recognition of foreign judgements, the Appeal of Munich followed the findings of Spanish court as to the validity of the award and refused to relitigate the same issues in the recognition and enforcement stage. ①

In contrast, even though the defendant had been unsuccessful in challenging the arbitral award on the ground of due process violation in the seat (Russia), the Swedish Supreme Court still refused the enforcement of the award on the ground of the due process defence. ②

(ii) The Effects of Set-Aside Decisions

The second circumstance concerns the case in which the court of the seat confirms that procedural irregularities existed and sets aside the arbitral award. The various jurisdictions show different opinions on whether the forum court should defer to the findings of the court of the arbitral seat in a due process defence.

Some jurisdictions refuse to recognise or enforce a set-aside award. The main argument for this approach is that an award that has been set aside ceases to exist, and therefore, there is no award left to recognise or enforce. ③ In the *Malicorp* case, the English High Court held that the word "may" in Article Ⅴ of the New

---

① Oberlandesgericht Munich [Court of Appeal Munich], 34 Sch 26/08, 22 June 2009 in (2010) XXXV Yearbook Commercial Arbitration 371, 373 [9].

② Belaya Ptitsa-Kursk v. Robot Grader AB, Högsta Domstolens [Supreme Court], Ö 3626 - 17, 4 May 2018 reported in the Arbitration Institute of the Stockholm Chamber of Commerce, 8 [23] <https://www. arbitration. sccinstitute. com/Swedish-Arbitration-Portal/Supreme-Court/The-Supreme-Court2/The-Supreme-Court/d_3259325 - judgment-in-the-swedish-supreme-court - 4 - may - 2018. - case-no. - o - 3626 - 17>.

③ See Albert Jan van den Berg, *The* 1958 *New York Arbitration Convention Revisited*, Swiss Arbitration Association Special Series 15, 2001, p. 125; Hamid G. Gharavi, *The International Effectiveness of The Annulment of An Arbitral Award*, Kluwer Arbitration International, 2002, p. 114; Georgios Petrochilos, *Procedural Law in International Arbitration*, Oxford University Press, 2004, p. 336.

York Convention[①] and s 103 (2) of the Arbitration Act (1996)[②] gave the enforcement court the discretion to enforce an award even though the award had been set aside by a decision of a competent court within s 103 (2) (f). However, the judge stated that it was not right to exercise that discretion to enforce the annulled award if, applying the general principles of English private international law, the set-aside decision was one to which the enforcement court would give effect.[③] Germany also shows deference to the annulment decision of arbitral seat. Article 1061 (3) of German Code of Civil Procedure provides "where the arbitration award is reversed abroad, after having been declared enforceable, a petition may be filed that the declaration of enforceability be repealed".[④]

However, some scholars[⑤] and jurisdictions, such as France, consider that the decision of annulment in the arbitral seat does not affect the enforcement court. First, Article 1525 of the French Code of Civil Procedure does not regard annulment as possible grounds for refusing enforcement of a foreign award.[⑥] Besides, according to Art Ⅶ's more-favourable-right provision in the New York Convention, the enforcement court may recognise or enforce an annulled foreign award. Last, the French courts consider that the foreign award concerning

---

① *Convention on the Recognition and Enforcement of Foreign Arbitral Awards*, open for signature 10 June 1958, 330 UNTS 3 (entered into force 7 June 1959) art Ⅴ.

② *Arbitration Act* 1996 (UK) c 23, s 103(2).

③ Malicorp Ltd. v. Government of the Arab Republic of Egypt, Egyptian Holding Co. for Aviation & Egyptian Airports Co. [2015] EWHC 361 (Comm) (19 February 2015) [21].

④ *Zivilprozessordnung* [Code of Civil Procedure] (Germany) § 1061(3).

⑤ Jan Paulsson, *Arbitration Unbound: Award Detached from the Law of Its Country of Origin*, International and Comparative Law Quarterly 30, 1981; Jan Paulsson, *Delocalisation of International Commercial Arbitration: When and Why it Matters*, International and Comparative Law Quarterly 32(1), 1983; Emmanuel Gaillard, *Enforcement of Awards Set Aside in the Country of Origin: The French Experience*, in Improving the Efficiency of Arbitration Agreements and Awards: 40 Years of Application of the New York Convention, Kluwer Law International, 1999, p.505.

⑥ *Code civil* [Civil Code] (France) art 1525.

"international commercial interests" is not integrated into the legal system of the arbitral seat. Hence, the standing award would not be affected by an annulment decision in the arbitral seat.① Accordingly, the set-aside decision of the court in the arbitral seat should not be binding on other jurisdictions which remain free to decide whether to recognise or enforce an award according to the New York Convention.

Besides France, the Netherlands also takes the approach that the Dutch court can enforce the award which has been set aside by the court of the arbitral seat. For instance, the Amsterdam Court of Appeal enforced the award which had been annulled by the court of the seat (Russia) and held that the enforcing court was not compelled to deny leave for recognition of an annulled arbitral award if the foreign decision annulling the arbitral award cannot be recognised in the Netherlands.② First, the Appeal Court held that neither Article Ⅴ(1)(e) nor other provisions of the New York Convention compelled the Dutch enforcement court to recognise such annulment decision of the Russian civil court directly. The question whether the Russian civil court decision annulling the arbitral award could be recognised in the Netherlands was reviewed under the general rules of the private international law.③ Subsequently, the Appeal Court held that the annulment decision of Russia had no impact on the enforcement proceedings as the Russian judges were not impartial and independent, thereby violating the general rule of the private international law — due process.④

① Courd' Appel [Court of Appeal], Paris, 2003/09894, 10 June 2004 in 2005 (XXX) Yearbook Commercial Arbitration 499, [1] - [2]; Courd'Appel [Court of Appeal], Paris, 23 October 1997 in (1998) XXIII Yearbook Commercial Arbitration 644, [25].

② Gerechtshof [Court of Appeal] of Amsterdam, 200, 005, 269, 28 April 2009 in (2009) XXXIV Yearbook Commercial Arbitration 703, [5].

③ Ibid., [4].

④ Ibid., [6].

(iii) Critical Analysis of the Effects of the Seat Court

For this paper, the decision of the supervisory jurisdiction concerning the validity of an award will be referred to as an award decision. The award decisions include the court decision recognising① or refusing the validity of an award. Although the aforementioned Amsterdam Court of Appeal enforced the set-aside award, it still applied the foreign judgment principles to the award decision. In other words, if the Russian judges were impartial and independent, the Amsterdam Court of Appeal would have enforced this set-aside award decision and further denied enforcement of this award. Even though the Amsterdam Court of Appeal and French courts do not grant effect to set-aside award decisions, they follow different routes. The critical issue is whether the award decisions can have extra-territorial effects in the enforcement forum, and the enforcement forum shall apply the foreign judgment principles to award decisions.

The fact that these award decisions are ancillary to arbitration awards means that they depend on the previous adjudication in the award. The distinction between a procedural review and an appeal on the merits should be emphasised. In other words, the court of the arbitral seat does not relitigate the merits of the dispute before the arbitrators. Instead, the award decisions focus on the validity of the award and its effects in the territory of the seat. ② Because of the ancillary nature of such award decisions, it is not advisable for the enforcement forum to give effect to the award decisions. The only subject of examination by the enforcement forum is the foreign arbitral award itself rather than the award decision. Consequently, the award decision should not apply the requirements for the recognition of foreign judgments.

① The recognising decisions include the situations the national court enters a judgment in the terms of the award or simply declares the award enforceable in the arbitral seat.

② Maxi Scherer, *Effects of Foreign Judgments Relating to International Arbitral Awards: Is the "Judgment Route" the Wrong Road?*, Journal of International Dispute Settlement 4(3), 2013, p. 606.

Firstly, the award decision by the supervisory court and the enforcement forum court's decision have different aims and apply different standards. The award decision determines whether the award is effective in its territory of arbitral seat. Given the sovereign nature of award decisions, the court of the arbitral seat decides the validity of an award under its national standards rather than the New York Convention. Even for the jurisdictions which adopt the UNCITRAL Model Law for setting aside awards on grounds similar to those under the New York Convention, the court of the arbitral seat must apply the grounds in the domestic approach to decide whether to set aside an award. In contrast, the recognition and enforcement forum determines whether a particular award can be enforced within its territory. The forum court should apply only the grounds for refusing recognition or enforcement prescribed in the New York Convention.

Secondly, owing to the sovereign nature of court judgments, the court of the arbitral seat can decide the effects of the validity of an award only within its territory. Hence, such award decisions by the arbitral seat jurisdiction upholding or setting aside an award have only a territorially limited effect, i. e., the territory of the State in which it is rendered, and cannot produce extra-territorial effects in other jurisdictions. As the Court of Appeal of Paris stated: "[j]udgments delivered pursuant to an annulment proceeding, like execution orders, do not have an international effect because they apply only to defined territorial sovereignty, and no consideration can be given to these judgments by a foreign judge in an indirect proceeding."①

Thirdly, if the international arbitral award is not independent of an award decision by the court of the arbitral seat, the parties would be subjected to more than one enforcement procedure (enforcement of award decision and enforcement

① Courd' appel de Paris [Court of Appeal of Paris], 29 September 2005 in (2006) XXXI Yearbook Commercial Arbitration 629, 633 [5].

of award *per sei*) before the forum courts. This duplication of proceedings amounts to judicial harassment of the parties. Therefore, the forum court should examine only the award itself and not take into account the award decisions by the arbitral seat jurisdiction in regard to the validity of arbitral awards.

Further, granting effect to award decisions poses a severe risk of proceedings, parallel to recognition or enforcement proceedings, being conducted elsewhere, which may result in different decisions on the validity of an arbitral award between the court of the seat and the court of the forum. As the High Court of Hong Kong Special Administrative Region held, the award debtor could challenge the award in the arbitral seat based on the grounds for annulment, or could wait until the recognition and enforcement stage to raise the grounds for defence under the New York Convention.① However, it is submitted that the award debtor should make this choice only before the commencement of recognition and enforcement proceedings. The award debtor should not be encouraged to seek the setting aside of an award after the recognition or enforcement proceedings have commenced. Imposing a stay on the recognition and enforcement proceedings pending the setting-aside proceedings at the seat would waste judicial resources and undermine the efficiency and economy of international arbitration awards. The better option is to allow the forum court to have the final word in the examination of the rufual grounds under the New York Convention.

Moreover, the main progress of the New York Convention was to abandon the doctrine of double-exequatur which required the award creditor to first obtain confirmation of the finality of an award in the seat before its recognition and enforcement.② If the forum court gives effect to the award decisions upholding the

---

① Paklito Investment Ltd. v. Klockner East Asia Ltd., [1993] 2 HKLR 39, 48 -49.

② Christoph Liebscher, *Non-Binding Award*, *Article* V (1)(*e*), in Reinmar Wolff (ed.), New York Convention: Convention on the Recognition and Enforcement of Foreign Arbitral Awards of 10 June 1958: Commentary, C. H. Beck · Hart · Nomos, 2012, p. 357 -358.

validity of an award, this policy will encourage the award creditor to seek confirmation of the finality of an award in the seat, resulting in the double-exequatur for the recognition and enforcement of international arbitral awards.

Last, it seems unreasonable to deprive the forum court of control over the examination of the validity of an award given that the forum has the assets of the award debtor and therefore has more interests than does the arbitral seat.

Based on the aforestated arguments, the better option for a forum court is to examine awards without taking into account the award decisions made by the court of the arbitral seat. In other words, the decision regarding the validity or otherwise of the award based on the grounds for annulment by the courts at the arbitral seat, does not eliminate or exclude the forum courts' control of the award's validity. Also, given the ancillary character of the award decision, such an award decision shall not be subject to the requirements for the enforcement of foreign judgments. This conclusion is consistent with the ancillary and sovereign characters of award decisions, the interests of the forum courts, and the spirit of the New York Convention.

Ⅲ. The Pluralism Theory

As discussed earlier, a foreign arbitral award may be enforced by an enforcing court even though the court of the arbitral seat has set it aside. The rationale underlying this approach is the pluralism theory. Pluralism theory perceives that the validity of arbitral award does not derive from a single legal order—the law of the seat—but from all jurisdictions that are willing to recognise the effectiveness of the award on certain conditions. ①

---

① Emmanuel Gaillard, *Legal Theory of International Arbitration*, Martinus Nijhoff Publishers, 2010, p. 24 – 31; Jan Paulsson, *Arbitration in Three Dimensions*, International and Comparative Law Quarterly 60 (2), 2011, p. 296 – 301; Jan Paulsson, *The Idea of Arbitration*, Oxford University Press, 2013, p. 35 – 39.

A. Delocalisation

According to Emmanuel, each State can decide on the recognition and enforcement of a foreign arbitral award irrespective of other States' decisions. No State enjoys an exclusive right to deal with the award, and the decision of one sovereign State has no decisive effects on other States. ① Because countries have different *lexarbitri*, some of these laws may be unfair and arbitrary. However, there is a delocalisation trend in the international arbitration domain, signifying the detachment of international arbitration from control by the law of the place of arbitration.

There are two developments in terms of delocalisation. First, the notion that the role of national courts should be more supportive rather than interventionist has been established by the modern national arbitration laws,② especially by the UNCITRAL Model Law. Specifically, Article 5 of UNCITRAL Model Law provides that "[i]n matters governed by this Law, no court shall intervene except where so provided in this Law."③ Second, it is suggested that the dual system of control (first by the law of the arbitral seat and then by the law of the enforcement forum) should be replaced with the end system of control by the law of enforcement forum. The end system of control is favoured by the New York Convention. The main progressive step taken by the New York Convention was to abandon the doctrine of double-exequatur prescribed by the 1927 Geneva Convention which required the award creditor to first get the finality confirmation

---

① Emmanuel Gaillard, *Legal Theory of International Arbitration*, Martinus Nijhoff Publishers, 2010, p. 28.

② Regarding the regulations of supportive role rather than supervision in modern arbitration law in the major arbitration jurisdictions, see the discussion in Julian D. M. Lew, *Achieving the Dream: Autonomous Arbitration*, Arbitration International 22, 2006, p. 192 - 193.

③ United Nations Committee on International Trade Law, *UNCITRAL Model Law on International Commercial Arbitration*, GA Res 61/33 (4 December 2006) art 5.

of an award in the seat before seeking the recognition and enforcement of the award.①

B. The Legislations Adopting the Law of Forum

The representative of delocalisation is France. The French Cour de Cassation, for instance, enforced an award set aside by the English High Court and held that:

[A]n international arbitral award, which is not anchored in any national legal order, is a decision of international justice whose validity must be examined according to the rules applicable in the country where its recognition and enforcement are sought.②

Moreover, France is but one representative of national courts enforcing awards that have been set aside by the courts in the place of arbitration. Courts in the United States have been prepared, on occasion, to recognise and enforce arbitral awards even though these have been annulled by the courts at the seat of arbitration. For instance, the District Court in Washington DC granted enforcement of an award annulled by the Egyptian court at the seat of arbitration in favour of an American corporation.③ Similarly, the District Court in the Southern District of New York enforced an award that had been set aside in the seat of arbitration—Mexico City.④ The District Court held that giving effect to the annulment of the award in Mexico would run counter to United States public policy and would be "repugnant to fundamental notions of what is decent and just

---

① *Convention on the Execution of Foreign Arbitral Awards*, open for signature 26 September 1927, 92 LNTS 301 (entered into force 25 July 1929) art Ⅰ(d); see also Christoph Liebscher, *Non-Binding Award, Article* Ⅴ(1)(*e*), in Reinmar Wolff (ed.), New York Convention: Convention on the Recognition and Enforcement of Foreign Arbitral Awards of 10 June 1958: Commentary, C. H. Beck · Hart · Nomos, 2012, p.357 –358.

② PT Putrabali Adyamulia (Indonesia) v. Rena Holding, Cour de Cassation [Supreme Court], First Civil Chamber, 29 June 2007 reported in (2007) XXXII Yearbook Commercial Arbitration 299, 302.

③ Chromalloy Aeroservices Inc. v. Arab Republic of Egypt, 937 F Supp 907 (D DC, 1996).

④ Corporación Mexicana de Mantenimiento Integral, S de RL de CV v. PEMEX-Exploration y Produccin (2nd Cir., No 13 –4022, 2 August 2016).

in the State where enforcement is sought."①

With the development of delocalisation, the pluralism theory emerged to provide a more theoretical basis for this trend. ②Delocalised awards do not mean that they are independent of any legal order. Instead, delocalisation refers to the possibility that an award may be enforced by the legal order of an enforcement forum whether or not the arbitral seat has accepted it. ③ As Emmanuel Gaillard observed, this representation considers that international arbitration is anchored in a plurality of national legal orders. In other words, the legitimacy of an international arbitral award does not merely derive from the legal system of the seat, but rather from all legal orders that would like to, on certain conditions, recognise the effectiveness of the award. ④

The delocalisation shows that owing to the sovereign nature of court judgments and decisions, the court of the arbitral seat can decide the effects of the validity of an award only within its territory. Hence, court decisions by the arbitral seat jurisdiction setting aside an award have only a limited territorially effect, which means they have legal effects only within the territory of the State in which they are rendered and cannot produce extra-territorial effects in other jurisdictions.

---

① Corporación Mexicana de Mantenimiento Integral, S de RL de CV v. PEMEX-Exploration y Produccin (2nd Cir., No 13 -4022, 2 August 2016) slip op 28, quoting Tahan v. Hodgson, 662 F 2d 862, 864 (DC Cir, 1981).

② Jan Paulsson, *Arbitration Unbound: Award Detached from the Law of Its Country of Origin*, International and Comparative Law Quarterly 30, 1981; Jan Paulsson, *Delocalisation of International Commercial Arbitration: When and Why it Matters*, International and Comparative Law Quarterly 32(1), 1983.

③ Jan Paulsson, *The Idea of Arbitration*, Oxford University Press, 2013, p. 36; Jan Paulsson, *Arbitration in Three Dimensions*, International and Comparative Law Quarterly 60(2), 2011, p. 298.

④ Emmanuel Gaillard, *Legal Theory of International Arbitration*, Martinus Nijhoff Publishers, 2010, p. 24.

Ⅳ. Autonomous Arbitration Legal Order

Among the international commercial arbitration community, the idea of autonomous international arbitration — independent of any national law and free of alocalised perspective (*lexarbitri or lexfori*) — appears popular in current theory and practice.① More members in the community of international commercial arbitration have favoured the transnational or international attribute of international arbitration. They argued that "the juridicity of arbitration is rooted in a distinct, transnational legal order, that could be labelled as the arbitral legal order, and not in a national legal system, be it that of the country of the seat or that of the place or places of enforcement."② They considered that international commercial arbitration has the transnational foundations that are comprised of national and international law, of statutes and private contracts, which create the normative infrastructure of international arbitration to function as an autonomous legal order.③

① Regarding the proponents of autonomous international arbitration, see Emmanuel Gaillard, *The Emerging System of International Arbitration: Defining System*, American Society of International Law Proceedings of Annual Meetings 106(1), 2012; Emmanuel Gaillard, *Sociology of International Arbitration*, Arbitration International 31 (1), 2015; Emmanuel Gaillard, *Legal Theory of International Arbitration*, Martinus Nijhoff Publishers, 2010; Jan Paulsson, *Delocalisation of International Commercial Arbitration: When and Why it Matters*, International and Comparative Law Quarterly 32 (1), 1983; Jan Paulsson, *Arbitration in Three Dimensions*, International and Comparative Law Quarterly 60(2), 2011; Jan Paulsson, *The Idea of Arbitration*, Oxford University Press, 2013; Gabrielle Kaufmann-Kohler, *Globalization of Arbitral Procedure*, Vanderbilt Journal of Transnational Law 36, 2003; Gabrielle Kaufmann-Kohler, *Soft Law in International Arbitration: Codification and Normativity*, Journal of International Dispute Settlement 1 (2), 2010; Julian D. M. Lew, *Achieving the Dream: Autonomous Arbitration*, Arbitration International 22, 2006; Julian D. M. Lew, *Is There a Global Free-Standing Body of Substantive Arbitration Law*, in Albert Jan van den Berg (ed.), International Arbitration: The Coming of a New Age?, Kluwer Law International, 2013.

② Emmanuel Gaillard, *Legal Theory of International Arbitration*, Martinus Nijhoff Publishers, 2010, p. 35.

③ Stephan W. Schill, *Developing a Framework for the Legitimacy of International Arbitration*, in Albert Jan van den Berg (ed.), Legitimacy: Myths, Realities, Challenges, Wolters Kluwer Law & Business, 2015, p. 808; Julian D. M. Lew, *Achieving the Dream: Autonomous Arbitration*, Arbitration International 22, 2006, p. 202.

However, the idea of an autonomous (or delocalised) international commercial arbitration law lacks an adequate theoretical foundation for the creation and infrastructure of normative rules, which makes this theory less convincing and inadequate. For instance, Julian Lew, the leading proponent of autonomous international arbitration legal order, considered that delocalised arbitration is merely a dream.① Lew is not the only scholar who is a dreamer. Gabriele Kaufmann-Kohler based her views on dreams, faith and visions as well.②

Michaels scriticised this dream of delocalised law, seeing it as utopian literature which seems to depend mainly on the will to believe.③ Although the international arbitration scholars tried to justify the autonomy of international commercial arbitration based on globalisation,④ soft law,⑤ international arbitration community⑥ or international arbitration culture,⑦ most of them did not consider the legitimacy of arbitration which only the philosophy of law can address. Therefore, such efforts to theorise and to further conceptualisc the autonomy of international commercial arbitration require much more extensive inquiry into the

① Julian D. M. Lew, *Achieving the Dream: Autonomous Arbitration*, Arbitration International 22, 2006, p. 179.

② Gabrielle Kaufmann-Kohler, *Globalization of Arbitral Procedure*, Vanderbilt Journal of Transnational Law 36, 2003; Gabrielle Kaufmann-Kohler, *Arbitral Precedent: Dream, Necessity or Excuse?*, Arbitration International 23 (3), 2007; Gabrielle Kaufmann-Kohler, *Soft Law in International Arbitration: Codification and Normativity*, Journal of International Dispute Settlement 1(2), 2010.

③ Ralf Michaels, *Dreaming Law without a State: Scholarship on Autonomous International Arbitration as Utopian Literature*, London Review of International Law 1(1), 2013, p. 39.

④ Gabrielle Kaufmann-Kohler, *Globalization of Arbitral Procedure*, Vanderbilt Journal of Transnational Law 36, 2003.

⑤ Gabrielle Kaufmann-Kohler, *Soft Law in International Arbitration: Codification and Normativity*, Journal of International Dispute Settlement 1(2), 2010.

⑥ Ibid., p. 295.

⑦ Joshua Karton, *International Arbitration Culture and Global Governance*, in Walter Mattli and Thomas Dietz (eds.), International Arbitration and Global Governance: Contending Theories and Evidence, Oxford University Press, 2014, p. 74 – 116; see also Joshua Karton, *The Culture of International Arbitration and the Evolution of Contract Law*, Oxford University Press, 2013.

concept of law.

There are still some intelligent scholars facing the most challenging part of international commercial arbitration law. ①The progressive trend in the legal theory of international arbitration was the theory of delocalisation that started in the 1980s following the publication of Jan Paulsson's and William Park's articles, and the emergence of French scholars' autonomous theory about international arbitration. William and Paulsson proposed the theory of transnational arbitration, namely, a delocalised legal system that is neither subject to the national law (substantive or procedural) nor the national courts of the seat of the arbitration (*lexarbitri*). ② In civil law systems, the influential work of French scholars, especially Emmanuel Gaillard, promulgated the notion of an autonomous arbitral order. ③

A. Gaillard's Autonomous Arbitral Legal Order

Emmanuel Gaillard is regarded as one of the foremost proponents of the transnational legal order. According to Gaillard, the pluralism proposition highlights the plurality of States while the transnational and autonomous arbitration legal order emphasises the collectivity of States. ④ Gaillard based his proposition regarding autonomy on the notion that the common rules of arbitration laws can be deduced from various jurisdictions. He also considered that such international, transnational rules of arbitration, although based on the States' normative

① Emmanuel Gaillard, *Legal Theory of International Arbitration*, Martinus Nijhoff Publishers, 2010; Jan Paulsson, *The Idea of Arbitration*, Oxford University Press, 2013; Joshua Karton, *The Structure of International Arbitration Law and the Exercise of Arbitral Authority*, Contemporary Asia Arbitration Journal 8 (2), 2015.

② William W. Park, *The Lex Loci Arbitri and International Commercial Arbitration*, International and Comparative Law Quarterly 32(1), 1983; William W. Park and Jan Paulsson, *The Binding Force of International Arbitral Awards*, Virginia Journal of International Law 23(2), 1983; Jan Paulsson, *Arbitration Unbound: Award Detached from the Law of Its Country of Origin*, International and Comparative Law Quarterly 30, 1981; Jan Paulsson, *Delocalisation of International Commercial Arbitration: When and Why it Matters*, International and Comparative Law Quarterly 32(1), 1983.

③ Emmanuel Gaillard, *Legal Theory of International Arbitration*, Martinus Nijhoff Publishers, 2010.

④ Ibid., p. 37.

activities, do not belong exclusively to any specific State. [①] Further, he suggested using the comparative method to ascertain transnational rules from the various States.

Moreover, he highlighted the active role of arbitrators in international commercial arbitration. He did not consider arbitrators as the agents of a specific national legal order but as the central actors of an autonomous, transnational legal regime. [②] This understanding of arbitration does not deny that sources of national law or international law can influence the substantive and procedural law of international commercial arbitration, but denies that these sources exclusively determine the outcome. Instead, the actors (primarily arbitrators but also arbitral institutions) of international commercial arbitration play the determinative role in interpreting the legal sources applicable to the disputing parties.

Gaillard based his notion of an autonomous arbitration legal order on the positive law of nations (the collectivity of national statutes). In other words, the existence of an arbitral legal order derives from the collective will of the States rather than from the autonomous arbitration legal order itself. In this sense, the autonomous theory of Gaillard is not fully independent of national statutes.

Furthermore, there are no significant distinctions between the autonomous legal order proposed by Gaillard and the pluralism theory. The arguments of the autonomous proposition are not stronger than the pluralism theory. He presented three arguments to support the existence of an autonomous arbitral legal order, but these demonstrations can merely justify the rationality of the pluralism theory rather than an autonomous arbitral legal order.

His first argument concerns the application of international public policy in

---

① Emmanuel Gaillard, *Legal Theory of International Arbitration*, Martinus Nijhoff Publishers, 2010, p. 59.

② Ibid., p. 35.

certain jurisdictions.[1] Gaillard cited Swiss Federal Tribunal's statement as follows:

An award is considered to be incompatible with public policy if it does not comply with the essential and widely accepted values that, according to the conceptions prevailing in Switzerland, should constitute the foundation of all legal orders.[2]

It is evident that the Swiss Federal Tribunal adopts international public policy. However, as the legal organ of a specific jurisdiction, no matter how "international" the public policy may be, the court must apply the public policy which reflects the local understanding (in this case, it is 'the conceptions prevailing in Switzerland'). Gaillard built his autonomous arbitral legal order on the endorsement of the forum States, which is as same route taken by pluralism. In other words, it is still based on the national legal orders rather than on an autonomous arbitral legal order.

Further, Gaillard's second argument that the courts of certain jurisdictions enforce a set-aside award[3] can demonstrate only the delocalised trend from the seat, i. e., the pluralism theory based on the plurality of national legal orders, rather than the existence of a transnational arbitral legal order based on the common rules or shared pratice of national legal orders. Even the stance of French courts that are regarded to hold the most autonomous arbitration attitude is substantially pluralist. For instance, in the *Putrabali* decision rendered on June 29, 2007, concerning the enforcement of a set-aside award, the French Court of Cassation held that:

An international arbitral award, which is not anchored in any national legal

---

① Emmanuel Gaillard, *Legal Theory of International Arbitration*, Martinus Nijhoff Publishers, 2010, p. 60 - 61.

② Ibid., p. 61.

③ Ibid., p. 61 - 66.

order, is a decision of international justice whose validity must be ascertained with regard to the rules applicable in the country where its recognition and enforcement are sought. ①

Even though the French court noted that the international arbitration award is not integrated into the jurisdiction of the seat, it stated that the validity of an arbitration award should be reviewed by the country in which the recognition and enforcement are sought (here France). The set-aside award is enforced not because of its autonomous legitimacy from the arbitral legal system itself, but because the French legal system takes an autonomous arbitration view. In other words, the rule enforcing the set-aside award is an international rule of French law and not a transnational rule. This has more in common with pluralism rather territorial theory.

Additionally, Gaillard's observation that national jurisdictions, such as Switzerland,② Sweden③ and Belgium,④ may enable parties to opt out of any judicial review of awards made within their territory involving only foreign interests, can merely support the delocalised trend from the seat which pluralism asks for, not indicate any about the autonomy of arbitral legal order.

According to Gaillard, pluralism might result in arbitrators having to consider all requirements of any legal system which might be called upon to enforce the award, which is burdensome and impossible. ⑤ Paulsson admitted such

---

① PT Putrabali Adyamulia (Indonesia) v. Rena Holding, Cour de Cassation [Supreme Court], First Civil Chamber, 29 June 2007 reported in (2007) XXXII Yearbook Commercial Arbitration 299, 301.

② *Federal Act on Private International Law* (Switzerland) 18 December 1987, art 192(1).

③ *Swedish Arbitration Act* (Sweden) SFS No. 1996:116, s 54(2), § 51 [Joel Dahlquist Cullborg trans, *The Swedish Arbitration Act* (2019) < https://sccinstitute.com/media/408924/the-swedish-arbitration-act_1march2019_eng.pdf >].

④ *Code Judiciaire* (Belgium), art 1717 (4).

⑤ Emmanuel Gaillard, *Legal Theory of International Arbitration*, Martinus Nijhoff Publishers, 2010, p. 33.

unpredictability might arise from pluralism theory and arbitrators had no obligation to apply the cumulated requirements under the laws of each jurisdiction that might be called upon to enforce an award.① However, Paulsson contended that in most cases, the plurality model would not necessarily result in unpredictability because most arbitral awards obtain the voluntary performance of parties without any involvement of national legal orders from beginning to end.②

As far as Paulsson is concerned, it is difficult to see how the autonomous arbitral legal order archives anything not already available under the pluralistic proposition if the competent authorities embraced more international norms or international trade practice under the conceptions of their domestic laws.③

In summary, Gaillard's representation of autonomous arbitral legal order, building its theory on the collectivity of national legal orders, is circular and unsatisfactory. He sought to establish this autonomous arbitral legal order by attributing its recognition to the endorsement of national legal orders, which adds no more to the pluralism theory. His three arguments supporting the existence of an autonomous arbitral legal order justify merely the rationality of the pluralism theory rather than an autonomous arbitral legal order.

B. Jan Paulsson's Three-dimensional Pluralism Thesis

Paulsson was not satisfied with Gaillard's autonomous legal order theory and traditional pluralistic theory and proposed another approach—the three-dimensional pluralism which merged with and expanded the pluralism theory, suggesting that arbitration may be effective under conventional arrangements that did not depend

① Jan Paulsson, *Arbitration in Three Dimensions*, International and Comparative Law Quarterly 60 (2), 2011, p. 301 – 302.

② Ibid., p. 300 – 301.

③ Ibid., p. 303.

on national law or judges at all. ①

Paulsson perceived that in its simplest sense, pluralism might be called horizontal as it envisages the cooperation of a multiplicity of territorial legal orders. However, Paulsson considered this horizontal pluralism is too restrictive and needs reform. Paulsson's revised pluralism includes a vertical dimension — where private legal order occupies the same space other than the State normative orderings. ②

Paulsson built his three-dimensional pluralism upon Santi Romano's theory. According to Santi Romano, the law must ultimately be based on social reality. The social reality may create a legal order without the formality required by national legal orderings. Moreover, every organised social group is a kind of legal order which might be superior, inferior or even parallel to a sovereign legal order, such as the international community, professional and trade organisations and even an institutionalised church. ③

Romano's contribution allows us to see the legitimacy of arbitration from the perspective of legal orderings different from those of the sovereign State. However, neither Romano nor Paulsson built the legitimacy of a legal order on an abstract normative system. Instead, they highlighted that the existence of a legal order was a matter of fact. Paulsson stated:

Once one sees that the ultimate rule depends on the fact of its social acceptance, the vision of a legal order cannot be reduced to an abstract normative system. Pretentions of legitimacy are not the real thing. It is necessary, and

---

① Jan Paulsson, *The Idea of Arbitration*, Oxford University Press, 2013, p. 30; Jan Paulsson, *Arbitration in Three Dimensions*, International and Comparative Law Quarterly 60(2), 2011, p.292.

② Jan Paulsson, *Arbitration in Three Dimensions*, International and Comparative Law Quarterly 60 (2), 2011, p.321.

③ Ibid., p.307.

sufficient, that the relevant body of norms be acknowledged as a matter of social reality. ①

In summary, the vertical dimensional pluralism proposed by Paulsson accounts for the fact that legal orders (national legal orders and non-national legal orders) in modern international society overlap and there are cases where the arbitration proceeds from beginning to end without the assistance of national courts. However, Paulsson did not seek the legitimacy of international arbitration in the sense of abstract normative orderings. The three-dimensional pluralism proposed by Paulsson is just an observation of fact and a depiction of the present trend, not examined from the perspective of a more extensive legal theory, i. e. , the notion of law essentially. From Paulsson's perspective, pluralism is merely an observation rather than a theory. ②

C. The Sources of Autonomous Arbitral Legal Order

Albeit in different ways, Gaillard and Paulsson sought to demonstrate that arbitration may be effective under arrangements independent of national laws or judges at all. However, from the above analysis, neither Gaillard's nor Paulsson's propositions are tenable.

The current literature theorising international arbitration cannot provide a sufficient and concrete legal structure to explain the legitimacy of international arbitration and how the international arbitration rules③ are created and evolve. It does not thoroughly explore the legitimacy of international arbitration from the perspective of legal philosophy.

---

① Jan Paulsson, *Arbitration in Three Dimensions*, International and Comparative Law Quarterly 60 (2), 2011, p. 309.

② Ibid. , p. 300.

③ "International arbitration rules" here do not refer to the arbitration rules of institutions. Instead, they refer to all arbitration rules (international conventions, domestic arbitration laws applicable to international arbitration, rules of arbitral institutions, even the soft law) in general meaning.

Redfern and Hunter criticised the idea that the consent of parties, together with an appropriate set of rules, was sufficient to turn international arbitration into an autonomous, delocalised process that took place independently of national law. They further argued that this autonomous view attached too much importance to the wishes of parties and ignored the significance of national laws within which the arbitral process must take place. Nevertheless, they admitted that the consent of parties remains the essential basis of a voluntary system of international arbitration. ①

Based on the contributions of Gaillard and Paulsson, some scholars have proposed alternative theoretical explanations for this autonomous arbitral legal order. ② Although Schill thought that Gaillard's notion of legitimacy of international arbitration, understood as a transnational legal order, acknowledged a plurality of domestic perspectives on legitimacy and the transnational practice in international arbitration, it could not stand up against the constitutional critiques. ③ He proposed a multidimensional legitimacy of international arbitration. It encompasses "party legitimacy", "community legitimacy", "national legitimacy" and "global legitimacy", designating the conditions under which international arbitration was considered legitimate from the perspectives of disputing parties, all

① Nigel Blackaby et al., *Redfern and Hunter on International Arbitration*, Oxford University Press, 6th ed., 2015, p. 71.

② Stephan W. Schill, *Developing a Framework for the Legitimacy of International Arbitration*, in Albert Jan van den Berg (ed.), Legitimacy: Myths, Realities, Challenges, Wolters Kluwer Law & Business, 2015; Stephan W. Schill, *Conceptions of Legitimacy of International Arbitration*, in David D. Caron et al. (eds.), Practising Virtue: Inside International Arbitration, Oxford University Press, 2015; Julian D. M. Lew, *Is There a Global Free-Standing Body of Substantive Arbitration Law*, in Albert Jan van den Berg (ed.), International Arbitration: The Coming of a New Age?, Kluwer Law International, 2013, p. 53.

③ Stephan W. Schill, *Conceptions of Legitimacy of International Arbitration*, in David D. Caron et al. (eds.), Practising Virtue: Inside International Arbitration, Oxford University Press, 2015, p. 809.

members of the arbitration, States and global society respectively. ①

Schill's multidimensional legitimacy of international arbitration does not distinguish between international commercial arbitration and international investment arbitration. His study concentrates specifically on the constitutional dimension of legitimacy, such as what the principles of democracy, the rules of law, and protection of human rights mean for international arbitration in the perspective of comparative constitutional analysis. In other words, he focused on the legitimacy of international arbitration informed by the values outside international arbitration, such as democracy, the rule of law and human rights, and the effects of the decisions and activities of arbitral tribunals on the actors beyond the disputing parties. Unlike the investment arbitration that may have consequences for non-parties such as the people of the host State, international commercial arbitration is more pertinent to the competing parties and potential users of international commercial arbitration. Thus, the analysis of the legitimacy of international commercial arbitration here is not very relevant in terms of constitutional concerns and do not refer to constitutional legitimacy. Nevertheless, Schill rightly acknowledged the significant roles of parties, actors from the international commercial arbitration community, and international society.

The foregoing discussion of autonomous arbitration legal order shows that this transnational international arbitration legal order encompasses the national law and international law, the private contracts and public statutes. ② In this transnational legal order, the actors, such as parties, counsel, arbitrators, arbitral institutions, professional associations, courts and legislatures, interact through a variety of instruments to create the normative expectations in a variety of forums.

---

① Stephan W. Schill, *Conceptions of Legitimacy of International Arbitration*, in David D. Caron et al. (eds.), Practising Virtue: Inside International Arbitration, Oxford University Press, 2015, p. 789 – 816.

② Ibid., p. 809.

There is no exclusive single source of law which determines the conditions under which international commercial arbitration is legitimate. This is because of the plurality of actors of international commercial arbitration who are parties, counsel, arbitrators, arbitral institutions, professional associations, legislatures, courts, etc. Consequently, the normative expectations are created by the combination of party agreements, activities of arbitral institutions and arbitrators, national law and international conventions. Therefore, the sources of this autonomous arbitration legal order derive from party autonomy, international practice (soft law represented by the UNCITRAL Model Law and IBA Guidelines and Rules), institutional arbitral rules, national law (including the enacted law and the decisions of the court concerning arbitration) and international treaties (e.g., the New York Convention).

First, party autonomy is the starting point and cornerstone of international commercial arbitration. It is their agreement to arbitrate that brings the proceedings into being. Parties have the freedom to play a direct role in the design of their arbitration, especially in the arbitral proceedings. In terms of arbitral procedure, the New York Convention gives preference to the will of parties, the law of the seat only being applied in the absence of an agreement.① International commercial arbitration is regarded as a normative order by the parties because the parties use it as creating normative expectations. Consequently, arbitration may be effective under private arrangements that do not depend on the national legal orders.② Moreover, the parties' agreement is the primary source of the tribunal's power. The tribunal has the duty to ensure that parties' agreement is

---

① *Convention on the Recognition and Enforcement of Foreign Arbitral Awards*, open for signature 10 June 1958, 330 UNTS 3 (entered into force 7 June 1959), art V (1)(d).

② Jan Paulsson, *The Idea of Arbitration*, Oxford University Press, 2013, p. 30.

not frustrated.① The principle that the States shall recognise and give effect to an arbitration agreement has been confirmed in Article Ⅱ (3) of the New York Convention.

Additionally, the activities of arbitral institutions play a significant role in the arbitration proceedings. The arbitral institutions reshape the expectations of the participants in international commercial arbitration by issuing the arbitral rules and practical directions. The fact that the common standards of a variety of institutional arbitration rules have been accepted by the international arbitration community gives more credibility to the institutional arbitration rules which *per sei* are used with the mutual consent of parties. Due to amendments made to them in recent years, arbitration rules of leading institutions include many similarities which lead to a certain degree of convergence and harmonisation in the treatment of arbitral proceedings.

However, institutional arbitral rules are not intended to, and cannot, regulate the procedural details of each arbitration.② Unless agreed to by the parties, it is usual for the arbitrators to determine the procedural issues which they consider appropriate to the circumstances, provided that the fundamental principle of due process is observed. Usually, arbitrators exercise their discretion by considering international arbitration practice, such as IBA Rules and Guidelines and Redfern schedule. These soft law instruments reshape arbitral proceedings and create normative expectations among participants of international commercial arbitration. Also, they address gaps in national arbitration laws and arbitration rules of institutions and respond to the need for the harmonisation and uniformity of the

---

① Antonio Crivellaro, *Note — Award of* 7 *December* 2001 *in Case No.* 10623, ASA Bulletin 21(1), 2003, p. 74 - 75.

② Nigel Blackaby et al., *Redfern and Hunter on International Arbitration*, Oxford University Press, 6th ed., 2015, p. 65.

standards applied. ①

Most arbitrations are conducted under the aforementioned private institutions—party agreement, arbitrators' discretion, international arbitration practice and rules of arbitral institutions—without any reference to the law of arbitral seat or the law of an enforcement forum. Nevertheless, the national law, either the law of arbitral seat or that of the place of enforcement, plays a role. *Lex arbitri* fills the gaps in the composition of the arbitral tribunal if there is no other mechanism, orders interim measures, exercises the supervisory jurisdiction on arbitration. By contrast, the law of the place of enforcement facilitates the enforcement of international arbitration awards and protects its own interests through the refusal grounds of arbitrability and public policy. Although anchored by domestic legal orders, national courts have interpreted arbitration-related concepts and have set the specific standards for refusal of recognition or enforcement of foreign arbitral awards and the standards for setting aside awards. Thus, the decisions of courts have contributed to the identification of the standards of enforcement, setting aside awards and challenging the arbitrators. The existing divergence and the emerging convergent standards of the above issues among national jurisdictions interact with the above private instruments (party autonomy, institutional arbitration rules and international arbitration practice), together order the rights and obligations of parties.

Last, the New York Convention is the cornerstone of international treaties in international commercial arbitration. It has promoted the standards to be followed and the uniform proceedings for the conduct of arbitrations reflected in the grounds for the recognition and enforcement of foreign and non-domestic awards.

---

① Julian D. M. Lew, *Is There a Global Free-Standing Body of Substantive Arbitration Law*, in Albert Jan van den Berg (ed.), International Arbitration: The Coming of a New Age?, Kluwer Law International, 2013, p. 60.

V. Fuller's Interactionism Theory and Its Implications on the Concept of International Commercial Arbitration

The current scholarship in international commercial arbitration, nevertheless cannot provide a sound theoretical framework to explain the creation and operation of the above normative systems (party autonomy, rules of arbitral institutions, soft law, domestic legal orders, international conventions) and their interaction with one another within an autonomous arbitral legal order. Although both Gaillard and Paulsson sought to establish a foundation for the international arbitration legal order and demonstrated that international commercial arbitration legal order can occupy the same space other than the State normative orderings, neither of their theories is satisfactory.

The theory of an autonomous arbitral legal order, proposed by Gaillard, is based on the collectivity of national legal orders, which adds no more to the pluralism argument. Meanwhile, the pluralism proposition depicts the delocalised award which is not thought to be independent of any legal order but refers to the possibility that an award may be accepted by the legal order of an enforcement jurisdiction whether or not the arbitral seat has also embraced it. Paulsson rightly pointed out that private instruments can create normative rights and obligations and operate without the involvement of sovereign legal orders, which is described as the three-dimensional pluralism. Unlike Gaillard's theory which concentrates on the autonomous aspect of international commercial arbitration, Paulsson's three-dimensional pluralism tries to combine the national legal systems and private normative arrangements in the international commercial arbitration legal orders. However, the three-dimensional pluralism is just an observation of fact and a depiction of the present trend. Neither Emmanuel Gaillard nor Jan Paulsson proposed their theories from the perspective of a more extensive legal theory,

i. e. , the notion of law essentially. Paulsson regarded pluralism as the result of an observation rather than based on a theory. ① However, the theory based on the observation cannot explain the creation of normative expectations and the interaction of various normative orderings in international commercial arbitration.

As the above discussion has shown, the underlying controversy regarding the notion of international commercial arbitration is, essentially, the notion of law. It is necessary to discuss the legitimacy of international arbitration by performing position oneself somewhere in a more extensive sphere of legal theory. The scholarship can be enriched by borrowing from Fuller's interactionism theory. Lon L. Fuller is undoubtedly one of the foremost jurists to have inspired the progress of process pluralism. As Carrie Menkel-Meadow put it, "in many ways, Lon [L.] Fuller remains the only legal philosopher to take theorising about dispute resolution processes seriously." ② Fuller is recognisedas the father of ADR, ③ and the "only legal philosopher to take theorising about dispute resolution processes seriously". ④ Although some arbitration scholars have called for more attention to be paid to Fuller's writings and their implications for international arbitration and even more extensive transnational legal order, ⑤ very rarely have arbitration scholars attempted to situate international arbitration legal order within Fuller's interactional perspective. The following section explores Fuller's interactionism

① Jan Paulsson, *Arbitration in Three Dimensions*, International and Comparative Law Quarterly 60 (2), 2011, p. 300.

② Carrie Menkel-Meadow, *Mothers and Fathers of Invention: The Intellectual Founders of ADR*, Ohio State Journal on Dispute Resolution 16(1), 2000, p. 13.

③ Ibid., p. 4.

④ Ibid., p. 13.

⑤ Thomas Schultz, *The Concept of Law in Transnational Arbitral Legal Orders and some of Its Consequences*, Journal of International Dispute Settlement 2(1), 2011; Ralf Michaels, *A Fuller Concept of Law Beyond the State? Thoughts on Lon Fuller's Contributions to Jurisprudence of Transnational Dispute Resolution — A Reply to Thomas Schultz*, Journal of International Dispute Settlement 2(2), 2011; Peer Zumbansen, *Debating Autonomy and Procedural Justice: The Lex Mercatoria in the Context of Global Governance Debates — A Reply to Thomas Schultz*, Journal of International Arbitration 2(2), 2011.

theory and develops the jurisprudent foundation for international arbitration legal order.

A. The Implications of Fuller's Eunomics and Interactionism for International Arbitration

(i) The Concept of Law-Eunomics

A less explored area of Fuller's ideas is that of "eunomics" — a term that refers to "the science, theory or study of good order and workable social arrangements". ①Eunomics theory aims to understand the phenomenon of social ordering in its diverse expressions. Fuller is a legal pluralist and process pluralist. He recognised various processes that contribute to social ordering, including legislation, adjudication, managerial direction, mediation, contractual agreement, and customary law. ② Given their norm-producing and order-generating capacity, Fuller considered them as legal processes and regarded the subsequent arrangements as law. Such systems of law operate simultaneously with national law in customary, informal and non-governmental domains.

Fuller's concept of law is very broad. It has been extended to include not only the legal systems of States but also the smaller systems such as the labour unions, professional associations, clubs, churches and universities. ③ Fuller opposed the view of legal positivism whereby the authority of law derives from the coercive power of the State to force compliance. Instead, Fuller attributed the authority of law to the stabilised expectancy derived from social interactions. ④ Fuller believed that the law has authority only if based on general societal

---

① Lon L. Fuller, *American Legal Philosophy at Mid-Century*, Journal of Legal Education 6, 1954, p. 477.

② Lon L. Fuller, *Mediation — Its Forms and Functions*, in Kenneth I. Winston (ed.), The Principles of Social Order: Selected Essays of Lon L. Fuller, Hart Publishing, 2001, p. 171 - 172.

③ Lon L. Fuller, *Human Interaction and the Law*, American Journal of Jurisprudence 14, 1969, p. 1.

④ Ibid., p. 1 - 36.

acceptance arising from the dynamic interactions of social actors. Fuller's interactional concept of law provides us with a powerful conceptual lens for our understanding of the significance of stabilised expectancies. Specifically, a sense of obligation that members of the community have towards a given social ordering depends on its compatibility with social expectancy and practices born out of everyday dealings.① Accordingly, a sense of obligation will occur when stabilisation of interactional expectancies has occurred, so that the parties have come to guide their conduct towards one another according to these expectancies.

Fuller's concept of law is not tied to the State and thus provides much inspiration for the legitimacy of international commercial arbitration. The authority of international commercial arbitration cannot arise from an exclusive single source. Instead, it arises from party autonomy, rules and codes of arbitral institutions, international arbitral practice, national law and international conventions.② The social actors of international commercial arbitration comprising parties, counsel, arbitrators, arbitral institutions, courts, national legislatures and international convention drafters interact with one another through the above systems of law. In international commercial arbitration, the stabilisation of interactional expectations may arise from parties' agreement, the activities of arbitrators and arbitral institutions, the decisions of courts, and international conventions. Thus, party autonomy, rules and codes of arbitral institutions, international commercial arbitration practice, national law and international conventions together and simultaneously can create normative rights and obligations among actors and generate ordering effects in the domain of international commercial arbitration.

---

① Kenneth I. Winston, *Introduction to the Revised Edition*, in Kenneth I. Winston (ed.), The Principles of Social Order: Selected Essays of Lon L. Fuller, Hart Publishing, 2001, p.3.

② See subsection Ⅳ(C).

If the sources of authority are pluralistic, this does not mean that they will have force in each international commercial arbitration. For instance, in most cases, the award debtor usually voluntarily complies with the award without the coercive force of States. According to the Queen Mary Report on International Arbitration, the corporate counsel stated that the non-prevailing party honoured more than 90% of awards. ① The award debtor complies with the award voluntarily because such expectancies arise from the parties' agreement.

(ii) The Interactionism Theory

Fuller, in his *Human Interaction and the Law*, developed the "standardised expectancy arising from social interaction" into the interactionism theory. ② Fuller considered that this interactionism theory of law was his essential disagreement with legal positivism:

I have tried to show that our differences... stem from a basic disagreement about law itself. This disagreement I have attempted to express by contrasting a view of law that sees it as an interactional process and one that sees in it only a unidirectional exercise of authority. ③

Fuller considered that laws, in whatever form, arise out of human interaction and serve to order and facilitate interaction. ④ On the one hand, the authority of law, that is, the stabilised expectancy, arises from social interactions. On the other hand, the purpose of law is to facilitate social interaction. Fuller's idea is not consistent with the pre-existing, autonomous, and static notion of law typically

---

① School of International Arbitration at Queen Mary University of London and Price Waterhouse Cooper, *International Arbitration: Corporate Attitudes and Practices*, Queen Mary University of London and Price Waterhouse Cooper, 2008, p. 8.

② Lon L. Fuller, *Human Interaction and the Law*, American Journal of Jurisprudence 14, 1969, p. 1 - 36.

③ Lon L. Fuller, *The Morality of Law*, Yale University Press, 1969, p. 223.

④ Lon L. Fuller, *Human Interaction and the Law*, American Journal of Jurisprudence 14, 1969, p. 7, 9, 14, 20.

found in the natural law tradition,① nor is it congruent with the positivist insistence on the indeterminacy of law and the extra-legal nature of adjudication.② This interactionism theory is central to Fuller's notion of law.

However, Fuller's interactionism theory goes beyond being a challenge to legal positivism and shines light on the institutional design and the authority of international commercial arbitration. Fuller's interactionism perspective gives rise to a pluralistic notion of law and social orderings — the one that considers social orderings to be diffuse and dispersed at multiple levels of society, and that might include private social orderings, such as contract law and customary law, other than the sovereign national legal order (enacted law and case law).

In *Human Interaction and the Law*, Fuller explored the relationship between human interaction and three distinct kinds of laws: contract law, customary law and enacted law, respectively. Fuller believed that laws, including contract law, customary law and enacted law, arise out of human interactions and serve to order and facilitate these interactions. According to the aforementioned authorities on international commercial arbitration, party agreement falls within the domain of contract law while the rules of arbitral institutions and international commercial arbitration practice mainly constitute customary law. These private normative arrangements operate together with State legal order (enacted law and case law of courts). The following sections analyse the mechanism of interaction within these normative orderings and their impact on international commercial arbitration.

B. The Interactional Foundations of Contract Law

Fuller regarded contract law as one means of establishing "stable interactional expectancies". Fuller employed the term "contract law", referring primarily not

---

① See Suri Ratnapala, *Jurisprudence*, Cambridge University Press, 3rd ed., 2017, p. 141 – 142.

② Ibid., p. 27.

to the law of or about contracts, but to the "law" a contract itself brings into existence.①

Fuller highlighted the "consensual element" in contract law.② Fuller cited Section 90 of the *American Law Institute's Restatement of Contracts* whereby the promise may become enforceable when the promisee has seriously and reasonably taken its anticipated performance into account in the arrangement of his own affairs. For instance, if by action towards B, A has given the other party B reasonably to understand that A will act similarly in the future in similar situations, and B has prudently adjusted his affairs to that expectation, then A is bound to follow the pattern set by his past actions toward B.③ This creates an obligation by A to B.

Fuller's contract theory provides the tool whereby parties' agreement can be regarded as a private normative system in international commercial arbitration. The parties' interaction with each other can create normative expectations concerning their mutual rights and obligations. Under this theory, international arbitration is a normative order that can be implemented voluntarily and independently of State institutions and domestic laws.

Fuller further argued that if we extended the pattern of interaction followed by A and B to the relevant community, then a rule of general customary law would have been created. During the process of this extension (from contract law to customary law), Fuller insisted that where C and D had been familiar with the rules between A and B, where C adopted this pattern between A and B, it was not because this model had any aptness for their matters, but because C knew D would

---

① Lon L. Fuller, *Human Interaction and the Law*, American Journal of Jurisprudence 14, 1969, p. 14.

② Ibid., p. 13.

③ Ibid., p. 16.

understand the meaning of his actions and would know how to react to it. [①]

We can see that reciprocal expectation plays a critical role in the process by which the obligations are created in contract law and customary law. This is the essence of the interactional mechanism. The potential extension from contract law to customary law applies to international arbitration rules as well. From the very beginning, the specific procedural rule was created between the parties in a particular case. Where this rule is compatible with the arbitration principles, it is likely to spread to other arbitration proceedings, by the wisdom of counsel and arbitrators, and even be confirmed by institutional arbitral rules, soft rules and Guidelines, Model Law, or national arbitration laws, achieving a widespread force in the community of international commercial arbitration. In other words, the legitimacy of international commercial arbitration can derive from the disputing parties and the acceptance by the community of participants in arbitral proceedings for whom international arbitration is a means of interacting with one another and creating normative rights and obligations. This vision broadens the understanding of international arbitration based merely on national and international law. It rightly highlights that not only can national laws or international conventions generate normative expectations but also that a private system itself can produce such expectations and enforce them through the private institutional infrastructure.

It is the opinion of this researcher, that the legitimacy of international commercial arbitration cannot be derived only from the party autonomy without the involvement of the international commercial arbitration community and national courts, such as set-aside and recognition or enforcement proceedings safeguarding the public interest. Party autonomy is inadequate as the exclusive source of legitimacy because it cannot account for legitimate effects from the community of

---

① Lon L. Fuller, *Human Interaction and the Law*, American Journal of Jurisprudence 14, 1969, p. 16 – 17.

international commercial arbitration, national courts and international treaties. Nevertheless, Fuller's contract theory justifies the possibility that in most cases, the operation of arbitration relies on party autonomy and the normative effects on parties through their interaction and mutual consent.

C. The Implications of Fuller's "Customary Law" Theory

Fuller paid particular attention to the analysis of customary law. According to Fuller, much of international law, and perhaps the most vital part of it, is mainly customary law.① This perspective provides a new theoretical perspective on international commercial arbitration. Fuller's theory on customary law provides the legal basis for the normativity of soft law in international commercial arbitration.

Although the interaction plays a significant role in the generation of normative rights and obligations in different forms of law, this role is remarkably reflected by customary law. First, Fuller emphasised that rights or obligations do not arise through mere repetition of actions by subjects. Instead, they would arise when a set of stable interactional expectancies have occurred so that parties' conduct toward one another would be guided by these expectancies.②

Second, Fuller disagreed that the force and meaning of what we call "customary law" lies in mere habit or usage. Instead, customary law could best be described as "a language of interaction".③ He argued that customary law originates from interaction and serves the purpose of organising and facilitating interaction.④ To explain the operation of human interaction in customary law, Fuller imported the term "complementary expectations". He suggested that customary law provides the members with a predictable pattern for their actions in a social setting. These expectations let members know how their counterparts

---

① Lon L. Fuller, *Human Interaction and the Law*, American Journal of Jurisprudence 14, 1969, p. 2.

② Ibid., p. 9.

③ Ibid., p. 2.

④ Ibid., p. 4.

would respond to their behaviours.[1] Accordingly, the members act and adjust their conducts based on their counterparts' reactions. This means that members' decision can be directed by a tolerably accurate estimate of costs in advance. In a word, the customary law directs members' actions through a quite stable set of interactional expectations, and these expectations also facilitate the interaction.

In terms of international commercial arbitration, the customary law is international commercial arbitration practice. The actors of international commercial arbitration community (parties, counsel, arbitrators and arbitral institutions) direct their actions through the stabilisation of interactional expectations arising from international commercial arbitration practice. Such international commercial arbitration practice codified by institution arbitral rules, soft law (e. g., IBA Rules and Guidelines), UNCITRAL Model Law and the like are increasingly substantially convergent. The international arbitration practice designates the conditions under which arbitration is seen as legitimate from the perspective of all members of international commercial arbitration.

Unlike the legitimacy deriving from party autonomy discussed earlier, international arbitration practice is less concerned with party-specific questions and individual results of arbitrations. Instead, it is focused on the entrenched practices that are broadly accepted by the members of international commercial arbitration. In other words, international arbitration practice reflects the degree of acceptance concerning particular practice by the whole community of international commercial arbitration.

According to Fuller, there are two characteristics of customary law. Firstly, the customary law is not declared or enacted but grows or develops through time. Secondly, the rules of customary law are not first brought into being and then

---

① Lon L. Fuller, *Human Interaction and the Law*, American Journal of Jurisprudence 14, 1969, p. 2.

project upon the conduct they are intended to regulate. Instead, they find their implicit expression in the conduct itself. ①

Here we may ask whether the representative of international commercial arbitration practice, soft law, can still be regarded as customary law, given the increasingly quasi-codification trend. Firstly, other than the national arbitration statutes, soft rules of international commercial arbitration (e. g. , rules of codes of arbitral institutions, IBA documents and UNCITRAL documents) develop over time, unlike sovereign enactment. This characteristic aligns with the first requirement of customary law. Secondly, even though most of the soft law is explicit, it derives from the well-accepted conduct of practitioners, by which it satisfies the second requirement of customary law. The significant difference between the made law and customary law is that the former comes from sovereign enactment while the latter is based on conduct. The soft law of international arbitration, whose normativity arising from the well-accepted conduct of the international arbitration community rather than the legislatures and courts of law, can be regarded as customary law under Fuller's theory.

Compared with enacted law, soft law engages with the international arbitration community in a better dynamic interplay, because soft law is always interacting with the community of international arbitration. Moreover, it is influenced and shaped by the participation of actors engaged in this international interplay among parties, counsel, arbitrators, arbitral institutions and professional associations. In short, soft law is more efficient and even adaptive in responding to the diverse and changing needs of the community of international arbitration than are legal systems of sovereign States.

---

① Lon L. Fuller, *Anatomy of the Law*, Frederick A Praeger, 1968, p. 44.

D. The Interactional Foundations of Enacted Law

In the above analysis, Fuller posited that customary law and contract law arise out of interaction and serve to order and facilitate interaction. In terms of enacted law, Fuller disagreed with the positive law's idea that the general purpose of the enacted law is to the effect that "law serves as an instrument of social control" and that the way law is conceived to come into existence is by an exercise of authority. ① Instead, Fuller contended that enacted law is dependent on the development of "stable interactional expectancies" between lawgiver and subject and serves the purpose of ordering and facilitating the interactions of citizens with one another as well. ②

The dependence on interactive practice is the same essential element of enacted law as customary law and contract law. The existence of a national legal order depends on the effective interaction between lawmaking, law-applying officials and subjects. As Fuller explained, the law is "the product of an interplay of purposive orientations between the citizen and his government... [not] a one-way projection of authority originating with government and imposing itself upon the citizen." ③ Fuller further argued that a substantial degree of congruency between enacted law and the background in which *informal social practices and conventions* govern the relations among citizens is essential for the existence of legal order. ④ It shows that the law has social depth and is deeply implicated in the

① Lon L. Fuller, *Human Interaction and the Law*, American Journal of Jurisprudence 14, 1969, p. 20.

② Ibid. At the same time, Fuller admitted that law did not always serve the purpose of ordering exclusively and facilitating human interaction in its actual formulation and administration. For instance, in the area of "crimes without victims", legal restraint appears most unequivocally as an "instrument of social control". See Lon L. Fuller, *Human Interaction and the Law*, American Journal of Jurisprudence 14, 1969, p. 22.

③ Lon L. Fuller, *The Morality of Law*, Yale University Press, 1969, p. 20.

④ Gerald J. Postema, *Implicit law*, Law and Philosophy 13(3), 1994, p. 368 (emphasis added).

practices and conventions of the communities it governs. In other words, the enacted law could not survive, and its norms would not be intelligible to the citizens as laws if such norms were at odds with or radically isolated from the well-accepted standard practices and conventions. ①

In terms of international commercial arbitration, the enacted law includes national arbitration statutes and international conventions. In the context of recognition and enforcement foreign awards, the forum courts must shape the refusal defences they interpret in anticipation of how arbitral actors are likely to understand and expect their fellow actors to understand, the language they use and the decisions they make. In this case, the arbitral actors, especially the parties and counsel, will understand forum courts' decisions in light of how they expect judges and other fellow actors to interpret and follow the rules. It will be meaningless if the forum courts apply the law in a way that parties cannot understand.

In international commercial arbitration that is strongly dependent on international practice and conventions, it is necessary for the courts to recognise such informal international arbitration practice among the arbitral actors and to be consistent with it. Fuller highlighted that "the creation of an effective interaction between them [lawgiver and subjects] is an essential ingredient of the law itself."② Such interaction will be effective only if most of the arbitral actors involved can reasonably expect that most of the others will identify and understand the applicable law in roughly the same way as they do, and can be relied upon to comply with them.

Fuller argued that we cannot understand the enacted law unless we rightly understand the customary law. ③ The UNCITRAL Model Law is a good example

① Gerald J. Postema, *Implicit law*, Law and Philosophy 13(3), 1994, p. 374.

② Lon L. Fuller, *The Morality of Law*, Yale University Press, 1969, p. 193.

③ Lon L. Fuller, *Human Interaction and the Law*, American Journal of Jurisprudence 14, 1969, p. 2.

showing the impacts of international arbitration practice on enacted law and the enacted law's consistency with international arbitration practice. UNCITRAL Model law codified the well-accepted international commercial arbitration practice and reflected the latest development and progress in international commercial arbitration. Even though the UNCITRAL Model Law itself has no legal force in states unless they adopt it, 80 States have national statutes based on the Model Law. ①

Compared with statutory law, Fuller considered that the common law (adjudicative law) projected its roots more deeply and intimately into human interaction by its unique way of proceeding case by case. ② According to Fuller, the interactionism is dynamic, and law derives its content through ongoing social interaction. ③ This view recognises the reciprocal expectancy between the law and its subjects, engaging with each other in a dynamic interplay. On the one hand, the adjudicative law directs members' actions through judgements. In this sense, the adjudicative law gives the meaning to the behaviours of subjects. On the other hand, the case law is likely to be more intelligently responsive to the needs of society than abstract enacted law. ④ The standardised interactional expectations are reflected by the adjudicative law through the judicial decisions. ⑤

In the context of the recognition and enforcement of foreign arbitral awards, although the judges decide the particular case before the court, they articulate the

---

① For the status of implementation of the Model Law in different jurisdictions, see *Status: UNCITRAL Model Law on International Commercial Arbitration* (1985), *with Amendments as Adopted in* 2006, UNCITRAL, https://uncitral.un.org/en/texts/arbitration/modellaw/commercial_arbitration/status.

② Lon L. Fuller, *Human Interaction and the Law*, American Journal of Jurisprudence 14, 1969, p. 26.

③ Ibid., p. 1 – 13.

④ Lon L. Fuller, *Anatomy of the Law*, Frederick A Praeger, 1968, p. 90.

⑤ Lon L. Fuller, *Human Interaction and the Law*, American Journal of Jurisprudence 14, 1969, p. 26.

rule on which the decision rests and justify that rule in deeper and broader issues of principle, which can be referred to by other Convention jurisdictions. Additionally, the adjudicative law of the signatory jurisdiction has the edge on the enacted New York Convention in keeping with the ongoing social interaction. In the UK, the courts consider that the UK decisions of due process defence, the opinions of the judges in other convention jurisdictions, the soft law and even the *lexarbitri*, are all sources of the due process exception. In the case of *Anthony*, the UK court held that the statutory language must be given an *autonomous meaning* [emphasis added], which may be informed by the *travaux* preparatoires, the decisions on it of *foreign courts and the views on it of foreign jurists—la jurisprudence* and *la doctrine*. ①Besides, the court referred the ICCA Guide to the Interpretation of the 1958 New York Convention: A Handbook for Judges which is representative of soft law as admissible material. ②

E. Interaction Between Law and Its Social Context

Fuller proposed that a given kind of law would not only act upon but also be influenced and shaped by the established forms of interaction which formed law's social context. This indicates that their application of the Convention needs to be rooted deeply in the social interactions of the international arbitration community they purport to serve. He further suggested that for a given social environment, one kind of law might be more appropriate than another. ③

Fuller observed that the very purpose of enacted law is to impose rules that set the limits men must follow in their interactions with another, leaving them free within those boundaries to pursue their own goals. Accordingly, the enacted law

---

① *Anthony Lombard-Knight & Jakob Kinde v. Rainstorm Pictures Inc.* [2014] EWCA Civ. 356 (27 March 2014) [3] (emphasis added).

② Ibid.

③ Lon L. Fuller, *Human Interaction and the Law*, American Journal of Jurisprudence 14, 1969, p. 27.

must be explicit and deal with defined acts.[①] In the private domains, enacted law is secondary to the horizontal interactions among parties. The object of enacted law is "providing the citizenry with a sound and stable framework for their interactions, the role of government [that is the formal institutions of authority] being that of standing as a guardian of the integrity of this system."[②]

As mentioned earlier, although the sources of international commercial arbitration include party autonomy, international arbitration practice, institutional arbitration rules, national law (including the enacted law and the case law) and international conventions, they have different roles and weight in international commercial arbitration.

International commercial arbitration is fundamentally based on party autonomy and operated by the activities of private arrangements that are controlled either by arbitrators or rules of arbitral institutions. The international conventions and national law (including the enacted law and decisions of the courts concerning arbitration) are secondary to the private institutional infrastructures such as party autonomy, international arbitration practice and institutional arbitration rules. The national law and international conventions are the guardians of international commercial arbitration and set the boundaries for the conduct of arbitration, and function only when the private arrangements are out of order.

On the one hand, the private institutional arrangements are freely and fully used to create the normative expectations between parties without the violation of public interest. They are capable of reshaping and rewording the rules in light of the actual situations. They are the primary tools for arbitral actors to participate in the arbitration practice. Unlike the legal ordering of a sovereign State, private

---

① Lon L. Fuller, *Human Interaction and the Law*, American Journal of Jurisprudence 14, 1969, p. 34.

② Lon L. Fuller, *The Morality of Law*, Yale University Press, 1969, p. 210.

institutional arrangements are more flexible and responsive to the needs of international arbitration practice. On the other hand, the private institutional arrangements, primarily through the interpretation of the arbitrators concerning the substantive and procedural law of arbitration, interpret and establish the meaning of the national law and international conventions.

In the context of recognition and enforcement of foreign arbitral awards under the New York Convention, it is necessary to discuss which applicable law is more appropriate to the defences of refusal. As Fuller observed, the enacted law sets the boundaries which persons must follow in their conduct, while in other free domains, people may develop rights and obligations with others by party agreement and customary law. In the enforcement fora, the provisions of Article V(2), arbitrability and public policy defences, have set limits for parties to protect the public interest. Article V(2) sets out the conditions under which the enforcement forum considers the arbitral award is legitimate according to its standards. Article V(2) of the New York Convention leaves it to the discretion of the enforcement fora to evaluate the conformity of an award according to their particular standards of arbitrability or public policy. Therefore, it is not necessary and may even be impossible to impose the uniform application of Art V(2) on different enforcement forums.

In contrast, the defences under Article V(1) are more pertinent to international arbitration practice, which mainly fall within the private institutional infrastructure. They are based on the specific characteristics of international arbitration, especially on the global practice followed by the transnational arbitration community. Hence, international arbitral practice must be taken into account when the defences prescribed in Article V(1) are decided.

Regarding the ability of a court to review a foreign award on the grounds for refusal, there is a notable difference in wording between Article V(1) and Article

V(2) of the New York Convention. Article V(1) provides that recognition and enforcement of an award may be refused "at the request of the party against whom it is invoked". However, Article V(2) states that recognition and enforcement may be refused "if the competent authority in the country where recognition or enforcement is sought finds that [...] the recognition and enforcement of the award would be contrary to the public policy of that country." Only the grounds for refusal contained in Article V(2) can be raised by the court's *ex officio* while due process defence under Article V(1) cannot be raised by the court on its own motion.

The difference in the burden of proof required by Article V(1) and Article V(2) can be attributed to the different purposes of these two rules. Specifically, Article V(1) is based on the specific characteristics of international arbitration practice, while Article V(2) is dominated by the enacted law of enforcement forum for the public interest. Because of such different purposes of the law, the defences under Article V (1) may be waived by the parties, while those under Article V(2) cannot.

Ⅵ. Conclusion

Even though the *lexarbitri* plays a significant role in arbitral proceedings, the supervisory court alone cannot decide the validity of an international arbitral award. The court of the arbitral seat can decide the effects of the validity of an award only within its territory. Hence, an award decision by the arbitral seat jurisdiction upholding or setting aside an award has territorially-limited effects only in the State in which it is rendered, and cannot produce extra-territorial effects in other jurisdictions. There are no grounds for the enforcing courts to apply the standards of the arbitral seat when deciding whether to recognise or enforce a foreign award.

Under the pluralism theory, a foreign arbitral award set aside by the court of the arbitral seat may be enforced by an enforcing forum. However, pluralism theory highlights the plurality of each State which is willing to recognise the legitimacy of the arbitration. This approach would result in the burdensome obligation for arbitrators to meet the potential requirements of each State in which enforcement is likely to be sought, which is unfeasible. Most importantly, the pluralism theory does not consider the normative function of private institutional infrastructures in international commercial arbitration, such as party agreement and international arbitration practice.

Neither Gaillard nor Paulson provided a concrete theoretical framework to explain the legitimacy of international arbitration and how the international arbitration rules are created and evolve under their autonomous arbitral legal order or three-dimensional pluralism. The autonomy of international arbitration theory proposed by Gaillard adds no more than to the pluralism. Although Paulsson recognised the limitations of traditional horizontal pluralism which envisages only the cooperation of a multiplicity of territorially sovereign legal orders and extended pluralism to include vertical dimension where private legal order occupies the same space other than the State normative orderings, he based his theory on the facts rather than on more extensive and concrete legal theory.

Fuller's conception of law, especially in terms of "eunomics" and interactionism, provides insight into the legitimacy of international commercial arbitration. Fuller is a legal pluralist and process pluralist. He recognised various processes that contribute to social ordering, including but not limited to contract law, customary law, enacted law and case law. Given their norm-producing and order-generating capacity, Fuller considered them as legal processes and regarded the subsequent arrangements as "law". Such systems of law operate simultaneously with national law in customary, informal and non-governmental domains. Fuller attributed the authority of law to the stabilised expectancy deriving from the social interaction. In Fuller's opinion, the law has authority only if based on general societal acceptance arising from the dynamic interactions of social actors.

In international commercial arbitration, the stabilisation of interactional expectancies can arise from parties' agreement, the activities of arbitrators and arbitral institutions, enacted law, decisions of courts concerning arbitration and international conventions. Thus, the authority of international commercial arbitration cannot be derived from an exclusive single source. Instead, it arises from party autonomy, rules and codes of arbitral institutions, international arbitral practice, national law and international conventions.

Meanwhile, Fuller's interactionism theory provides us with a dynamic interplay between the law and its subjects. According to Fuller, laws, in whatever form, arise out of human interaction and serve to order and facilitate interaction. In international commercial arbitration, on the one hand, the actors create normative rights and obligations through party agreement, international arbitration practice, national law (enacted law and decisions of courts on arbitration) and international conventions. On the other hand, these normative infrastructures must be rooted deeply in the social interaction of the international arbitration community they purport to serve.

Additionally, an effective interaction depends on a substantial degree of congruency between enacted law and the background in which informal social practices and conventions govern the relations among actors. From the very beginning, the specific procedural rule was created between the parties of a particular arbitration. Where this rule is compatible with the arbitration principles, it is likely to spread to other arbitration proceedings, by the wisdom of counsel and arbitrators, and may even be confirmed by institutional arbitral rules, Guidelines,

Model Law, or national arbitration laws, and get the broad force in the international arbitration community. Hence, the national law needs to recognise such informal international arbitration practice and ensure consistency with it given that international commercial arbitration strongly depends on international practice and conventions.

This congruence between the forum courts and international arbitration practice is the aim of the New York Convention as well. The application of the New York Convention requires not merely understanding the meaning of the words, but also understanding the institutions, practices, and attitudes of the international arbitration community to which it is addressed. The New York Convention can guide the recognition and enforcement of foreign arbitral awards only if its application is congruent with the generally accepted practice and patterns of interaction in the arbitration community. The forum courts, along with other arbitral actors (parties, counsel, arbitrators, arbitral institutions), together develop and reflect the international arbitration practice. Thus, the forum court should apply the international standards based on the well-accepted international arbitration practice to the interpretation of the refusal grounds of foreign awards.

域外 参考

非洲商事仲裁:现状和未来

宝拉·霍奇斯(Paula Hodges)等* 著 朱伟东** 艾昕语*** 译

译者摘要:商事仲裁的发展对非洲大陆经济发展具有重要意义,它不但可以通过为国际当事人提供优良的争议解决环境,吸引外来投资,而且商事仲裁本身也可成为一种重要的资金来源。近年来,许多非洲国家通过签署或批准《承认及执行外国仲裁裁决公约》(以下简称《纽约公约》)以及根据联合国国际贸易法委员会《国际商事仲裁示范法》制定现代化的立法,极大改善了本国的仲裁立法环境。此外,非洲国家和地区还设立了许多设施完善的仲裁机构,这也在一定程度上促进了仲裁的发展。但由于非洲还存在很多不利于进行国际商事仲裁的因素,是否选择在非洲进行仲裁是很多国际当事人需要思考的问题。

关键词:非洲 商事仲裁 OHADA 仲裁地

---

* 史密斯斐尔律师事务所(Herbert Smith Freehills)合伙人、御用大律师,利昂、迪文戴尔和帕克都是史密斯斐尔律师事务所律师。史密斯斐尔律师事务所是公认的非洲法律事务领导者,包括交易和争议解决项目。2016 年 9 月,律所发布了其更新版《非洲争议解决指引》,对非洲 54 个国家的诉讼和仲裁事务提供见解。

** 中国社会科学院西亚非洲研究所非洲法律研究中心主任、研究员。

*** 湘潭大学法学院国际法专业研究生。本文最初发表在 2017 年 2 月的史密斯斐尔律师事务所 *Inside Arbitration* 杂志上。在翻译成中文时,译者对文中部分内容和脚注稍微作了技术处理。

非洲经济正在不断增长。据国际货币基金组织(the International Monetary Fund, IMF)的预测,撒哈拉以南非洲地区2016年经济增长率为4%,北非为3.6%。[①] 但是由于商品价格的波动,其增长幅度并不能够得到保障,且所有非洲国家的经济部门都需要或寻求投资。在本文中,史密斯斐尔律师事务所合伙人霍奇斯(Paula Hodges,御用大律师)、利昂(Peter Leon)律师、迪文戴尔(Craig Tevendale)律师和帕克(Chris Parker)律师认为,在非洲争端的解决对于促进投资以及使其作为投资来源均具有重要意义。他们还分析了仲裁在非洲的发展,讨论了当事人是否应在非洲"岸上"(on-shore)还是"离岸"(off-shore)解决争端的问题。

一、争端解决:促进投资和其本身作为一种投资来源

关于影响新兴市场区域投资的因素,已多有论述。有些人可能会认为,一个重要的影响投资决定的相关因素是一国的法律制度和法律结构。如果一个国家具备以下条件,它将会成为更具吸引力的投资地点:一套清晰而确定的、规范投资行业的立法框架,从而表明其具有稳定的监管环境;一个高效、务实、中立的司法系统;国家认可投资者对稳定的投资环境和法制实施的关注,了解国际上优先采用的争议解决实践。

第三条标准要求相关国家认识到,对于国际或者国内投资者来说,国内法院不一定是解决争端的首要选择或合适方式。这也反过来要求接受仲裁作为争端解决的方式。[②] 仲裁被认为是一个国家商业开放程度和了解投资者关注和

---

① http://www.imf.org/external/pubs/ft/weo/2016/update/01/pdf/0116.pdf, June 6, 2016.

② 一个国家接受仲裁可以有多种形式。这可能意味着:

允许国际当事人在与国家订立合同时选择进行国内或国际仲裁:例如,拥有丰富的石油或其他自然资源的国家可以允许国际石油公司与该国石油公司签订含有仲裁条款的协议。但是,这并不一定意味着其所允许的仲裁程序是符合目的的。

允许仲裁裁决得以执行:这可以通过签署和批准或加入《纽约公约》来实现。然而,这么做从本身来说是不够的。投资者需要确信当地司法机构会支持仲裁并遵守《纽约公约》,按照公认的国际实践来解释该公约的规定。

积极鼓励在该国进行仲裁:也许可以通过制定现代化的国内和国际仲裁法(可以联合国国际贸易法委员会《国际商事仲裁示范法》或其他现代仲裁立法为基础)。该国还可以支持或资助在当地设立的仲裁机构,而且欢迎和支持国际仲裁机构。同时,确保司法人员获得仲裁方面的培训并支持仲裁是非常重要的。

市场实践的一个标志。

接受仲裁不仅对鼓励更广泛的投资进入一国经济具有重要意义,争端解决市场特别是在仲裁领域,其本身就是一种经济活动来源,从而可以成为经济增长和繁荣的动力。如果一个国家能够成为一个“安全”的仲裁场所(作为仲裁地)或举行仲裁庭审的合适场所,将会有外国公司和律师事务所在那里投入大量资金。会议中心、酒店、翻译、庭审速记员和当地律师都能从中受益。

这不仅有助于非洲成为一个解决与自己国家有关的争端的理想地方,一旦成为一个“仲裁友好型”的法域,它就有可能吸引来自整个非洲,甚至在适当时候吸引来自全世界的国际争端在此地解决。正如与法语非洲①相关的许多争端目前往往通过设立在巴黎的仲裁机构来解决一样,今后这些争端可能越来越多地在某一个法语非洲国家内得到解决。

许多非洲国家已经意识到这种投资和机会所蕴含的潜力,整个非洲大陆都在努力将仲裁发展成为一个产业。尽管有一些国家雄心勃勃地想要发展成为“非洲争端解决”的中心,但花落谁家还不可知,包括埃及、卢旺达、肯尼亚和摩洛哥在内的许多非洲国家正在努力争夺。非洲境内的毛里求斯岛在地理上与许多亚洲国家很接近,也是这方面的一个竞争者。当然,非洲大陆面积广阔,可以拥有不止一个仲裁中心。

二、商业仲裁在非洲的成长和发展

一个国家在完善其司法制度和“接受”仲裁方面的潜在利益是明显的,毫

成为一个安全的仲裁庭审地:为了成为一个安全的仲裁庭审地,投资者希望得到保证,他们在该国进行仲裁不会受到来自该国法院的干预。当事人还希望能够平安、便利地进出该国,能够自由地选择律师代理他们进行仲裁,希望该地拥有优质的商业酒店和必要的基础设施。

成为一个可靠的仲裁地:这需要上面的所有因素,而且当地司法机构积极支持或至少不干预仲裁程序。这种名声需要长期形成,当地应表现出一种亲仲裁的立场,对仲裁裁决的异议能够做出独立、公正的决定,并且要求司法机构介入以支持仲裁的进行。

① “法语非洲”为译者的直译,是将法语当作第一语言和第二语言的国家的统称。

无疑问,非洲许多国家正竞相发展成为非洲仲裁中心。但这是否能带来非洲近年来仲裁的发展和完善?

我们必须界定清楚"非洲仲裁"(arbitration in Africa)的概念。这可能意味着选择仲裁(而不是其他解决争端的方法)来解决与非洲的项目、合同或者其他投资有关的争端,或是指涉及非洲当事人的仲裁,或是指在非洲进行仲裁或以非洲为仲裁地的仲裁。

至少在目前,我们看到与非洲有关的仲裁案件在增加。然而,这些争议往往发生在非洲大陆之外其他国家或地区的投资者之间或涉及此类投资者。虽然非洲当事人也参与仲裁,但纯粹非洲当事人之间通过国内或国际仲裁解决的争议并没有大幅增加。但是,一些仲裁当然是在非洲当事人之间而提起的,而且当地的仲裁机构也受理了许多案件。例如,基加利国际仲裁中心自成立以来已登记了52个案件,它受理的案件包括非洲大陆的当事人之间或涉及非洲大陆当事人的仲裁。

就国际仲裁机构而言,2014年国际商会仲裁院受理的来自撒哈拉以南非洲地区的案件数量大幅提升,但2015年这一水平并未持续。在2014年和2015年,来自北非的当事人数量保持稳定。来自尼日利亚和南非的当事人是国际商会仲裁院最常见的非洲用户,几乎占了来自非洲大陆的所有当事人的一半。

但从长期来看,人们预计这种情况将会改变,无论就非洲当事人选择解决争议的机构而言,还是就当事人选择通过仲裁解决争议的范围而言,非洲仲裁都会有极大发展。在非洲某些地区,情况尤其如此,在这些地区我们可以看到持续的投资和仲裁的发展。

史密斯斐尔律师事务所编写的《非洲争端解决指南》强调了过去几年许多非洲法域在立法、态度和方法方面的变化。笔者注意到,在非洲有很多政府主导的、旨在将本地区打造成争议解决中心的方案,如肯尼亚、卢旺达和毛里求斯。一些非洲国家如南非正在对仲裁立法进行现代化改革。非洲商法协调组织(Organization pour l'harmonisation du Droit des Affairs en Afrique,

OHADA)成员方也一直在努力构建一套一致的、稳定的仲裁框架。① 与此同时,其他非洲国家面向国际,批准或加入了《纽约公约》,以表明它们对仲裁的认可程度。安哥拉就在最近加入了《纽约公约》。

(一)签署、批准或加入《纽约公约》

许多非洲国家已经或正在采取国际上规定的措施,使本国成为符合《纽约公约》规定的批准国。截至2016年年底,非洲54个国家中已有35个国家批准了《纽约公约》。除少数国家在签署《纽约公约》时提出保留外,大部分国家在签署该公约时并未作出任何保留。比如,最近加入《纽约公约》的刚果民主共和国在批准《纽约公约》时提出了创纪录的4项保留意见:(1)限制该公约使之仅适用于在另一缔约方领土内作出的裁决;(2)该公约的适用不具有溯及力;(3)该公约只适用于根据国内法被认为是商业性质的法律关系所引起的争端;(4)该公约不适用于涉及不动产的案件。

安哥拉推动加入《纽约公约》的立法于2016年8月12日起生效。据报道,

---

① "非洲商法协调组织"成立于1993年,旨在协调非洲法郎区域内的商法。正如我们在《非洲争端解决指南》中所解释的那样,17个非洲国家签署了《OHADA条约》,该条约是增加该区域对潜在投资者吸引力的项目一个的核心内容之一。OHADA是非洲大陆法律迅速增长和发展的一个例子:它表明愿意对外接触,同时发展内部制度和法律,以建立一个投资者可以依靠的一贯和稳定的机构。加强对国际仲裁作为解决各缔约国之间商业争端的一种手段的信心,是OHADA的核心宗旨之一。OHADA建立了仲裁的双重轨道:由司法与仲裁共同法院(Cour Commune de Justice et d'Arbitrage,CCJA)管理的机构仲裁和司法与仲裁共同法院作为最高法院的临时仲裁。司法与仲裁共同法院提供了一个机构仲裁的机制。它为现代化和提高透明度做出了相当大的努力,包括公布与仲裁有关的决定和若干文件。在最近的发展中,司法与仲裁共同法院撤销了"GETMA v. Republic of Guinea(几内亚共和国)案"的仲裁裁决,理由是审理该案的国际仲裁机构获得的报酬高于司法与仲裁共同法院所规定的标准。这一决定是一把"双刃剑"。它可能会使国际当事人不愿意参与OHADA仲裁,因为国际仲裁员可能不乐意接受司法与仲裁共同法院规定的报酬。但也有一些积极的方面。首先,司法与仲裁共同法院强调有必要在整个仲裁过程中保持透明度。其次,司法与仲裁共同法院已经表明,它将坚持自己对仲裁员收费的决定。鉴于许多欧洲仲裁机构的收费在非洲被认为是不可承受的,司法与仲裁共同法院的决定将使当事人感到能够接受,即仲裁员单独协商的结果不会超过规定的费用。《统一仲裁法》(Uniform Arbitration Act,UAA)为在17个OHADA成员方内进行的仲裁提供了基础,并保证所有OHADA管辖的仲裁裁决包括临时仲裁裁决将可以在所有会员方内得到强制执行。这非常有用,因为OHADA的一些国家并不是《纽约公约》的缔约方。《统一仲裁法》还存在一些不足之处,并且我们了解到OHADA已经开始着手修订该法。2016年6月,OHADA还与国际商事仲裁院签署了一项合作协议,旨在加强两个机构之间的合作,并在OHADA的17个成员方之中促进仲裁实践的专业化和标准化。

安哥拉总统于2016年8月12日签发了正式批准书，该批准书被发布在2016年12月19日的政府公报上。然而，在2017年2月，安哥拉加入《纽约公约》尚未生效，在联合国国际贸易法委员会的网站上还没有记录和体现。

2016年6月，索马里宣布有意加入《纽约公约》并采纳联合国国际贸易法委员会的《国际商事仲裁示范法》(以下简称《示范法》)。

需要注意的是，批准或加入《纽约公约》只是一个步骤，而司法机关是否能够遵守公约义务才是至关重要的。对于公约中规定的拒绝承认和执行仲裁裁决的有限理由，可能存在一种广泛认可的国际方法，除非有关司法机构认识到并愿意遵循同一方法，否则即便加入或批准了公约，亦不会产生实际的差异。

(二)根据《纽约公约》在非洲执行仲裁裁决

对非洲的一种普遍性看法是，在非洲国家申请强制执行仲裁裁决非常困难。这种看法一部分源于缺乏证据，更多是因为信息不对称。通常因为一些已经公布的案例难以查询，从而导致数据跟踪记录难以建立。

对一些非洲国家来说，原因很简单：几乎没有当事人向它们提出承认和执行仲裁裁决的申请。如果没有，就很难确认这些国家会执行仲裁裁决。在另一些非洲国家，案件可能受到限制且持续数年，因此这些案例可能就会出现前后不一致或含糊之处。例如，2002年在肯尼亚高等法院审理的“阿波罗保险公司案”(Christ For All Nation v. Apollo Insurance Co.)中，当肯尼亚高等法院驳回公共政策抗辩时，对拒绝执行仲裁裁决设置了较高标准，并且该法院认为仲裁当事人应总体上“毫无保留”地接受仲裁裁决。然而，在“科比尔石油公司案”[Kenya Shell v. Kobil Petroleum (2006)]中，肯尼亚上诉法院维持了执行程序中的上诉权，理由是其国内立法没有禁止上诉权，或没有限制法院的监督管辖权。当然，人们也不应必然认为仲裁裁决不能在非洲得到执行。正如《非洲争端解决指南》表明的，在许多法域，即使不是《纽约公约》签署方的法域，仲裁裁决也可能得到执行。更重要的是，获得执行过程和执行程序的精确信息，包括执行过程会花费多长时间。

（三）非洲仲裁机构

1. 北部非洲

在摩洛哥，设立了卡萨布兰卡国际调解和仲裁中心（Casablanca International Centre Mediation and Arbitration Centre，CICMAC）。2014年，该中心组织了年度仲裁大会——"卡萨布兰卡仲裁日"，吸引了全球仲裁界许多知名嘉宾前来发言。该活动得到了国际商会仲裁院、国际争端解决中心（International Center for Dispute Resolution，ICDR）和伦敦国际仲裁院（London Court of International Arbitration，LCIA）的支持。但是，卡萨布兰卡国际调解和仲裁中心目前还处于初期阶段，很难找到它的相关信息，包括该中心的仲裁规则。

埃及首都是非洲最古老的仲裁机构开罗地区国际商事仲裁中心（The Cairo Regional Center For International Commercial Arbitration，CRCICA）的所在地，该中心是在1979年由亚非法律协商组织成立的。[①] 2014年4月，非洲开发银行（African Development Bank）发布了一份调查报告，将开罗地区国际商事仲裁中心列为非洲大陆领先的仲裁中心之一。[②] 截至2016年6月30日，开罗地区国际商事仲裁中心共受理了1109起案件。在2015年，有13个非埃及当事方参与了该中心管理的仲裁案件，而且在该中心管理的案件中，有10名被指定的仲裁员来自其他国家。其中，非阿拉伯国家的仲裁员来自美国、英国、德国、法国和西班牙。阿拉伯国家的仲裁员来自埃及、黎巴嫩、沙特阿拉伯、利比亚和突尼斯。

2. 东部非洲

在卢旺达，基加利希望通过设立基加利国际仲裁中心（Kigali International Arbitration Center，KIAC）在仲裁市场分一杯羹。[③] 该中心可以根据其本身的规则和联合国国际贸易法委员会的规则管理案件，它既有国内仲裁员名单，也有

---

① 关于该中心的介绍，参见该中心网站，http://crcica.org.eg/。

② 迪文戴尔律师指出："许多人认为开罗地区国际商事仲裁中心是非洲领先的仲裁机构，随着其成立40周年的临近，它将产生一个经验丰富的团队、高质量的设施以及在案件管理方面的良好记录。"

③ 关于该中心的介绍，参见该中心网站，http://www.kiac.org.rw。

国际仲裁员名单。基加利国际仲裁中心正在积极寻求吸引国际知名仲裁员。自该中心成立以来,已受理了52起案件。

3. 南部非洲

南部非洲仲裁基金(Arbitration Foundation of Southern Africa,AFSA)为国际投资者提供了一种国内选择。该机构成立于1996年,总部设在南非,虽然它受理的案件主要源于国内,但它也受理了20多起国际仲裁案件,涉及来自欧洲、英国[①]、美国、澳大利亚、亚洲和非洲的当事人。南部非洲仲裁基金拥有一个700多名专家的名单,在约翰内斯堡、开普敦、德班和比勒陀利亚设有办事处。为扩大国际影响力,2015年6月南部非洲仲裁基金与中国上海国际仲裁中心达成协议,成立中非联合仲裁中心(China-Africa Joint Arbitration Centre,CAJAC)。中非联合仲裁中心旨在成为解决涉及中国和非洲当事人的争议的主要仲裁机构之一。

毛里求斯虽然在地理上属于非洲,但它并不构成非洲大陆的一部分。它的岛屿位置比许多其他非洲地区更靠近亚洲国家。因此,毛里求斯可以作为"岸上"和"离岸"仲裁地。毛里求斯为能够成为"非洲仲裁地"也作出了很多努力,其中包括在2008年根据《示范法》通过了一项新的仲裁法。2011年7月,毛里求斯共和国政府、伦敦国际仲裁院和毛里求斯国际仲裁中心(Mauritius International Arbitration Centre,MIAC)达成协议,共同成立并运营一家新的仲裁中心——"伦敦国际仲裁院—毛里求斯国际仲裁中心仲裁中心"(以下简称LCIA-MIAC仲裁中心)。[②] 该中心可以根据自己的规则、联合国国际贸易法委员会的规则或当事人约定的任何其他程序规则来管理仲裁和其他形式的替代争议解决机制(Alternative Dispute Resolution,ADR)。

---

① 英国人常常只认为自己是英国人而非欧洲人,欧洲大陆国家的人在日常生活中也不把英国视为他们口中的"欧洲"国家,因此英文原文把"欧洲"和"英国"分开来写。

② 关于该中心的介绍,参见该中心网站,http://www.lcia-miac.org。

4. 西部非洲

该地区在采用外国投资者通常寻求的争端解决机制方面发展相对缓慢。尼日利亚是该区域唯一一个根据《示范法》制定现代仲裁法即《仲裁和调解法》的国家。尼日利亚拥有各种仲裁机构,包括拉各斯地区国际商事仲裁中心和拉各斯仲裁院。拉各斯仲裁院成立于1989年,并于2013年修订了规则,引入了紧急仲裁员程序。虽然尼日利亚力求创造一个有利于仲裁的环境,但法院处理仲裁事项的方式极不统一。法院对仲裁程序的介入将会减缓争端的解决。

如果考虑选择上述这些仲裁机构(或其他一些不熟悉的机构)进行仲裁,重要的一点是,检查它们的仲裁规则或仲裁协议中是否允许指定经验丰富的国际仲裁执业者,以及其收费水平是否能够确保一个高水平的仲裁庭愿意解决争议;同时,还需认真考虑仲裁机构和仲裁地的组合问题。

三、在非洲进行仲裁是一种选择吗?

选择仲裁机构与选择仲裁地不同。机构会管理仲裁事项,只要仲裁机构健全并且有一套现代化的仲裁规则,这种管理就会非常有效。但当你选择仲裁地时,你同时也选择了仲裁地国的法院对仲裁进行监督,并且该国法院可能会对临时救济等问题作出决定,而且最终可能会对仲裁裁决提出的异议进行审查。这就需要当地有一部现代化的、符合目的的仲裁法,而且当地需要有中立公正且通过培训或经历并对仲裁事项具有专业技能的法官。当事人可以选择委托国际律师在仲裁中代表自己行使权利,大多数国家对此问题没有规定。为了吸引优质仲裁员,需要让仲裁员享有豁免权,并且还得保证各方当事人和律师能够进出仲裁地国。

在一些拥有现代化仲裁机构的地区,也可能没有上述这些必要的基础法律结构。一些国家还没有现代化的仲裁立法,此类立法规定通常与仲裁友好型国家的仲裁立法规定一致,如在对仲裁裁决提出异议的理由等方面。一些阿拉伯语国家或地区法院要求向法院提交的仲裁文件必须使用阿拉伯语,这可能会使当事人不愿选择在这些地区进行非阿拉伯语的仲裁。在其他一些法域，立法的发展可能超出了包括司法人员在内的经验和知识。

在所有法域，程序上的障碍或缺陷可能只有依靠经验才能发现。这正是《解决非洲争端指南》的目的所在。它在阐明每一法域争端解决结构的同时，也旨在指明当地的实际情况。

对许多国际客户和投资者来说，仅确保某一特定法域拥有良好仲裁所需要的全部要素还不够，他们还想要证据来证明。为此，你需要证明在该地有过令人满意的经历和法院裁判，以表明该地持有一种倾向仲裁的立场，而且该地法院对仲裁裁决的异议作出过明智的裁判。

对于许多非洲国家来说，这就是问题之所在。它形成一种恶性循环：为了发展出倾向仲裁的法理，当事各方需要把该地选择为仲裁地，但他们又不愿意这么做，因为他们不愿相信一个缺乏相关仲裁记录的法域。如伦敦、巴黎和纽约这样的老牌仲裁地已经形成了支持仲裁的悠久历史，但对于非洲国家来说无论政府和司法部门对仲裁如何支持，在短期内也很难复制，除非有足够多的案件量。虽然这具有一定的挑战性，但也并非完全不可能。关键在于持之以恒地、积极地对仲裁采取友好的做法。[①]

目前，最有可能在竞争者中成为非洲“可靠的”仲裁地的领先者是毛里求斯。该国政府在打造仲裁中心形象方面进行了大量投资，而且它在世界银行（World Bank）的“营商便利化”排名中位列第32位。[②] 毛里求斯法院关于仲裁的判例法也很有前瞻性（尽管案例数量仍然有限）。毛里求斯最高法院曾指

---

① 在非洲当地进行仲裁是否恰当取决于议价能力、交易的性质、可能发生争议的金额、财产所在地、仲裁裁决的可能执行地以及所提议的仲裁地。如果对方当事人所关切的是争端不要“出口”到非洲以外的地方，则有可能就下列事项达成一致意见：

选择适用“非洲的”法律，但选择一个离岸仲裁地和仲裁机构；

选择适用“国际性”的法律和离岸仲裁地，但由“非洲的”仲裁机构仲裁；

选择适用“国际性”的法律、岸上仲裁庭审地但离岸的法律上的仲裁地，仲裁机构是“非洲的”仲裁机构；

在少数一些非洲法域，有可能争议的所有方面都在岸上进行但确保国际当事人可以相信争议能够得到有效处理。

② See http://www.doingbusiness.org/rankings, August 19, 2016.

出，仲裁裁决执行申请必须向该法院的仲裁分庭（由3名法官组成的专门法庭，旨在创建一个在国际仲裁方面具有专业知识的单一机构）提出，即使仲裁不受毛里求斯2008年仲裁立法的调整。

液化天然气及欧盟天然气价格审查:给日本的启示

安娜·斯塔尼克(Ana Stanič)[*] 著

王子越[**] 译 孙巍[***] 校审

摘要:欧盟大部分天然气销售遵循长期液化天然气买卖协议,协议双方通常会商定一种定价机制,允许天然气价格随其市场价值波动。典型的价格审查条款为,在发生特定事件并影响用户终端市场的天然气价值时,任何一方有权启动价格审查协商,若未能协商成功,可请求仲裁庭决定。自2005年以来,受欧盟天然气市场自由化、欧盟电力行业对天然气需求增加、跨大西洋地区液化天然气交易量增加、2008年金融危机后欧盟天然气需求下降、欧盟枢纽的流动

* 英国E&A Law律师事务所创始人。

** 北京市中伦律师事务所律师助理。

*** 北京市中伦律师事务所合伙人;中国国际经济贸易仲裁委员会、北京仲裁委员会、上海仲裁委员会、上海国际经济贸易仲裁委员会、深圳国际仲裁院、广州仲裁委员会、石家庄仲裁委员会及宁波仲裁委员会等10余家中国内地仲裁委员会仲裁员,香港国际仲裁中心(Hong Kong International Arbitration Centre, HKIAC)、新加坡国际仲裁中心(Singapore International Arbitration Centre, SIAC)、亚洲国际仲裁中心(Asian International Arbitration Centre, AIAC)、南部非洲仲裁基金会(Arbitration Foundation of Southern Africa, AFSA)、塔什干国际仲裁中心(Tashkent International Arbitration Centre, TIAC)等国际仲裁机构仲裁员;中国政法大学兼职教授、联合国贸易法委员会第二工作组中国国家代表团成员、国际商会中国国家委员会仲裁和替代争议解决委员会委员、国际商会“一带一路”委员会大使、中国国际经济贸易仲裁委员会建设工程业务小组召集人、《中国建设工程法律评论》主编、常设中国建设工程法律论坛秘书长、全国青联委员。

性增强因素影响,欧盟出现了3轮天然气价格审查仲裁的浪潮,天然气的定价机制也随之从与石油产品的价格挂钩转变为参考天然气基准价格。在未来,欧盟的价格审查仲裁数量会逐渐减少,日本等亚洲国家将成为价格审查仲裁的下一个主战场。对日本来说,欧盟在价格审查中形成的经验殊值借鉴,例如,应慎重起草价格审查条款、重视准据法的影响、在价格审查仲裁中专家密切合作、谨慎指定仲裁员、注重竞争法立法等。

关键词:天然气定价机制　欧盟天然气价格审查仲裁　经济销售条款　日本天然气市场

一、引言

如今大部分销往日本的液化天然气仍依靠长期液化天然气买卖协议供应,液化天然气价格与石油价格挂钩。2005 年天然气价格审查仲裁开始之前,欧盟的情况也是如此。

来自美国和澳大利亚的供应商正与其他传统供应商(来自卡塔尔、马来西亚和印度尼西亚)竞争有利可图的日本市场,他们正提出石油指数化的替代定价机制,[①]包括将液化天然气价格与煤炭价格、电力价格或其他市场的天然气价格挂钩。[②]

同时,由于日本市场液化天然气供过于求,日本公平贸易委员会(Japan Fair Trade Commission)调查了液化天然气买卖协议中所包含的目的地条款是否违反日本竞争法(Japanese Competition Law)。据估计,日本 80% ~90%的液化天然气买卖协议规定了交货地点,并阐明了交货地点变更的限制条件。尽管区域性套利交易(Regional Arbitrage Opportunities)由此受限,但许多行业人士认为,取消目的地限制将为液化天然气购买者带来更多灵活性和机会,从而便于他们转售其持有的过剩天然气。2017 年 6 月,日本公平贸易

① 在日本,天然气价格与公布的“一揽子”进口原油价格指数(日本原油综合价格)挂钩。

② Inajima T., Murtaugh D., *Gas Sellers Flip the Script to Hook Customers Spoilt for Choice*, Bloomberg, May 10, 2018.

委员会表示,FOB 合同中的目的地条款可能违反了日本竞争法。但与 21 世纪初欧洲委员会(European Commission)的做法不同,日本公平贸易委员会并未将目的地条款从现有液化天然气买卖协议中删除。①

本文回顾了过去 15 年欧盟的天然气价格审查以及由此引发的天然气定价方式的改变,从而为日本液化天然气定价的讨论提供参考。过去 15 年,由于天然气市场的结构性变化、取消目的地限制、电力行业天然气使用量的增加、液化天然气供应增加以及通过立法开放天然气市场,欧盟开展了对天然气的价格审查。目前,日本天然气市场也正面临许多类似变化,通过分析欧盟的情况,本文试图为日本提供可供借鉴的经验。

本文共由十部分组成。紧接着第一部分引言,第二部分从历史角度概述了欧盟液化天然气买卖协议和定价机制。第三部分讨论了欧盟价格审查条款的典型措辞。第四部分和第五部分详细介绍了自 2005 年至今欧盟天然气价格和液化天然气价格审查仲裁背后的原因,以及价格是如何随之进行调整的。第六部分讨论了欧盟价格审查条款的一部分——"市场经济"条款的执行。第七和第八部分描述了天然气在欧盟的价格审查仲裁浪潮,以及欧盟未来可能发生的变化。最后,也是本文的重点,第九部分列举了日本应从欧盟价格审查仲裁中吸取的 6 点教训。第十部分为本文结论。

二、欧盟液化天然气买卖协议和定价机制的历史概述

20 世纪 60 年代,在荷兰发现了大量天然气。为对其进行开发,项目开发商和天然气购买者签订了长期液化天然气买卖协议。② 根据长期液化天然气买卖协议,无论是否需要,天然气购买者承诺 15 ~ 30 年内购买约定数量的天然气。这便为卖方(项目开发商)提供了稳定的收入来源,以负担天然气生产所需的大量资金。作为回报,项目开发商承诺以合同约定的价格和数量向买方出

① 日本公平贸易委员会:《关于液化天然气交易情况的调查》,载日本公平贸易委员会官方网站,https://www.jftc.go.jp/houdou/pressrelease/h29/jun/170628_1.html。

② Stanic A., Weale G., *Changes in the European Gas Market and Price Review Arbitrations*, Energy and Resource Law, (2007) J.

售天然气,从而使买方能通过签订背对背协议制订销售计划。换言之,在传统的液化天然气买卖协议中,卖方承担价格风险;因必须购买约定数量的天然气,买方也承担一定风险。

到21世纪初,欧盟大部分天然气的销售都遵循长期液化天然气买卖协议。[①] 由于持续时间长,协议各方通常会商定一种定价机制,允许天然气价格随其市场价值波动。[②] 这向买方确保了在协议有效期内,天然气相对于其他能源仍具有价格优势。同时,这一定价机制也便于卖方掌控天然气在用户终端市场的价值,而这一价值也会在协议期内发生变化。

作为用户终端市场中天然气的替代品,石油及石油产品的价格通常会影响天然气在液化天然气买卖协议中的定价。因此,典型的液化天然气买卖协议定价机制也涵盖了石油、汽油和燃油的价格指数。

这一定价机制从数学角度体现了各方在协议商定时如何看待天然气与石油产品间的关系。各方希望在协议期内,天然气和石油产品间的价格关系能视情况而变化,如果发生特殊情况,则会审查并调整原有的定价机制。

三、欧盟中的典型价格审查条款

欧盟不同的液化天然气买卖协议中,各价格审查条款的措辞也各不相同。有些协议规定,定价机制可定期自动调整。而大部分的价格审查条款则规定,协议各方有权要求定期(通常为3年)对价格进行审查而非调整。

除定期审查价格外,有些于20世纪90年代中期制定的液化天然气买卖协议也规定了一系列的特殊价格审查。这使天然气价格能够更快地根据市场的变化进行调整。将这些特殊价格审查纳入液化天然气买卖协议,其目的是通过立法放开欧洲天然气市场。

---

① 在美国,液化天然气买卖协议中的天然气价格参考了天然气基准价格,通常为亨利中心(Henry Hub)基准价格。

② "天然气价格"与"天然气价值"非同一概念。"天然气价格",是指液化天然气买卖协议中根据定价机制确定的天然气价格。而"天然气价值"则是一个相对概念,即在传统的定价机制下,天然气的价格是参照其他能源(通常是石油产品)的价格确定的。

以下便是典型的价格审查条款：

“双方约定，若在液化天然气买卖协议生效期间时常出现超出双方控制能力的事件，导致买方能源市场与约定之时相比大不相同（或第一次价格审查之后的所有审查，与本条款签订时最近的审查相比均出现重大变化），影响了谨慎高效的天然气公司在用户终端市场上可以获取的天然气价值，则任何一方都可要求进行如下的定期价格审查或特殊价格审查……若在价格审查的通知发出后（X）日内，当事双方未达成书面协议修改定价机制，则另一方有权在向对方发出价格审查通知（Y）日内，通过仲裁庭对价格进行审查……”

（一）价格审查是一个分“两步走”的过程

如上述价格审查条款所示，典型的价格审查通常包括两个阶段。首先，提出价格审查要求的一方必须证明发生了价格审查事件，即超出双方控制能力的事件。其次，只有当价格审查事件影响用户终端市场的天然气价值时，价格审查程序才会被启动，价格也将得以调整。因此，在欧盟大部分的液化天然气买卖协议中，价格无法自动调整，价格审查事件是调整价格的必要条件。

从程序角度看，价格审查也分为两个阶段——谈判和仲裁。根据上述价格审查条款，审查在一方发出审查通知后生效。在审查的第一阶段，收到请求后，当事双方开始谈判，以确定审查事件是否已经发生，如果是，则调整价格；如果双方未能在约定的时间内（通常为请求发出后的60～120天）达成协议，则一方有权要求对定价机制进行审查，并在必要时由仲裁法庭对定价机制进行调整。

（二）价格审查的客观依据

在讨论价格审查背后的原因之前，需要注意的是，审查的原因和依据都是客观的。只有当价格审查事件发生时，才能进行审查。并且，只有当审查事件影响了谨慎高效的燃气公司在客户终端市场获取的天然气价值时，才能对价格进行调整。换言之，如果审查事件的发生仅使协议一方经济负担加重,并不构成价格审查的依据。调整定价时,也不会考虑买方在终端市场的天然气变价。因此,价格审查条款与“艰难条款”①(hardship clause)在执行上有所不同。*

四、欧盟价格审查背后的原因

如上所述,若要展开价格审查,当事方必须证明:(1)“买方市场”出现变化;(2)变化具有重大影响;(3)变化发生于“审查日期”之前;(4)变化超出了价格审查提请方的控制能力。

变化必须具有重大影响,这一点从基本上保证了变化是举足轻重的,从而证明了价格审查的合理性。在一般情况下,价格审核条款不会界定何为“重大影响”。因此,当事方必须在欧盟价格审查仲裁中提交大量的专家意见,以证明质或量上出现了重大变化,或两者兼而有之。

至于审查时间,价格审核条款则进行了明确阐述。除第一次审查外,审查期从上次价格审查日开始至下一次审查通知日止。因此,作为价格审查依据,经济情况的变化应当发生在审查期内。

如果涉及特殊价格审查,则需对其提请审查时间进行细致的评估。通常而言,价格审查开始得越晚,经济情况的变化会变得越清晰。但推迟审查也有不利的一面,因为价格的调整只有在审查开始之后才能进行。

为防止审查提请方干预调价,经济情况的变化必须超出其控制能力,且审查必须开始于变化出现之后。

价格审核条款规定变化必须发生于买方市场中,这体现了价格审核条款的

---

① 在欧盟,许多液化天然气买卖协议都包含了“艰难条款”。因此,当发生超出各方控制的事件,给合同的履行造成困难时,可以对天然气价格进行调整。具体例子请参考如下链接:https://iccwbo.org/publication/icc-force-majeure-clause-2003icc-hardship-clause-2003/。在一些仲裁中,根据准据法,“艰难条款”是包含在液化天然气买卖协议中的。

* “艰难条款”与价格审查条款的不同之处在于:判断“艰难条款”是否触发的依据是,如果继续履行原合同是否对一方当事人造成不公;而判断价格审查是否触发的依据是,“真诚高效的经营者”在买方最终用户市场中获得的天然气价值是否受到了影响。前者考虑的是当事人的情况,后者则为客观标准。——译者注

地域限制。21世纪前的欧盟（详见前文第二部分的论述），企业只能在本国市场经营，用户终端市场的情况相对容易确定。但是，随着欧盟天然气市场逐渐放开，买方不再只和单个欧盟成员开展贸易往来，多数情况下，他们会在全球范围内开展业务。这给在欧盟的价格审查仲裁中的仲裁当事方和仲裁员都带来了各种挑战，并增加了仲裁结果的不确定性。

2005年以来，最常见且成功触发欧盟针对液化天然气买卖协议中管道气和液化天然气供应的价格审查的“情况发生重大变化”的事件主要有：（1）欧盟天然气市场自由化；（2）电力行业对天然气需求增加；（3）跨大西洋地区液化天然气交易量增加；（4）欧盟市场的液化天然气供应量增加；（5）2008年金融危机后天然气需求下降；（6）欧盟液化气枢纽的流动性增强。其中，许多变革是随着价格审查一起出现的，下文将对这些变革一一进行讨论。

（一）欧盟天然气市场自由化

为通过调价放开天然气市场，欧盟委员会发起了第一次价格调整。2000年以前，国有垄断企业负责生产、进口和运输天然气，并将天然气销往批发和零售市场。即使在上述所有权更多样化的欧盟国家，也很少存在市场竞争。由于缺乏跨境管道设施，各国运营商没有或少有机会在本国市场之外经营，欧盟各国间交易的天然气数量非常有限。

为建立单一的欧洲天然气市场，加强欧盟各国的内外竞争，欧盟于1998年6月通过了第一项天然气指令。[①] 随后，欧盟于2003年通过了第二项天然气指令，该指令要求欧盟各国在2007年之前完全放开其下游天然气市场以参与竞争。[②] 此外，第二项天然气指令要求第三方介入管道气市场，这使许多于该指

① 欧洲议会和理事会于1998年6月22日颁布的关于天然气内部市场共同规则的第98/30 / EC号指令，载欧盟委员会网站，http://ec.europa.eu/energy/ gas/legislation/legislation_en.htm。

② 某些于2004年加入欧盟的国家例外。

令之前生效的优先协议被迫中止①。

20 世纪 90 年代末和 21 世纪初,欧盟委员会开始执行与电力和天然气市场有关的竞争法,这深深地影响了此后能源公司的运作方式。② 值得一提的是,依据当时生效的《欧洲联盟职能条约》(Treaty on the Functioning of the European Union, TFEU,以下简称《欧盟职能条约》)第 101 条和第 102 条,欧盟委员会对法国燃气公司(GDF,现为 Engie)、埃尼集团(ENI)和意大利国家电力公司(ENEL)提出了竞争诉讼。③ 根据这些案例,若有公司为了子公司的利益而推迟管道投资或给予分销公司优先权以挤兑竞争者,均会视为滥用支配地位。除客观原因外,签订含有大量需求的长期合同也属于滥用支配地位。同时,欧盟委员会还采取了相应措施,迫使公司放弃目的地条款④。

尽管欧盟各成员能源市场的自由化步伐不同,但从 2003 年到 2006 年,自由化对整个欧盟天然气市场主要产生了两方面影响。首先,天然气开始与其他能源形成竞争关系。天然气的市场准入壁垒被移除以及联合循环燃气轮机的使用使天然气需求增加,而新出现的卖家则试图提供比以往更低的价格吸引买家,用户终端市场天然气间的竞争加剧。这意味着,在许多西欧市场上,天然气的价格不再完全由石油产品的价格决定。其次,由于法律不再强制买方仅在自己的市场上交易,而欧盟委员会也宣布目的地条款为非法,大多数天然气购买

---

① VEMW 等, C－17/03, 载欧洲法院网, http://curia. europa. eu/juris/showPdf. jsf; jsessionid = 9C726B04 5B25353F0544DCC07C3E5186? text = &docid = 60341&pageIndex = 0&doclang = en&mode = lst&dir = &occ = first&part = 1&cid = 2245086。

② Stanic A., *Overview of EU Energy Law*, *Legal Aspects of EU Energy Regulation*, edited by Cameron P., Heffron R., Oxford University Press, October 2016.

③ 欧盟委员会竞争总署第 38662 号案,载欧盟委员会网站, http://ec. europa. eu/competition/elojade/isef/case_details. cfm? proc_code = 1_38662。

④ 欧盟委员会在其 2002 年对尼日利亚液化天然气调查的和解中指出,"一旦天然气交易完成交付和付款,买方便可无条件地将天然气转售给他人"。参见欧盟委员会新闻稿,欧盟委员会针对尼日利亚天然气公司 NLNG 地域销售限制的调查, IP/02/1869,载欧盟委员会网站 2002 年 12 月 12 日, http://europa. eu/rapid/press-release_IP－02－1869_en. html。有关调查的详细信息,参见 Nyssens h., Cultrera c., Schnichels d., 天然气行业的地域限制的现状, 载欧盟委员会网站, http://ec. europa. eu/competition/publications/cpn/2004_1_48. pdf。

者越来越多地在欧洲乃至全球范围内开展业务。

2009年,第三项天然气指令通过,进一步开放和整合了欧盟市场。① 更重要的是,垂直整合后的天然气公司必须采取有效的方式将天然气的运输、生产和销售分开,燃气管道也必须允许天然气反向流动。此外,政府还出台了相关法规,鼓励建设跨境管道和液化天然气再气化终端,以提高欧盟各国间的互联互通性和互操作性。②

21世纪初,笔者曾参与了欧盟的第一轮价格审查仲裁。当时,以上述开放欧盟天然气市场为由,买方也借此成功地推动了第一项和第二项天然气指令的实施。

(二)电力行业对天然气需求增加

欧盟电力行业对天然气需求增加是引发第一轮价格审查仲裁的另一重要原因。自20世纪60年代以来,欧盟的天然气需求持续增长。到20世纪90年代,电力行业的联合循环燃气轮机使用天然气供能,天然气需求就此激增。如图1所示,描绘了从1990~2014年欧盟28国电力行业对天然气需求的变化。从1990年到2008年,此需求增长了269%。

时至今日,天然气仍为欧盟28国15%~20%的发电行业供能。未来,燃煤发电将转为燃气发电,而作为可再生发电能源的有力补充,天然气也将会因其可靠性和灵活性,更广泛地运用到电力行业中。

① 欧洲议会和欧洲理事会于2009年7月13日发布的2009/73/EC号指令,涉及天然气内部市场的通用规则并废除了2003/55/EC号指令,载欧盟法规速递,https://eur-lex.europa.eu/legal-content/EN/TXT/HTML/?uri=CELEX:32009L0073&from=EN。

② 欧洲议会和欧洲理事会于2013年4月17日发布的第347/2013号条例,关于跨欧洲能源基础设施的指导方针,废除了第1364/2006/EC号决定,并修订了第713/2009号、第714/2009号和第(EC)715/2009号条例,载欧盟法规速递,https://eur-lex.europa.eu/legal-content/EN/TXT/HTML/?uri=CELEX:32013R0347&from=en。

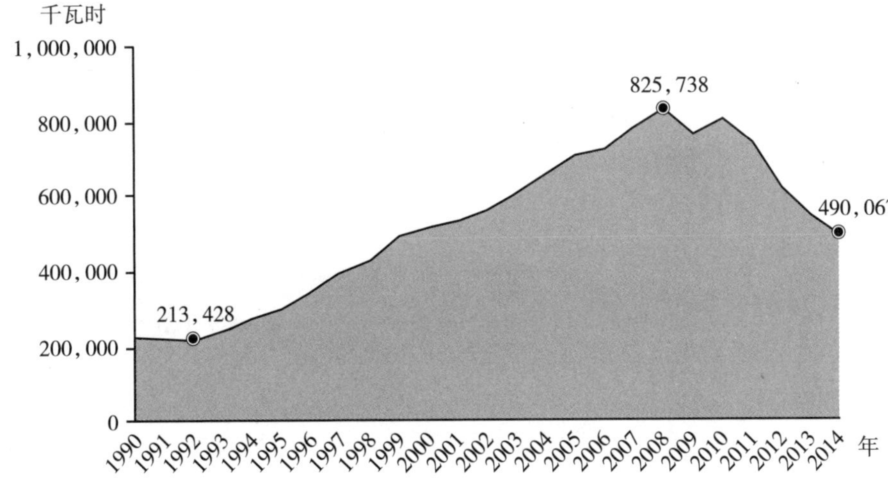

图1 1990~2014 年欧盟 28 国发电行业的天然气需求

资料来源：欧洲环境署，载 https://www.eea.europa.eu/data-and-maps/daviz/gross-electricity-production-by-fuel-2#tab-googlechartid_chart_11_filters=%7B%22rowFilters%22%3A%7B%7D%3B%22columnFilters%22%3A%7B%22pre_config_sector%22%3A%5B%22Natural%20and%20derived%20gas%22%5D%3B%22pre_config_ugeo%22%3A%5B%22European%20Union%20(28%20countries)%22%5D%7D%7D。

2000 年后，天然气在发电行业的使用量增加，这意味着除石油和石油产品，天然气也开始与其他诸多能源竞争。如图 2 所示，天然气开始与煤炭和核电形成竞争关系，这无疑是天然气市场上重大的结构性变化。2004~2008 年，许多欧盟买方以天然气需求增加为由，成功提请了价格审查。

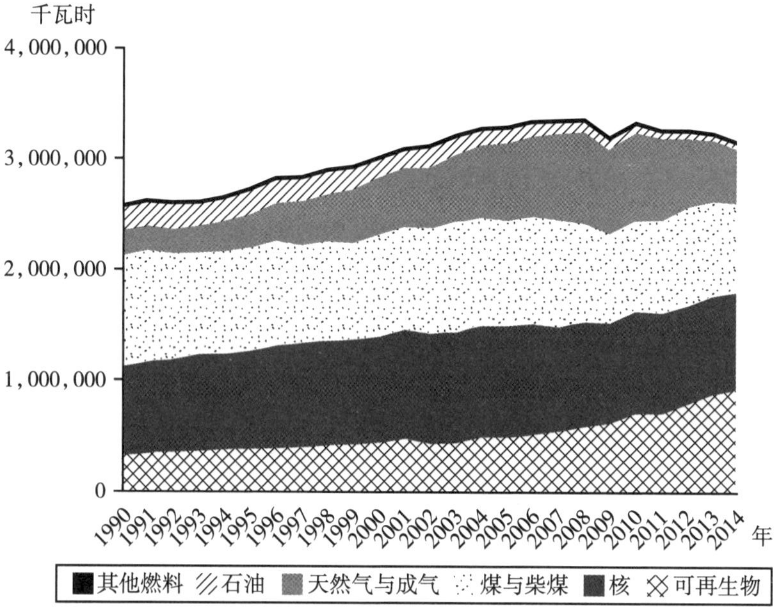

图2　1990～2014年欧盟28国各能源总发电量

资料来源：欧洲环境署，载 https://www.eea.europa.eu/data-and-maps/daviz/gross-electricity-production-by-fuel-2#tab-googlechartid_chart_11_filters=%7B%22rowFilters%22%3A%7B%7D%3B%22columnFilters%22%3A%7B%22pre_config_sector%22%3A%5B%22Coal%20and%20lignite%22%3B%22Natural%20and%20derived%20gas%22%3B%22Nuclear%22%3B%22Oil%22%3B%22Other%20fuels%22%3B%22Renewables%20%22%5D%3B%22pre_config_ugeo%22%3A%5B%22European%20Union%20(28%20countries)%22%5D%7D%7D。

（三）跨大西洋地区液化天然气交易量增加

2000年以前，跨大西洋地区天然气贸易量相对较小。尽管阿尔及利亚、尼日利亚、特立尼达和多巴哥的生产商在美国和欧洲市场上都销售过天然气，但这些市场均为独立市场，有自己的定价机制。天然气贸易都根据地域进行划分，大部分液化天然气买卖协议也包含目的地条款。如图3所示，2001年，美国本土天然气产量骤降，天然气市场供不应求，导致美国和欧洲的液化天然气销售价格差异悬殊。当欧盟委员宣布目的地条款为非法之后，大部分天然气购买者便利用价格差，将销往欧盟的天然气转运到美国，使跨大西洋地区的液化天然气交易量增加。

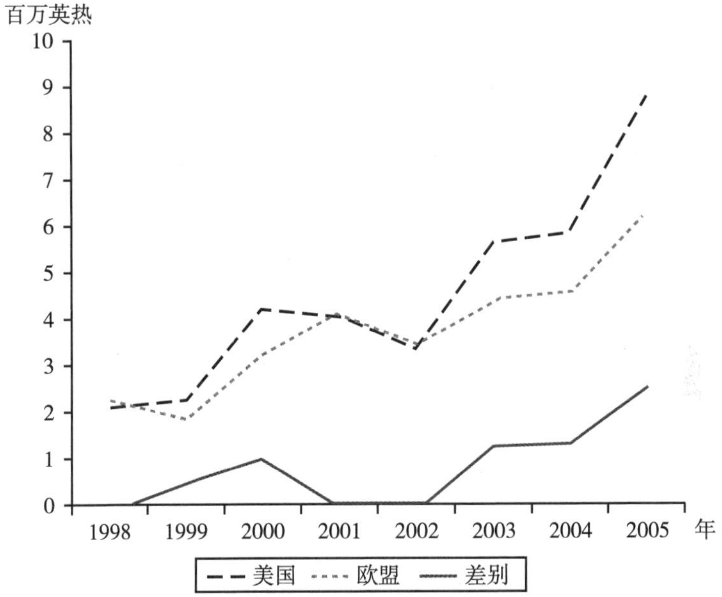

图 3 1998～2005 年欧洲和美国的天然气产量

资料来源：英国石油公司（BP）对世界能源的统计回顾，2006 年 6 月，载 https://www.bp.com/productlanding，16 & 31。

跨大西洋地区液化天然气交易量的增长给欧洲天然气市场带来了以下影响。首先，越来越多的欧洲天然气买家开始向美国市场出售产品并开展全球业务，以从传统市场外的价格套利和其他机会中获利。其次，2005 年前后，某些行业的天然气价格开始参考亨利中心（Henry Hub）基准价格进行定价。因此，卖方便以液化天然气交易量增加为由，提请了价格审查。

（四）2008 年金融危机后天然气需求下降

2008 年金融危机导致欧盟天然气需求大幅下降。如图 4 所示，2011 年欧盟 28 国的天然气需求量降至 478 亿立方米，与 2008 年相比下降了 9%，尚未达到危机前的水平。同一时期，卡塔尔和澳大利亚生产液化天然气，美国生产页岩气，这导致本该运往美国的液化天然气运到了欧盟新建的再气化终端。如上所述，这种转运只有当欧盟委员会根据欧盟竞争法（EU competition law）宣布目的地条款为非法之后方可进行。

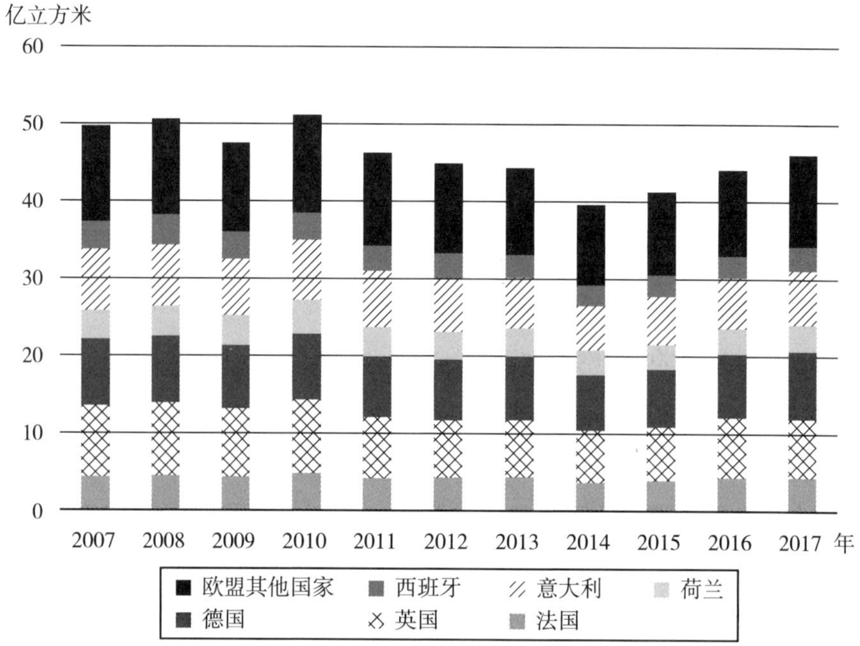

图 4 2007～2017 年欧盟 28 国的天然气总消耗量

资料来源：剑桥教育集团（CEG Europe）基于 2018 年英国石油公司（BP）的统计回顾作出的分析，载 https://www.bp.com/en/global/corporate/energy-economics/statistical-review-of-world-energy.html。

上述因素导致了 2009 年后欧盟天然气供过于求。另外，买方出售过剩的天然气，又促进了欧盟枢纽的流动性。因此，2009 年后，许多欧盟买方以部分欧盟市场天然气之间的竞争已进一步发展为由，再一次提出进行价格审查。

（五）欧盟市场的液化天然气供应量增加

2000 年后，美国因其天然气和页岩气的生产而成为天然气净出口国，从而确保了全球液化天然气供应的持续增长。此外，2017 年卡塔尔对北油田（North Field）新生产的天然气取消了 2005 年的强制性暂停措施，并提出到 2024 年将其液化天然气产能从每年 77 万吨增加到 100 万吨。[①] 如图 5 所示，显示了自 2004 年来，欧盟液化天然气供应量的增长。2011 年 3 月日本福岛核

① Cornot-Gandolphe S., *The Next Wave of Global LNG Investment is Coming*, https://www.ifri.org/en/publications/editoriaux-de-lifri/edito-energie/next-wave-global-lng-investment-coming, December 16, 2018.

事故发生后，日本一夜之间关闭了所有的核电站，使本该运往欧盟的液化天然气必须转运到日本，欧盟液化天然气的供应量才开始下降。

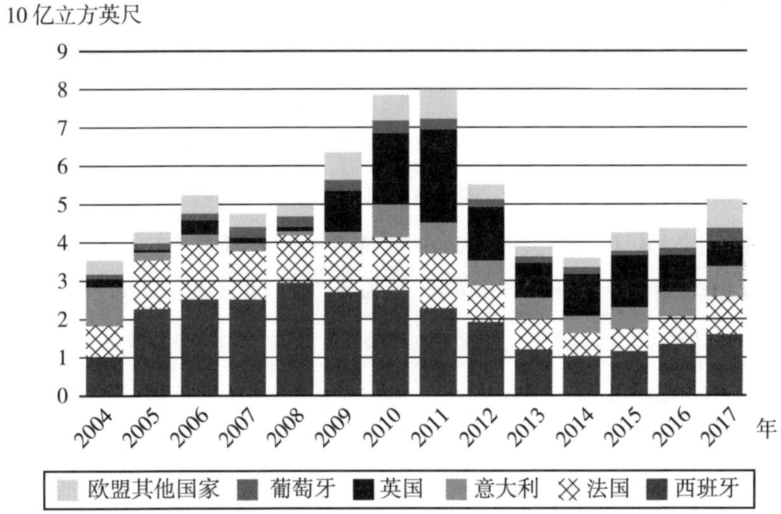

图 5　2004 ~ 2017 年欧盟 28 国液化天然气进口量

资料来源：https://www. eia. gov/todayinenergy/detail. php? id = 37354。

如上所述，全球液化天然气供应增加，而金融危机后欧盟经济衰退造成天然气需求下降，到 2009 年，欧盟天然气供过于求。① 从 2009 年开始，买方以此为由，成功发起了价格审查，标志着欧盟第二轮价格审查浪潮的开始。

（六）欧盟液化气枢纽的流动性增强

最近一轮价格审查，即第三轮价格审查浪潮始于 2012 年。当时，由于欧盟某些枢纽的流动性增强，买方呼吁将定价机制与基准价格完全挂钩。这主要因为 2008 ~ 2016 年，荷兰天然气交易中心（Title Transfer Facility，TTF）和英国天

① Wood Mackenzie, *Gas Outlook: European Oversupply and Low Prices*, https://www. woodmac. com/news/editorial/gas-outlook-european-oversupply-and-low-prices/, December 16, 2018. 2020 年后，全球天然气供过于求的局面可能会持续下去。

然气交易中心(National Balancing Point,NBP)的交易量分别增加了38倍和2倍,[①]其枢纽的流动性也随之增强,在天然气的竞争中,它们也为定价提供了更可靠的参考。表1显示了欧盟天然气枢纽的顾客流失率。

表1 欧盟天然气枢纽的顾客流失率(2008~2016年)

单位:%

枢纽	欧盟天然气枢纽的顾客流失率				
	2008年	2011年	2014年	2015年	2016年
荷兰天然气交易中心	3.3	13.9	36.0	45.9	57.1
英国天然气交易中心	14.4	19.8	26.2	26.2	22.1
中欧天然气枢纽公司	2.4	2.2	4.8	3.9	5.7
比利时天然气交易中心+比利时泽布鲁格贸易点	5.1	4.1	4.9	4.3	4.1
NetConnect Germany公司(NCG)	0.4	1.8	4.2	3.9	4.0
德国天然气交易中心		0.8	3.0	2.5	2.5
法国北部天然气交易点	法国0.4	法国1.0	1.6	1.7	1.7
意大利天然气虚拟交换点	0.2	0.2	0.8	1.0	1.2
捷克天然气交易中心	不适用	不适用	0.4	1.0	1.1
法国天然气南部贸易区	不适用	不适用	南部交易点1.0 法国道达尔基础设施天然气公司交易点0.1	0.6	0.6
西班牙天然气虚拟贸易点	不适用	不适用	不适用	<0.1	0.1

资料来源:牛津能源研究所(Oxford Institute of Energy Studies, *European Traded Gas Hubs: An Updated Analysis on Liquidity, Maturity and Barriers to Market Integration*, https://www.oxfordenergy.org/publications/european-traded-gas-hubs-updated-analysis-liquidity-maturity-barriers-market-integration/, December 16, 2018.)。

注:基于市场径流式计算,所有年份的计算方法有所不同。

---

① Oxford Institute of Energy Studies, *European Traded Gas Hubs: An Updated Analysis on Liquidity, Maturity and Barriers to Market Integration*, https://www.oxfordenergy.org/publications/european-traded-gas-hubs-updated-analysis-liquidity-maturity-barriers-market-integration/, December 16, 2018.

五、价格调整

如第三部分所述，在价格审查的第二阶段，审查提请方必须证明，出现的重大变化影响了谨慎高效的天然气公司在用户终端市场上获得的天然气价值。因此，如果要调整价格，首先，考量客观因素而非仅参考买方根据特定液化天然气买卖协议提供的天然气价格；其次，要根据用户终端市场的情况确定天然气的价值。

由于大多数价格审查条款并未对"用户终端市场"进行界定，欧盟的价格审查仲裁花费了大量专家的时间来确定其概念范围。大多数仲裁庭认同单一欧盟天然气市场情况并不能作为参考依据。尽管多年来天然气枢纽特别是西北欧枢纽实现了发展，但由于建设跨境互联器以及要求现有管道设施逆流，北欧建立起了内部的天然气市场、中东欧也建立了各自的市场，而伊比利亚半岛和波罗的海国家则仍相对孤立。因此，在价格审查仲裁中，定价机制是参照买方经营的一个或多个特定市场进行调整的。在美国，天然气价格主要根据亨利中心基准价格确定，但在欧盟，各国有不同的定价机制，这体现了欧盟天然气市场的复杂性。此外，目前 TTF 和 NBP 是欧盟流动性最强的枢纽，其定价机制也尤为复杂。[①] 那么，仲裁庭用何种方式确定变化因素影响了谨慎高效的天然气公司在用户终端市场上获得的天然气价值？可以看到，首先，价格审查条款没有说明是如何确定的；其次，为得到确定答案，必须进行定量评估。

按照行业惯例，在第一轮价格审查仲裁之前，需确定审查期内每次重大变化对天然气价值的影响，并由此确定调整的价格，以反映变化本身带来的影响。例如，如果某种石油产品的税收增长，而定价机制以此为参照，为了反映税收增长对天然气相对价值的影响，天然气价格也应相应提高。过去价格审查的目的在于在买方市场重建天然气及与天然气相竞争的石油产品的关系，因此，价格

---

① Oxford Institute of Energy Studies, *European Traded Gas Hubs: An Updated Analysis on Liquidity, Maturity and Barriers to Market Integration*, https://www.oxfordenergy.org/publications/european-traded-gas-hubs-updated-analysis-liquidity-maturity-barriers-market-integration/, December 16, 2018.

审查条款参考的是“天然气内在价值”而非“天然气外在价格”。由于不考虑非重大变化和由当事方引起的变化，显然每次都会单独考量各重大变化的影响。因此，在价格审查这一阶段，并不考虑用户终端市场中天然气的实际价格。

然而，第一轮价格审查仲裁反映了这种方法的复杂性。在这种情况下，需要修改价格公式以反映天然气间的竞争关系，抑或是天然气与石油、煤炭和核能间的竞争关系。第一轮价格审查仲裁期间，欧盟大陆还尚未形成液化气市场，仲裁法庭只是简单地降低价格水平（以“Po”著称），以反映市场上天然气间的竞争价格，而定价机制仍与石油产品的价格挂钩。

在第二轮价格审查浪潮中，西北欧天然气市场的定价机制经过调整，除包含石油指数外，还囊括了基准价格，以反映天然气间的竞争关系。根据买方所处的位置，审查中会选择 NBP、TTF、ZEE 或 GPL* 的基准价格纳入参考范围。

第三轮价格审查期间，基准价格机制变得更复杂。在如今的价格审查仲裁中，当事人一直认为，定价机制的调整仅需参考基准价格。然而，对于是否考虑运输成本以及相对于基准价格来说，应折价还是溢价，各方仍存在分歧。

六、经济销售条款

许多价格审查条款都包含经济销售条款。经济销售条款也称为“无论如何”条款（“in any case” clause），通常是这样规定的：“无论如何，买方都应当能够在买方的终端用户市场与所有能源供应商竞争、以经济的方式销售天然气……”

加入该条款后，对于该条款是否给予买方提请价格审查的独立权利，欧盟价格审查谈判和仲裁存在诸多争论。①

同时，关于该条款是否在液化天然气买卖协议执行期内保证买方保留其边际利润的权利，也存在诸多争论。有人认为，保留边际利润实际上相当于保留

---

* ZEE 是指比利时天然气交易中心；GPL 是指德国天然气交易中心 Gaspool Balancing Point。——译者注

① 但据作者所知，目前尚未有单独以该等条款触发价格审查的案例。

固定价格,这违反了《欧盟职能条约》第101条的规定。

七、欧盟天然气价格审查浪潮

液化天然气买卖协议的缔约方最常通过谈判调整价格,原因在于过去协议中的天然气定价机制是基于石油产品与天然气的价格的相互关系制定的,而触发价格调整的情形影响了二者之间的相互关系。[①] 例如,颁布法规禁止在买方能源市场中销售高硫燃料油也引发了价格审查。该禁令意味着在买方市场上,高硫燃料油无法再与天然气竞争。因此,将高硫燃料油价格作为参考的定价机制变得不再适合,需要对其进行调整。

然而,前述欧洲天然气市场的变化导致2005年之后,当事人以结构性变化为原因触发价格审查机制,而当时价格审查条款并未考虑到这一情形。因此,在过去的15年里,当事方不得不诉诸第三方来调整定价机制,价格审查仲裁的数量也随之激增。

正如第四部分中所述,通常会谈及的天然气价格仲裁有3轮:(1)2005~2008年进行的仲裁;(2)2008~2010年进行的仲裁;(3)从2012年开始持续至今的仲裁。[②]

八、天然气价格审查在[③]欧盟的未来之期望

诸多行业人士预计,由于目前大多数定价机制都已调整为与基准价格挂钩,未来欧盟针对天然气或液化天然气的价格审查将会变少。如图6所示,在西北欧地区,90%的天然气合同都依据基准价格制定,未来其价格审查数量必

---

① 更多2000年前的案例,详见 Stanic A., Weale G., *Changes in the European Gas Market and Price Review Arbitrations*, (2007) J. Energy and Resource Law。

② 更多有关三次价格审查仲裁的讨论,详见 Anway S. P., von Mehren G. M., *The Evolution of Natural Gas Price Review Arbitrations*, in The Guide to Energy Arbitrations edited by Rowley J. W., Global Arbitration Review (2nd edition), 2017。

③ 此为译者的补译,英文原文为"What can we expect in the EU going forward?"。

然变少。[①] 但在地中海及东南欧(SEE)地区,分别只有32%和10%的天然气合同依据基准价格制定,其情况则并非如此。

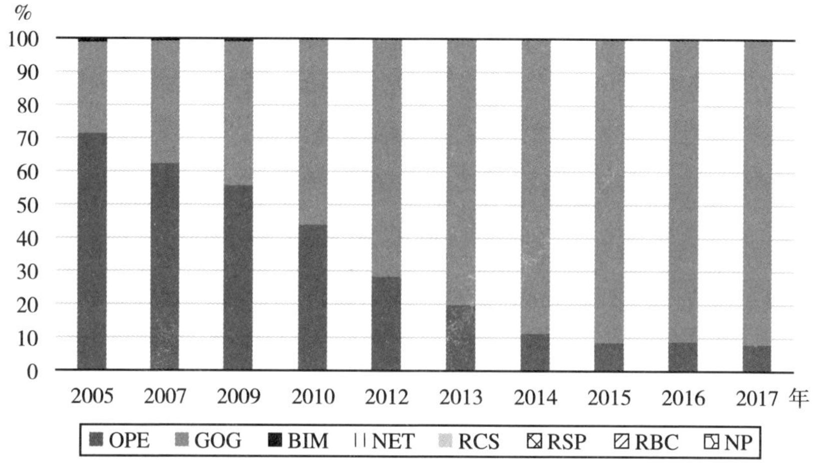

(a)西北欧地区的价格形成

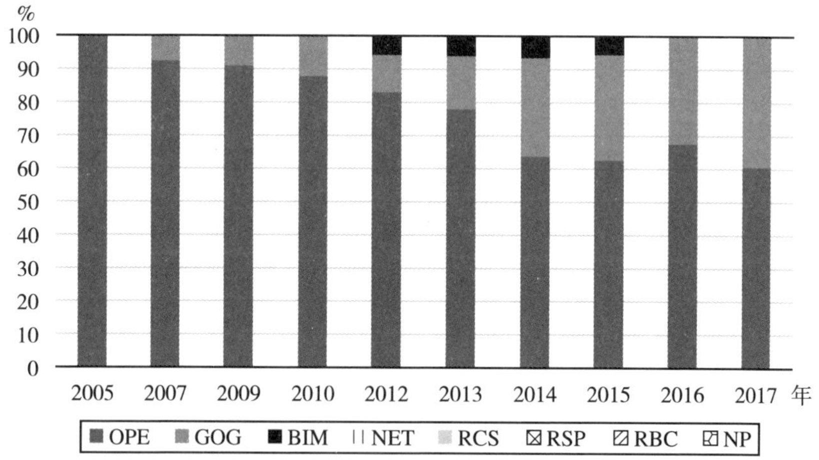

(b)地中海地区的价格形成

① International Gas Union, *Wholesale Gas Price Survey* 2018 *Final*, https://www.igu.org/sites/default/files/node-document-field_file/IGU_Wholesale%20Gas%20Price%20Survey%202018%20Final.pdf, December 24, 2008.

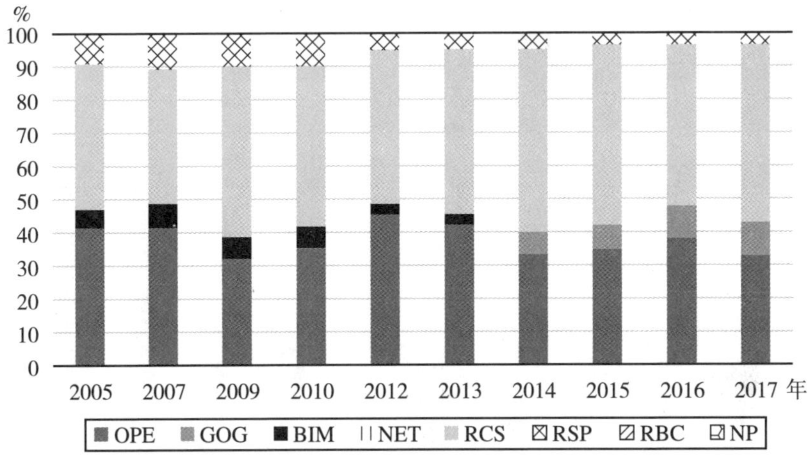

(c)东南欧地区的价格形成

图 6 欧洲价格形成

资料来源:国际气体联盟(International Gas Union,IGU)2018 年天然气批发价格调查最终版。

注:图 6 的 3 个图的简称指代如下:OPE 是指石油价格上涨(Oil-Price Escalation);GOG 是指石油对石油竞争(Gas-on-gas Competition);BIM 是指相互独占(Bilateral Monopoly);NET 是指市场净回值(Netback From Final Product);RCS 是指规制:服务费用(Regulation: Cost of Service);RSP 是指规制:社会与政治(Regulation: Social and Political);RBC 是指规制:成本以下(Regulation: Below Cost);NP 是指无价格(No Price)。——译者注

此外,能源监管机构合作局(Agency for the Coordination of Energy Regulators,ACER)的数据显示,尽管中东欧价格一体化程度已经有所提高,但至本文撰写之时,只有 40% 左右的天然气合同参照了基准价格。①

然而,笔者认为,未来欧盟的价格审查仲裁数量有可能减少,主要有以下两个原因:第一,目前许多东南欧和中东欧的液化天然气买卖协议都为短期协议,通常持续 1 ~3 年。第二,欧盟国家的天然气采购成本相差无几,几乎所有价格差都低于每兆瓦时 3 欧元,很多甚至低于每兆瓦时 1 欧元。②

① Acer, *Market Monitoring Report* 2017 – *Gas Wholesale Markets Volume*, https://www. acer. europa. eu/Official _ documents/Acts _ of _ the _ Agency/Publication/ACER% 20Market% 20Monitoring% 20Report% 202017% 20 – % 20Gas% 20Wholesale% 20Markets% 20Volume. pdf, December 16, 2018.

② Acer, *Market Monitoring Report* 2017 – *Gas Wholesale Markets Volume*, https://www. acer. europa. eu/Official _ documents/Acts _ of _ the _ Agency/Publication/ACER% 20Market% 20Monitoring% 20Report% 202017% 20 – % 20Gas% 20Wholesale% 20Markets% 20Volume. pdf, December 16, 2018, p. 18.

因此,笔者认为,和20年前的欧洲一样,亚洲将成为价格审查仲裁的下一个"主战场"。亚洲市场尚未开放,天然气价格仍与石油产品价格挂钩。如图7所示,亚洲只有不到20%的液化天然气买卖协议以基准价格为参考。

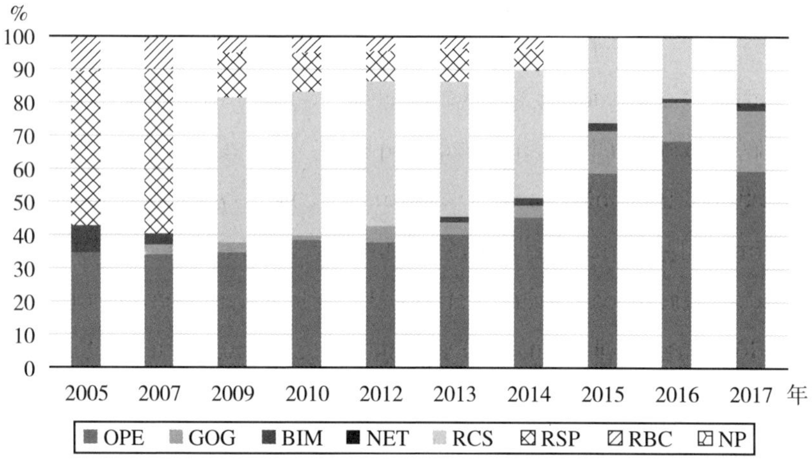

图7　亚洲价格形成

资料来源:国际气体联盟2018年天然气批发价格调查最终版。

如图8所示,2017年日本公平贸易委员会(Japan Fair Trade Commission)的调查显示,日本10%～15%的液化天然气售价是根据混合定价公式或市场指数公式确定的。到2025年,这一比例预计达到30%左右。[①] 如果日本买方提请价格审查谈判和/或仲裁,将有望在2025年前达到甚至超过这一比例。

日本、韩国预计将率先采取这种做法,而中国的价格审查仲裁预计很少,这是因为,也是令人意外的一点,[②]大多数中国的液化天然气买卖协议中均未包含价格审查条款。

---

① JFTC., *Survey on LNG Trades* (*Summary*), https://www.jftc.go.jp/en/pressreleases/yearly-2017/June/170628_files/170628-1.pdf, December 16, 2018.

② 尽管大多数液化天然气买卖协议都是在欧盟价格审查仲裁浪潮中谈成的,但大多数中国买家同意的液化天然气买卖协议均未包含价格审查条款。

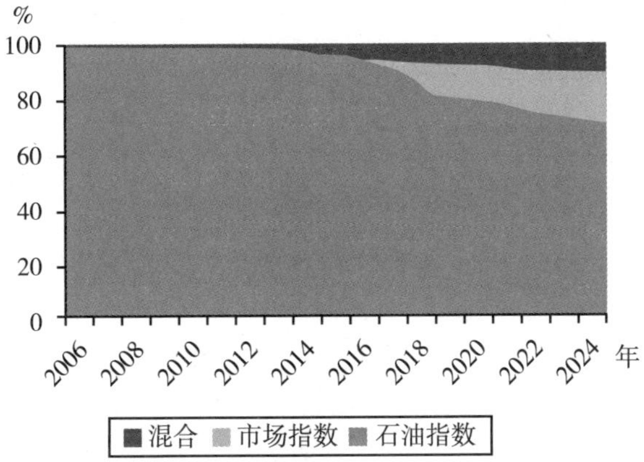

图 8 日本价格形成(容量比率)——日本公平贸易委员会

资料来源:日本公平贸易委员会液化天然气贸易调查。

九、给日本的启示

从 2005 年至今,欧盟共经历了 3 轮价格审查仲裁浪潮,下文将分析日本能从中借鉴的主要经验。

(一)价格审查条款的重要性和起草要点

第一,为使天然气价格的调整反映市场状况的变化,价格审查条款发挥了重要作用。也即与首次起草时相比,尽管欧盟天然气市场出现了难以预料的变化,但条款也发挥了其应有作用。

鉴于此,很难理解为什么许多在欧盟外国家和地区谈判签订的(有些甚至是最近签订的)长期液化天然气买卖协议都不包含价格审查条款。的确,许多非普通法司法管辖区都允许当事方重新谈判,在某些情况下甚至可以因实际困难而终止液化天然气买卖协议,即使液化天然气买卖协议中未明确包含此类条款。但是,在欧盟外,许多液化天然气买卖协议受英国法律或其他国家法律的管辖,而在这些国家内,并不能以困难为由终止协议。

第二,价格审查条款和价格审查仲裁已经被证明是开放欧盟天然气市场、增强市场流动性、确保合同稳定性和维护买卖双方长期关系的重要机制。

第三,欧盟的价格审查仲裁已证明了慎重起草价格审查条款的重要性。20

世纪60年代，为帮助荷兰开发其天然气，第一份价格审查条款得以谈判起草。此后，尽管天然气市场发生了重大的结构性变化，该审查条款的措辞也几乎没有改变。尤其令人意外的是，尽管欧盟之后的价格审查谈判和仲裁都暴露了条款的局限性，但亚洲最新的液化天然气买卖协议中引入的审查条款仍与欧盟的典型条款非常相似。之所以如此，一方面是由价格审查仲裁的保密性决定的，另一方面是因为参与制定液化天然气买卖协议谈判的律师通常不参与价格审查仲裁。

借鉴欧盟价格审查条款起草的经验，日本要考虑是否起草全新的价格审查条款。因为现存条款是根据20世纪60年代荷兰的情况制定的，不适应目前日本天然气市场的运作方式。如果双方都不能接受这种激进的方法，则至少应采取以下措施：

(1)明确定义"买方市场"和"终端用户市场"；

(2)明确价格调整程序；

(3)明确仲裁员的角色以及他们可在多大程度上修改定价机制；

(4)考虑是否将"经济销售条款"纳入价格审查条款中，如果是，需明确"经济销售"调查能否作为提请价格审查的单独依据；

(5)考虑是否应明确必须在无偏见的情况下进行谈判。

(二)准据法

欧盟价格审查仲裁强调了当事方选择准据法的重要性。液化天然气买卖协议的准据法将决定仲裁庭如何解释价格审查条款；决定艰难条款或不可抗力条款是否适用于液化天然气买卖协议；决定合同前谈判对于解释液化天然气买卖协议能发挥多大作用；决定当事人能否依据其在无偏见谈判时制定的文件和主张进行仲裁。

仲裁员的观点有可能会决定仲裁的结果，因此在起草价格审查条款时应更加重视准据法带来的影响。特别是在各国法律间作取舍时，要仔细权衡其中的利弊。

(三)价格审查是事实驱动的

有人强调价格审查是一个受事实驱动的过程，一个价格审查仲裁的结果是具体个案的结果。因此,价格审查成功与否在很大程度上取决于法律团队(由国内外律师及内部法律顾问组成)与专家的紧密合作程度,以得出连贯而令人信服的论点。这些论点涉及买方市场中经济情况变化的性质和范围,以及天然气的市场价值。在日本和其他亚洲国家,价格审查仲裁不能简单地照搬欧盟审查中所引用的论点,必须深入分析和了解欧盟天然气市场、欧盟能源和竞争法,充分了解日本市场的具体情况。这些对于认识审查背后的原因尤为重要,也有利于审查成功进行。

(四)找准"合适"仲裁员的重要性

当事各方在指定仲裁员时必须格外谨慎。价格审查仲裁与其他商业仲裁大不相同,因为仲裁员在价格审查中不是确定哪一方在法律上有过错,而是允许调整定价机制,从而使双方保持长期合同关系。因此,审查中的仲裁员应深入理解天然气市场和天然气价格公式的数学复杂性。

(五)确保无偏见谈判的重要性

欧盟价格审查仲裁还证明,确保谈判无偏见也尤为重要。通常而言,欧盟价格审查条款没有明确规定谈判必须不带任何偏见,这主要取决于液化天然气买卖协议的准据法。当事人双方需要明确谈判过程是否带有偏见,如果是,那么一方则有可能利用另一方在谈判过程中确定的文件或论点,要求仲裁法庭采纳和/或否决另一方的主张。为了避免出现有关的不确定情况,当事方应从一开始就保证其在价格审查中立场一致,从策略上解决此问题。因此,建议尽早让外部专家和律师参与价格审查,并促进律师、专家和内部工作人员间的密切合作。[①]

(六)改变欧盟天然气市场状况时,采取立法措施以及实施竞争法的重要性

欧盟机构采取的立法措施对开放欧盟天然气市场、带来价格趋同和降低天然气价格起到了重要作用。2000 年年初,欧盟委员会为执行竞争法而采取的行动,对改变天然气市场的运作来说,也是同样重要的。如前文"跨大西洋天然气贸易的增长"部分所述,2005 年,欧盟委员会认定目的地条款违背了市场

---

① 根据作者的经验,当事方一般都会在价格审查后期邀请专家、内部律师和内部人员介入,由此一来,上述各方间的合作常常不够理想。

竞争,使天然气买方能够将运往欧洲的天然气转运到美国,从而利用价格差套利,放开了欧盟天然气市场。几年后,目的地条款的废除又使天然气购买者能将运往欧洲的天然气转运到亚洲。因此,正是欧盟委员会采取的措施(包括废除目的地条款)和买方提请价格审查的意图,促成了如今欧盟天然气定价机制的变化。

十、结语

当前,全球天然气市场仍存在诸多不确定性。从中期来看,这种不确定性产生的原因是,在向零碳经济转型的过程中,天然气的作用尚不明确。从短期而言,美国页岩气在建立全球燃气市场中能发挥什么作用也仍不确定。而美国前总统特朗普试图迫使与美国存在较大贸易逆差的国家如日本,进口美国的天然气,天然气价格问题愈发带有了政治色彩。在这种高度政治化的环境中,天然气价格审查条款和天然气价格审查仲裁为化解纠纷、去政治化与和平解决争端提供了非常重要的途径。

图书在版编目（CIP）数据

仲裁与法律. 第146辑 / 中国国际经济贸易仲裁委员会，中国国际商会仲裁研究所主办. -- 北京 : 法律出版社，2021

ISBN 978-7-5197-5807-3

Ⅰ. ①仲… Ⅱ. ①中… ②中… ③中… Ⅲ. ①仲裁-研究-丛刊 Ⅳ. ①D915.704-55

中国版本图书馆CIP数据核字(2021)第153344号

仲裁与法律·第146辑
ZHONGCAI YU FALÜ · DI-146 JI

中国国际经济贸易仲裁委员会
中国国际商会仲裁研究所
主办

策划编辑 沈小英
责任编辑 沈小英 毛镜澄
装帧设计 汪奇峰

出版发行 法律出版社
编辑统筹 法治与经济出版分社
责任校对 周合芝
责任印制 吕亚莉
经　　销 新华书店

开本 710毫米×1000毫米 1/16
印张 14.75 **字数** 226千
版本 2021年9月第1版
印次 2021年9月第1次印刷
印刷 中煤(北京)印务有限公司

地址：北京市丰台区莲花池西里7号(100073)
网址：www.lawpress.com.cn
投稿邮箱：info@lawpress.com.cn
举报盗版邮箱：jbwq@lawpress.com.cn

销售电话：010-83938349
客服电话：010-83938350
咨询电话：010-63939796

书号：ISBN 978-7-5197-5807-3
定价：69.00元

凡购买本社图书，如有印装错误，我社负责退换。电话：010-83938349